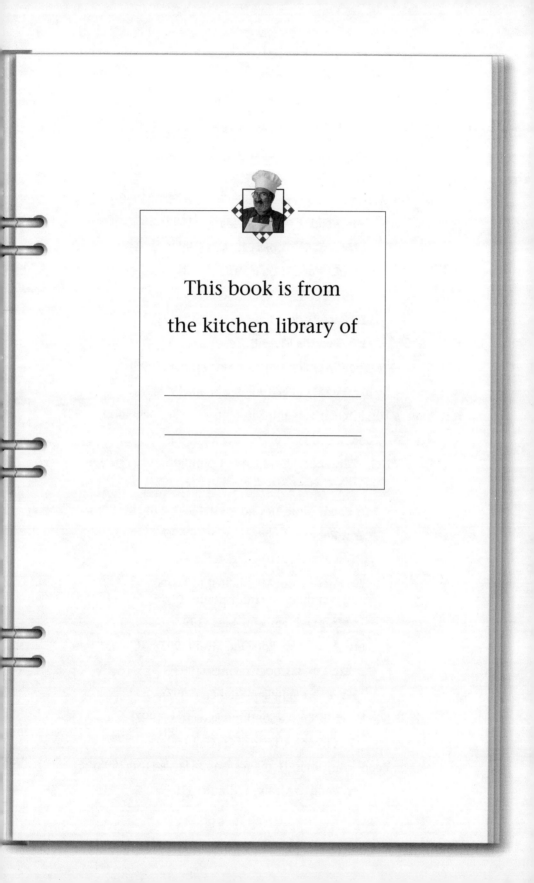

This book is from

the kitchen library of

_____

_____

ALSO BY ART GINSBURG, **Mr. Food**®

The **Mr. Food**® Cookbook, *OOH IT'S SO GOOD!!*® (1990)

Mr. Food® Cooks Like Mama (1992)

Mr. Food® Cooks Chicken (1993)

Mr. Food® Cooks Pasta (1993)

Mr. Food® Makes Dessert (1993)

Mr. Food® Cooks Real American (1994)

Mr. Food®**'s** Favorite Cookies (1994)

Mr. Food®**'s** Quick and Easy Side Dishes (1995)

Mr. Food® Grills It All in a Snap (1995)

Mr. Food®**'s** Fun Kitchen Tips and Shortcuts (and Recipes, Too!) (1995)

Mr. Food®**'s** Old World Cooking Made Easy (1995)

"Help, **Mr. Food**®! Company's Coming!" (1995)

Mr. Food® Pizza 1-2-3 (1996)

Mr. Food® Meat Around the Table (1996)

Mr. Food® Simply Chocolate (1996)

Mr. Food® A Little Lighter (1996)

Mr. Food® From My Kitchen to Yours:
Stories and Recipes from Home (1996)

Mr. Food® Easy Tex-Mex (1997)

Mr. Food® One Pot, One Meal (1997)

Mr. Food® Cool Cravings (1997)

Mr. Food®**'s** Italian Kitchen (1997)

Mr. Food®**'s** Simple Southern Favorites (1997)

Mr. Food® A Taste of QVC (1998)

A **Mr. Food**® Christmas: Homemade and Hassle-Free (1998)

Mr. Food®**'s** Meals in Minutes (1999)

FIFTY-TWO WEEKS OF
YEAR-ROUND FAVORITES

Mr. Food®
COOKING
BY THE
CALENDAR

Art Ginsburg
Mr. Food®

WILLIAM MORROW AND COMPANY, INC.
NEW YORK

Library of Congress Cataloging-in-Publication Data

Ginsburg, Art.
    Mr. Food cooking by the calendar / Art Ginsburg.
        p.   cm.
    ISBN 0-688-15678-9
    1. Cookery.   I. Title.
    TX714.G564   1999
    641.5—dc21   97-39184
                                                                    CIP

Printed in the United States of America

First Edition

1   2   3   4   5   6   7   8   9   10

BOOK DESIGN BY MICHAEL MENDELSOHN OF MM DESIGN 2000, INC.

www.williammorrow.com
www.mrfood.com

DEDICATED TO

J.G.,

WHO HELPED ME WITHOUT BEING ASKED

Acknowledgments

As I got more and more into this book, my awareness of calendars certainly heightened. Calendars seemed to be jumping out at me from everywhere! I couldn't go anywhere without seeing one . . . or two or three! Every desk in the Mr. Food offices has one. My kitchen, bank, dry cleaner—even the customer service area at the supermarket has a calendar displayed. And the bookstore—wow, what a selection they have!

Once I really paid attention to all these calendars, I discovered that each one has its own personality—and calendars are as diverse as the staff of talented people who helped me bring this book together. Now here's my chance to thank those special people. Once again, I get to applaud my kitchen staff, who works so closely with me—I have to say it—day in and day out. (Like my calendar humor?) As always, Janice Bruce, Patty Rosenthal, Cheryl Gerber, Joan Wolff, Cela Goodhue, and Ava Ray Bernardi added lots of color and taste to our calendar of foods. Joe Peppi, my director of recipe development, kept the pages of the calendar turning, always right on time, along with "Charlie" Tallant, who managed to keep up with us and all of the recipe information we needed entered into our computers.

I sure owe a big thank-you to Caryl Ginsburg Fantel and Howard Rosenthal! I can always count on these two to make sure that my books are fun, creative, high quality, and good value, full of recipes that are simple, tasty, and no-fuss.

I'm grateful to Helayne Rosenblum and Larissa Lalka, who helped organize my thoughts for each week's timely recipe-related stories. And a big thank-you to the rest of the Mr. Food team, who, as usual, brought interesting perspectives to the blend that became *Mr. Food® Cooking by the Calendar*: Ethel, Steve, Chuck, and Carol Ginsburg; Rhonda Weiss; Chet Rosenbaum; Tom Palombo; Marilyn Ruderman; Alice Palombo; Heidi Triveri; Robin Steiner; and Beth Ives.

It's hard to believe, but agent Bill Adler, publishing company William Morrow, and I have been together for over a decade now. That's a lot of seasons *and* seasoning! Thanks, Bill, and also Bill Wright, President and CEO of the Hearst Book Group; Michael Murphy, Morrow Publisher and Senior Vice President; Editor Zachary Schisgal; and Richard Aquan, Deborah Weiss Geline; Jackie Deval; Nikki Basilone, and all the other folks at Morrow who make my books come together. Michael Mendelsohn and Philip Scheuer have designed and illustrated quite a few of my books, and now more than ever I appreciate their senses of humor and good taste.

Throughout the creation phase of each of my books, there are always companies and organizations willing to help out with information and testing materials. I'm grateful for their support, as well as the ever-present encouragement of my viewers and readers. I love meeting you and hearing from you—it helps me know what you need to make your lives easier!

I started out here by discussing calendars . . . so now I'll tell you which is my favorite type—the ones with a different interesting quote for each day. They're enlightening and inspiring (just like all the people I've thanked!), but you know, no matter how many quotes I read, the one that rolls off my tongue the easiest is still, "OOH IT'S SO GOOD!!®"

Contents

Acknowledgments   vii

Recipes   xiii

Introduction   xxiii

A Note About Packaged Foods   xxvi

Week 1   New Year's Day Brunch: *A great way to start the year!*   1

Week 2   The Soup Pot: *Ladle after ladle brimming with good taste*   7

Week 3   Martin Luther King, Jr.'s Favorites: *A meal of southern classics*   13

Week 4   Super Bowl Munchies: *Just in time for kickoff*   19

Week 5   Midwinter Picnic: *Boy, do we need it now!*   27

Week 6   Canned Food Creations: *You'll love these long after National Canned Food Month*   33

Week 7   Valentine's Day Dinner: *A "hearty" meal for two*   39

Week 8   Presidents' Day Salute: *A tribute to our country's leaders*   45

Week 9   Homemade Takeout: *A Chinese New Year celebration*   51

Week 10   Mardi Gras Feast: *The next best thing to being there*   59

Week 11   March Madness Buffet: *Slam-dunk favorites*   67

Week 12   St. Patrick's Day Dinner: *Everybody's Irish this week*   73

Week 13   The Tastes of Spring: *Worth waiting for*   79

Week 14   April Foods That Fool 'Em: *You won't believe your eyes*   87

Week 15   Passover Seder: *Finally—matzo balls that float!*   95

Week 16   Easter Traditions: *For a "hoppy" holiday*   101

Week 17   Two Tasty Tributes: *Celebrating two things we can't live without*   107

Week 18   Kentucky Derby Winners: *No horsing around here*   113

Week 19   Cinco de Mayo: *A Mexican fiesta*   119

Week 20   Mother's Day Brunch: *Give Mom a well-deserved break today*   125

Week 21   College Graduation Party: *Hooray for the graduate!*   131

Week 22   Memorial Day: *A time to share with family and friends*   139

Week 23   Pre-Wedding Welcome: *A welcoming meal sure to impress the in-laws-to-be*   147

Week 24   Beefed-Up Dinners: *Celebrating beef*   155

Week 25   Fun Food: *School's out, so make the kids' favorites*   161

Week 26   Father's Day Barbecue: *This week, Dad's King of the Grill*   167

Week 27   Red, White, and Blue Birthday Bash: *Get 'em ready for the fireworks*   173

Week 28   Campfire Cookin': *More than just "burgers and dogs"*   179

Week 29   Le French Buffet: *In honor of Bastille Day*   185

Week 30   Ice Cream Sampler: . . . *As if we need an*   193
           excuse to eat ice cream!

Week 31   Rhode Island Sensations: *Vacation with me*   201
           at the shore

Week 32   Magic with Mustard: *Hats off to our favorite*   207
           yellow condiment

Week 33   Blueberry Bonanza: *The true taste of summer*   213

Week 34   Light 'n' Healthy Summer Celebration: 219
           Light 'n' luscious

Week 35   An English Tea: *Remembering Princess Di*   225

Week 36   Labor Day Get-Together: *Great food, little*   233
           work

Week 37   Back-to-School Favorites: *Don't forget* these   239
           school supplies

Week 38   Grandparents' Day Dinner: *What a way*   245
           to show you care

Week 39   State Fair Fare: *The tastes and smells of*   251
           the midway

Week 40   Oktoberfest: *The only thing missing is the*   259
           accordion

Week 41   Orchard Goodies: *Enjoy some apple goodness*   267
           every day

Week 42   Columbus Day Discoveries: *Old World*   275
           meets New World

Week 43   Chocoholic Fantasies: *Chocolate at its best*   281

Week 44   Halloween Treats: *No tricks here!*   289

Week 45   National Sandwich Week: *The sandwich*   297
           sure has come a long way

Week 46   Veterans Day: *Good food from hard times*   305

Week 47   Autumn Harvest Dinner: *Sure to warm your*   311
          tummy

Week 48   Turkey Time: *Thanksgiving as it was meant*   319
          to be

Week 49   Recipes for Romance: *Mr. and Mrs. Food's*   325
          anniversary dinner

Week 50   Holiday Open-House Nibbles: *Sure to make*   333
          everybody feel welcome

Week 51   Hanukkah Traditions: *Just bring along*   341
          a dreidel

Week 52   Christmas Dinner: *What a way to end*   349
          the year!

Index   357

Recipes

Appetizers

Buttermilk Dip	335
Chilled Shrimp with Lime	120
Creamy Salsa Two-Step	68
Easy Egg Rolls	52
Festive Crab Spread	334
Hazelnut-Crusted Brie	186
Picnic-Time Deviled Eggs	140
Pinecone Cheese Ball	88
Steaming Artichoke Dip	326
"Timeout" Stuffed Spuds	69
Touchdown Wings	20

Salads

Easy Caesar Salad	204
Fruity Chicken Salad	133
Hot Bacon 'n' Potato Salad	29
Maple Mustard Dressing	209
Marinated Flank Steak Salad	156
Marinated Salad	34
Mediterranean Green Salad	327
Mixed Berry Salad	174
Pineapple-Carrot Slaw	222
Presidential Honey Walnut Salad	46
Salad on a Stick	132
Strawberry Spinach Salad	148
Sweet-Pickle Potato Salad	169

Tossed Garden Salad 307
Toss-Together Corn Salad 180
Two-Hearts Salad 40
Veggie Cabbage Slaw 143

Soups

Carrot and Parsnip Soup 312
Creamy Clam Chowder 203
Creamy Corn and Potato Soup 9
Creamy Pumpkin Soup 350
Extra-Creamy Mushroom Soup 11
Hamburger Soup 8
Homemade Chicken Soup 97
Aunt Sarah's Matzo Balls 98
Macaroni and Cheese Soup 240
Speedy Bean Soup 10
Velvet Corn Soup 54
Vichyssoise 187
Victory Garden Soup 308

Breads

Bacon Corn Bread 14
Blueberry Muffins 214
Cranberry Irish Soda Bread 74
Derby Rolls 114
Dunkin' Bread Sticks 12
Honey Corn Bread 306
Honey-Mustard-Swirl Bread 208
Hot Cross Buns 103
Light 'n' Flaky Biscuits 220
Mint-Laced Popovers 80
Passover Rolls 96
Pumpkin Spice Bread 336

Shortnin' Bread 47
Sour Cream and Chive Biscuits 315
Strawberry 'n' Cream Roll-ups 3
Teatime Scones 226

Sandwiches

Bacon 'n' Blue-Cheese Burger 168
Baked Stuffed Tuna Sandwich 302
Barbecue Joe 157
Campfire Hot Diggity Dogs 182
Cheese Pretzel Sandwiches 242
Croissant Club 298
Cucumber Tea Sandwiches 229
Fresh Veggie Pita 300
Grilled Fluffwich 163
Halftime Hoagies 22
Ham and Nacho Cheese Roll-ups 241
Hot-Shot Meatball Hoagies 70
Italian Focaccia Sandwich 301
Jack-o'-Lantern Sandwiches 291
Monte Cristo 299
Sausage, Pepper, and Onion Sandwich 253
Steak Sandwiches with Black Bean Salsa 121
Super Stuffed Pizza 134
Taco Dogs 164
Upside-down Chicken Pizza Muffins 162
Watercress-Salmon Tea Sandwiches 228

Pasta

Citrus Twist Pasta 223
Halloween Pasta Salad 290
Linguine and Clams in Red Sauce 205
Pork Lo Mein 55

Rich and Creamy Fettuccine 276
Winner's Circle Shrimp Pasta Salad 115

Poultry

Apple-Glazed Chicken 270
Barbecue-Style Chicken 28
Buttermilk Fried Chicken 15
Chicken with Root Vegetables 108
French Country Chicken 328
Mincemeat-Crusted Turkey 320
Saucy Chicken 247
Simple Chicken Cordon Bleu 149
Walkaway Turkey Drumsticks 252

Meat

Beef Bourguignon 188
Bread Bowl Chili 21
Corned Beef and Carrots 75
Cozy Beef Stew 35
Diner-Style Salisbury Steak 160
Kung Pao Beef 56
Maple-Glazed Ham and Sweet Potatoes 105
Meat Loaf Cake 89
Orange-Grilled Strip Steaks 234
Orange Mustard Pork Tenderloin 211
Passover Brisket 99
Reuben Casserole 313
Roasted Holiday Prime Rib 351
Roasted Leg of Lamb 81
Sage Breakfast Sausage 128
Skillet Round Steak 159
Tangy Barbecued Spareribs 141
Tarragon Tenderloin 158

Traditional German Braten Stew   260
Veal Cacciatore Stew   277
Veal with Artichoke Hearts   41

Seafood

Crusted Baked Salmon   49
"Jazzed-Up" Shrimp Étouffée   61
Lemonade-Poached Salmon   221
New England Lobster Boil   175

Side Dishes

Apple Baked Beans   235
Apple Sauerkraut   261
Autumn Creamed Spinach   262
Baked Mashed Potatoes   249
Beet Mashed Potatoes   109
Buttery Squash   248
Christmas Peas   352
Chunky Applesauce   344
Colonial Spinach   48
Double Stuffers   329
Festive Rice   62
Grilled Caramelized Onions   171
Grilled Corn on the Cob   170
Grilled Veggie Kebabs   144
Hash-Brown Bake   4
Herb-Marinated Asparagus   84
Herbed Corn on the Cob   30
Homemade Cranberry Sauce   322
Hot Potato Packets   181
Irish Potatoes   76
Mashed Turnips   323
Mixed-up Roasted Vegetables   189

Onion Straws	236
Orchard Sweet Potato Bake	271
Parsley Buttered Potatoes	210
Popcorn Dressing	321
Potato Pancakes	342
Potato Roses	150
Praline Sweet Potatoes	353
Red Pepper Pilaf	42
Sautéed Greens	278
Seasoned Fries	254
Slow-Cookin' Collard Greens	16
Spaghetti Squash Scampi	91
Spring Vegetable Couscous	83
"Sweet Potato" Dumplings	263

Beverages

Black-and-White Soda	257
Café Mochaccino	153
Cap-and-Gown Punch	137
Eye of a Hurricane	60
Frozen Virgin Margaritas	123
Hot Chocolate Mix	184
Irish Coffee	78
Kickoff Punch	25
Mint Julep Iced Tea	117
Minted Lemonade	32
Orange Smoothie	129
Patriotic Milk Shakes	177
Pineapple Cran-Orange Refresher	238
Pineapple Wassail	317
Simmering Cider	274
Strawberry-Banana Smoothie	244
Sunrise Mimosas	2
Witch's Butterscotch Brew	295

Cakes and Pies

Awesome Blueberry Pie	216
Black Forest Cake Roll	264
Blueberry Custard Pie	218
Chocolate Mousse Tarts	331
Chocolate Pecan Fudge Pie	286
Coconut Chocolate Cake	282
Dreamy Orange Swirl Cheesecake	206
Easy King Cake	64
Fruit Cocktail Cake	37
Graduation Cake	135
Layered Watermelon Cake	172
Limesicle Pie	145
Minty Ice Cream Pie	77
Mud Pie	110
Peppermint Swirl Cheesecake	354
Pumpkin Custard Pie	324
S'more Brownie Pie	183
Strawberry Sweetheart Cake	43
Super Bowl Pennant Cakes	23
Sweet Potato Pie	17
Tart Cherry Pie	50
Toasted Blueberry Shortcake	217
Upside-down Apple Pie	272
Wedding Basket Cake	151

Cookies and Other Delights

Almond Cookies	57
Almond Gelato	279
Apricot Macadamia Snowballs	339
Blueberry Cobbler	215
Candied Popcorn Balls	292
Caramel Ice Cream Balls	31

Cherry Lasagna	92
Chocoholic's Parfait	285
Chocolate Almond Truffles	111
Chocolate Chip Bars	237
Chocolate Raspberry Tarts	100
Coconut Cream Pie Ice Cream	197
Cookies 'n' Ice Cream	166
Fabulous Chocolate Walnut Fudge	284
Frozen Mochaccino	199
Frozen Peanut Butter Cups	195
Fruit Pinwheels	250
Fruity Egg Nests	106
Hanukkah Butter Cookies	346
Honey Mousse	309
Jelly Donuts	345
Kentucky Bourbon Parfaits	116
Lemon Tart Cookies	85
Light and Easy Crepes Suzette	190
Nutty Caramel Corn	71
Nutty Meringues	280
Old-fashioned Candy Apples	255
Peanut Butter and Jelly Bars	243
Peanut Butter Chippies	72
Peanut M&M® Bars	165
Pecan Toffee Bars	316
Picture-Perfect Berries and Cream	126
Pistachio Ice Cream	194
Pumpkin Patch Chocolate Chip Cookies	293
Quick Beignets	63
Quick Mini Éclairs	112
Red, White, and Blue Ribbon Cookies	176
Simple Peach Sorbet	36
Snowflake Tea Cookies	230
Spanish Flan	122

Spumoni   198
Sugar Plums   338
Tropical Chocolate Fondue   6
Upside-down Pineapple Muffins   224
White Chocolate Macadamia Bars   287

Information and Other Goodies

Apple Chart   268
Breakfast in a Cup   5
Colored Eggs   102
Disappearing Stuffed French Toast   127
English Rose Jelly   227
Glazed Grapefruit   246
Parmesan-Garlic Oil   202

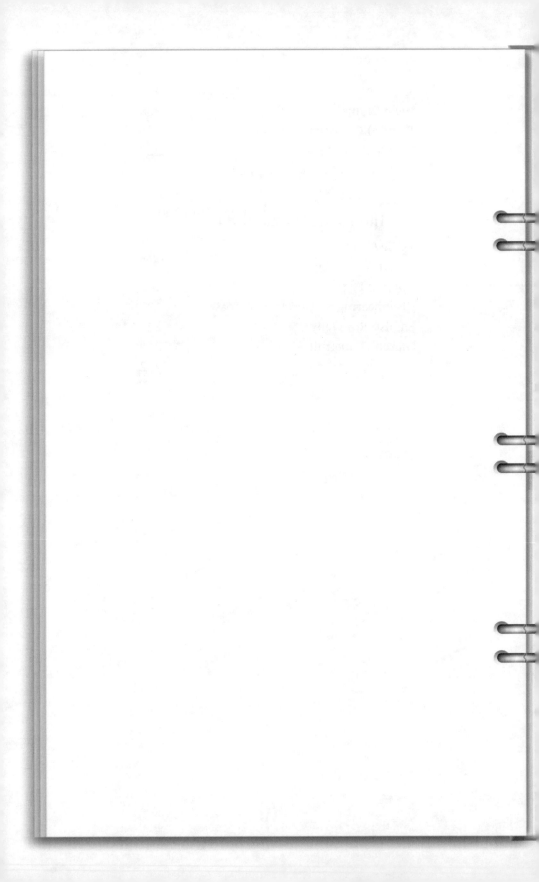

Introduction

If you're like me, you're always ready to go . . . anywhere! It's a rare occasion when I'm not up for a journey—whether it's across the country to visit one of my TV stations or to a festival featuring a particular food or culture, or even to the local farm stand, butcher shop, or supermarket. If you could check out my calendar, you'd see that I'm on the go quite often—I *have* to be to keep up with what's going on in the industry, in the field, and with you.

So this time I'm inviting you to take a journey with me—and I know you're up to it, 'cause you won't have to grab a passport or even pack a suitcase. Nope, this time we're taking a journey through the calendar . . . and it's a trip you won't want to miss!

It all started one day when I was looking over my schedule of appearances and started flipping through my calendar, noticing all the occasions listed there. Sure, there were all the "biggies"—you know, the seasons and the major holidays—but there were lots of lesser-known holidays noted, too, ones that deserve to be acknowledged and celebrated!

Sure, most Americans celebrate New Year's Day, Memorial Day, July Fourth, Labor Day, and Thanksgiving—so I have easy menu ideas to help make those celebrations more festive. But why not take other opportunities to celebrate, too? For example, in honor of National Soup Month, we can whip up some great soups. During National Beef Month, why not put together a super Marinated Flank Steak Salad or other great beef dishes? For National Mustard Day, it's easy to make a quick batch of Maple Mustard Dressing or another zippy recipe high-lighting mustard, and, of course, for National Ice Cream Month, we can have fun making sensational homemade treats.

Holidays *are* fun, but some weeks there aren't any . . . any that are well known, that is. So, to keep every week of the year exciting, I've come up with a few events that may not appear on any calendar, but are sure worth celebrating! Well, see what I did in January with a menu for a Midwinter Picnic ('cause in the middle of winter we need something sunny to pick us up!), and State Fair Fare—a bunch of recipes that bring home the flavors and fun of the midway.

It's easy to do! Honor your grandparents with a colorful back-to-basics menu for Grandparents' Day. Celebrate Earth Day by maybe planting a tree and then going inside to enjoy foods like Chicken with Root Vegetables, Ruby Mashed Potatoes, and, naturally, Mud Pie. And oh, what a bunch of goodies I have for Worldwide Chocolate Month!

Your graduation celebration will be a hit when you serve my Salad on a Stick, Super Stuffed Pizza, Cap-and-Gown Punch, and other party foods. And after the kids are out of school, you won't have to worry about keeping them happy till camp starts. They're gonna love helping you make Taco Dogs, Grilled Fluffwich, and Upside-down Chicken Pizza Muffins. And, of course, once they're back in school, I have ways to keep their lunch boxes filled with excitement and goodness every day of the week.

Got the picture now? There are fifty-two weeks of celebrations here! Why, besides providing creative solutions for Super Bowl Sunday, Easter, St. Patrick's Day, Hanukkah, and Christmas meals, I even have menus for Martin Luther King, Jr.'s Birthday,

Mardi Gras, and the Chinese New Year—and Recipes for Romance in honor of my own December wedding anniversary; use *those* goodies whenever you want to celebrate with *your* special someone. And that's what you can do with all of these menus and recipes—mix and match them and use one or a bunch of 'em whenever they'll help you make any day special.

So get going and flip the pages of my calendar of goodies for a timely, whimsical, seasonal, flavorful "OOH IT'S SO GOOD!!®"

A Note About Packaged Foods

Packaged food sizes may vary by brand. Generally, the sizes indicated in these recipes are average sizes. If you can't find the exact package size listed in the ingredients, whatever package is closest in size will usually do the trick.

WEEK 1

New Year's Day Brunch

Happy New Year! We can be like everybody else and welcome it in with a late-night party, or, for a change of pace, let's invite friends and family over for a festive New Year's Day brunch. We can get a good turnout if we schedule it just right—not too early, so whoever partied a bit too hard can sleep in, but early enough so that it doesn't interrupt the very important afternoon football games! Sure, it's still okay to put out party hats and noisemakers—after all, it *is* a New Year's celebration!

Sunrise Mimosas

Strawberry 'n' Cream Roll-ups

Hash-Brown Bake

Breakfast in a Cup

Tropical Chocolate Fondue

1

Sunrise Mimosas

6 servings

As the sun comes up for the first time in the New Year, let's welcome it with a colorful, refreshing drink that'll make our eyes open wide . . . our smiles, too!

> 2 cups chilled orange juice
> 1½ cups chilled cranberry juice
> 2 cups chilled Asti Spumanti or other sparkling wine
> 1 orange, cut into 6 slices

In a large pitcher, combine the orange and cranberry juices; mix well. Pour evenly into 6 champagne or wineglasses. Add ⅓ cup Asti Spumanti to each glass and garnish with the orange slices. Serve immediately.

NOTE: This is the perfect way to use up leftover Asti Spumanti or champagne from New Year's Eve.

Strawberry 'n' Cream Roll-ups

8 roll-ups

Why not prepare, wrap, and refrigerate these a day ahead? Then when morning comes, you can just crawl out of bed and pop 'em in the oven. They'll be ready in minutes!

¼ cup strawberry preserves (see Note)
2 ounces cream cheese, softened
1 package (8 ounces) refrigerated crescent rolls
1 teaspoon confectioners' sugar

Preheat the oven to 375°F. In a small bowl, combine the strawberry preserves and cream cheese; mix well. Unroll the crescent rolls and separate into 8 triangles. Spread the strawberry mixture evenly over each triangle. Roll each triangle from the wide end to the point and place seam side down on an ungreased baking sheet; curve into crescents. Bake for 12 to 15 minutes, or until golden. Allow to cool slightly, then sprinkle with the confectioners' sugar and serve warm.

NOTE: Make sure to use preserves rather than jam or jelly, 'cause they're chunkier and won't become too liquid.

Hash-Brown Bake

6 to 8 servings

Sure, we could serve the same old hash browns, but why would we when we can make this New Year's brunch extra special . . . with no extra fuss?!

¾ cup (1½ sticks) butter, melted, divided
1 garlic clove, minced
1 tablespoon dry mustard
1 package (32 ounces) hash brown potatoes, thawed
1 can (14 ounces) artichoke hearts, drained and chopped
¼ cup grated Parmesan cheese
1 teaspoon dried basil
1 teaspoon salt
¼ teaspoon black pepper
½ cup plain dry bread crumbs

Preheat the oven to 375°F. Coat a 9" × 13" baking dish with nonstick cooking spray. In a large bowl, combine ½ cup melted butter, the garlic, and mustard; mix well. Add the hash brown potatoes and toss. Add the artichoke hearts, Parmesan cheese, basil, salt, and pepper; mix well. Spoon into the baking dish. In a small bowl, combine the bread crumbs and the remaining ¼ cup melted butter; mix well. Sprinkle over the potato mixture and bake for 55 to 60 minutes, or until heated through and the topping is golden.

NOTE: If we have leftovers, we can cover, wrap, and refrigerate 'em for serving as a dinner go-along during the week.

Breakfast in a Cup

6 servings

I have an egg-cellent way to ring in the new year and it doesn't matter how large a brunch you're planning . . . it's perfect for just the family, or you can double the recipe for a New Year's brunch for a bunch!

    4 sheets phyllo dough
    6 eggs
    ½ cup processed cheese sauce
    ¼ cup heavy cream

Preheat the oven to 350°F. Coat a 6-cup muffin tin with nonstick cooking spray. Stack the phyllo dough sheets on a cutting board and cut into 6 squares. Place each square in a muffin cup, pressing down so it takes the shape of the cup. Without breaking the yolks, crack each egg into a phyllo cup. Bake for 15 to 18 minutes, or until the eggs are cooked and the cups are golden. Meanwhile, in a small saucepan, heat the cheese sauce and cream over medium heat, stirring until heated through. Pour over the egg cups and serve immediately.

NOTE: If you'd like, season the eggs with salt and pepper before baking.

"DARE I SAY IT? I'M EGG-CELLENT!"

Tropical Chocolate Fondue

6 to 8 servings

If you made a New Year's resolution, I hope it wasn't that you were giving up desserts! I would hate to see you break your resolution on day one, 'cause I know you won't be able to resist a dip or two . . . or more!

½ cup orange juice
¼ teaspoon coconut extract
1 pint strawberries, washed and hulled
1 pineapple, cut into bite-sized pieces
2 bananas, peeled and cut into bite-sized pieces
2 squares (1 ounce each) unsweetened chocolate
1 can (14 ounces) sweetened condensed milk
⅓ cup miniature marshmallows
1 teaspoon instant coffee granules
1 teaspoon hot water

In a large bowl, combine the orange juice and coconut extract; mix well. Add the strawberries, pineapple, and bananas; toss gently, cover, and chill for 30 minutes to marinate. In a small saucepan, combine the chocolate, sweetened condensed milk, and marshmallows over low heat, stirring until the chocolate and marshmallows melt and are well combined and smooth. In a small bowl, dissolve the coffee granules in the water. Add to the chocolate mixture, stirring to mix well. To keep the fondue hot, transfer to a fondue pot or a heat-proof serving bowl placed on an electric warming tray; stir occasionally. Serve with the marinated fruit for dipping.

NOTE: At other times of the year, feel free to use your favorite berries for dipping, along with peaches and nectarines, or apples and pears, depending on the season.

WEEK 2

The Soup Pot

Did you know that January is National Soup Month? Yup—that's why I've devoted a whole section to some of our simmering favorites—you know, some of them hearty, others spicy, and, you guessed it, all quick and easy! So what are you waiting for? Grab a bowl and spoon and dig in!

Hamburger Soup

Creamy Corn and Potato Soup

Speedy Bean Soup

Extra-Creamy Mushroom Soup

Dunkin' Bread Sticks

Hamburger Soup

No, this isn't a mistake—it really is hamburger soup! This is hamburger that we eat with a spoon . . . and serve with a bun for dunking. But I do recommend dishing it out with a ladle instead of a spatula!

   1½ pounds ground beef
   1 medium onion, chopped
   3 cans (14½ ounces each) ready-to-use beef broth
   1 can (28 ounces) diced tomatoes, undrained
   1 package (16 ounces) frozen peas and carrots
   1 teaspoon black pepper

In a soup pot, brown the ground beef and onion over medium-high heat for 5 to 8 minutes; drain. Add the remaining ingredients, reduce the heat to medium, and cook for 15 minutes, or until the vegetables are tender.

NOTE: To be truly burger-authentic, serve each bowl of soup with a dollop each of ketchup and mustard and a toasted sesame seed bun.

Creamy Corn and Potato Soup

10 to 12 servings

When I was young, my mom often made a big pot of tasty corn soup. . . . Mmm, mmm! Well, this recipe is a spin-off of Mom's that has become a favorite with our kids and their families. This is the first time that I've shared it, so please try it and, as I always tell the kids, "Enjoy!"

1 small onion, chopped

2 carrots, diced

2 tablespoons butter

3 cans (14½ ounces each) ready-to-use chicken broth

4 large potatoes, peeled and diced (see Note)

3 cans (14¾ ounces each) cream-style corn

2 cups (1 pint) half-and-half

1 teaspoon black pepper

In a soup pot, sauté the onion and carrots in the butter over medium heat for 5 to 6 minutes, or until tender. Add the chicken broth and potatoes. Bring to a boil and cook for 12 to 15 minutes, or until the potatoes are fork-tender. Add the remaining ingredients and cook for 8 to 10 minutes, or until heated through. Serve immediately.

NOTE: Give this some added color by using red-skinned potatoes and leaving the skins on.

Speedy Bean Soup

6 to 8 servings

Just because it's National Soup Month, it doesn't mean we want to spend hours in the kitchen making soup, so here's an extra-quick one that will have 'em saying, "You couldn't have made it—you were only in the kitchen a few minutes!"

> 2 cans (16 ounces each) navy beans, undrained
> 2 cups water
> 1 container (16 ounces) salsa
> 1 can (15¼ ounces) whole kernel corn, drained
> 1 can (14½ ounces) ready-to-use beef broth
> 2 teaspoons ground cumin

In a soup pot, bring all the ingredients to a boil over high heat. Reduce the heat to low and simmer for 15 minutes.

NOTE: How do you like it—mild or spicy? It's easy to adjust each potful to taste by using different-"temperature" salsas. Just make this with whichever one your family likes.

Extra-Creamy Mushroom Soup

8 to 10 servings

Thick and creamy and studded with loads of mushrooms, this is so good that you'd better start off with extra-big bowls!

¼ cup (½ stick) butter
2 pounds fresh mushrooms, sliced
1½ teaspoons onion powder
½ teaspoon black pepper
1 cup all-purpose flour
4 cans (14½ ounces each) ready-to-use beef broth
2 cups (1 pint) half-and-half

Melt the butter in a soup pot over medium heat. Add the mushrooms, onion powder, and pepper and sauté for 5 to 6 minutes, or until the mushrooms are tender. Stir in the flour for about 1 minute, or until absorbed. Add the broth and bring to a boil. Reduce the heat to medium, add the half-and-half, and simmer for 25 to 30 minutes, or until slightly thickened, stirring occasionally. Cover and let sit for 10 minutes to thicken before serving.

NOTE: Our markets have quite a variety of mushrooms available throughout the year, so go ahead and experiment with different kinds!

Dunkin' Bread Sticks

1 dozen

Yes, we love our soups, but we can't live on soup alone! We need some crusty bread sticks for dunkin'!

  1 loaf (12 ounces) French bread
  ½ cup (1 stick) butter, melted
  ¼ cup grated Parmesan cheese
  ½ teaspoon dried oregano
  ¼ teaspoon dried basil

Preheat the oven to 425°F. Cut the bread crosswise in half, then cut each half lengthwise in half. Cut each piece into 3 long strips. In a small bowl, combine the remaining ingredients and brush on the bread strips. Place on a baking sheet and bake for 5 to 6 minutes, or until golden. Serve warm.

NOTE: These easy-to-make bread sticks can be seasoned with any of your favorite fresh or dried herbs. If you'd like them extra-crunchy, just leave them in the oven for a few extra minutes.

WEEK 3

Martin Luther King, Jr.'s Favorites

It's time for our country to salute Dr. Martin Luther King, Jr. Every year we set aside the third Monday in January to celebrate the life and work of this remarkable man. The Martin Luther King, Jr., Center for Non-Violent Social Change, Inc., shared a list of Dr. King's favorite foods with me, so in honor of his birthday, let's make some of them. They're southern and tasty—just one more reason for him to be a hero in my book!

Bacon Corn Bread

Buttermilk Fried Chicken

Slow-Cookin' Collard Greens

Sweet Potato Pie

Bacon Corn Bread

6 to 9 servings

When you make this, you can tell the family you're "bakin' bacon corn bread." They're gonna think you're repeating yourself and that you're makin' "Bacon Bacon Corn Bread," . . . but that's okay. One slice and they'll agree that it's doubly good!

 1 cup yellow cornmeal
 1 cup all-purpose flour
 1¼ cups milk
 ¼ cup real bacon bits
 ¼ cup (½ stick) butter, melted
 1 egg
 1 tablespoon baking powder
 1 teaspoon salt

Preheat the oven to 425°F. Coat an 8-inch square baking dish with nonstick cooking spray. In a large bowl, combine all the ingredients; mix well and place in the baking dish. Bake for 30 to 35 minutes, or until a wooden toothpick inserted in the center comes out clean. Cut into squares and serve warm.

Buttermilk Fried Chicken

4 to 6 servings

Crispy, crunchy, incredible . . . those are just a few of the words that come to mind after just one bite. Maybe we should make a double batch 'cause it gets snatched up so quickly!

> 1½ cups all-purpose flour
> 1 teaspoon garlic powder
> ½ teaspoon ground red pepper
> 1 tablespoon salt
> 2 teaspoons black pepper
> One 3- to 3½-pound chicken, cut into 8 pieces
> 1 cup buttermilk
> 2 cups vegetable oil

In a large bowl, combine the flour, garlic powder, ground red pepper, salt, and black pepper; mix well. Dip the chicken pieces in the buttermilk and then in the flour mixture, coating completely. In a large deep skillet, heat the oil over medium heat until hot but not smoking. Fry the coated chicken in batches for 8 to 10 minutes per side, until golden and no pink remains. Drain on a paper towel–lined platter. Serve immediately.

NOTE: Make sure to fry some dark meat and some white meat in each batch to get the best flavor. And for spicier fried chicken, add additional ground red pepper to the flour mixture.

Slow-Cookin' Collard Greens

4 to 6 servings

I'll have to admit that I didn't used to be a big collard greens fan. But when they're cooked until really tender, with a little sugar in the water to cut the bitterness, it makes a big difference. Guess what? I'm enjoying my collards more and more these days.

> 1 bunch (about 2 pounds) collard greens, stems removed
>   and coarsely chopped
> 1 tablespoon sugar
> 2 teaspoons salt, divided
> ¼ cup (½ stick) butter
> ¼ teaspoon black pepper

In a soup pot, combine the collard greens, sugar, and 1½ teaspoons salt. Add enough water to cover and bring to a boil over medium-high heat. Cover and cook for 1½ to 2 hours, or until the greens are very tender, stirring occasionally. Drain off the liquid and stir in the butter, the remaining ½ teaspoon salt, and the pepper. Continue cooking until the collards are sizzling and coated with butter.

Sweet Potato Pie

6 to 8 servings

I refer to this as a "dump, blend, and bake" pie 'cause all you do is dump the ingredients in a blender, give 'em a whirl, then bake them in a pie plate. In no time you have a pie that's impossible to beat!

2 cans (29 ounces each) sweet potatoes or yams, drained
1 can (12 ounces) evaporated milk
2 tablespoons butter, softened
2 eggs
1 cup firmly packed light brown sugar
½ cup biscuit baking mix
2 teaspoons vanilla extract
¾ teaspoon ground cinnamon
½ teaspoon ground nutmeg

Preheat the oven to 350°F. Coat a 9-inch deep-dish pie plate with nonstick cooking spray. Combine the sweet potatoes and evaporated milk in a blender, in batches, and blend until smooth. Pour into a large bowl and set aside. Place the remaining ingredients in the blender and blend until well combined, scraping down the sides as needed. Add to the sweet potato mixture; mix well. Pour into the pie plate, mounding the center, and bake for 50 to 60 minutes, or until a wooden toothpick inserted in the center comes out clean. Allow to cool completely on a wire rack before serving.

NOTE: Top each slice with a dollop of whipped cream and a sprinkle of cinnamon.

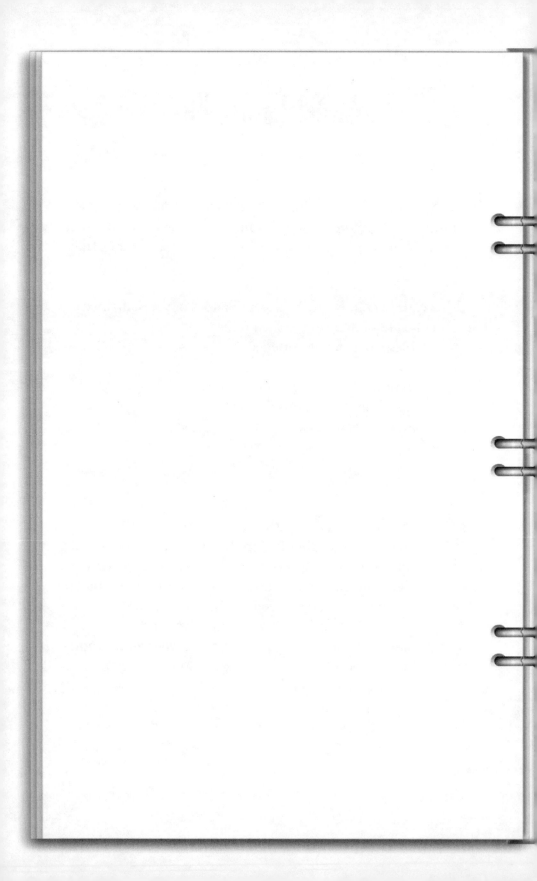

WEEK 4

Super Bowl Munchies

Can you believe it? It's the end of January already and the Super Bowl is here! We know what that means—a whole gang coming over to gather in front of the TV . . . and around the buffet table! Sometimes I wonder if maybe everybody just uses the game as an excuse to get together and eat! Well, it doesn't matter, 'cause with this menu, we're guaranteed to score big.

Touchdown Wings

Bread Bowl Chili

Halftime Hoagies

Super Bowl Pennant Cakes

Kickoff Punch

Touchdown Wings

4 to 6 servings

Let's put out a platter of these crispy wings to kick off our next Bowl game. Oh—don't forget lots of napkins!

    2 sticks (1 cup) butter, melted
    1 envelope (1 ounce) onion soup mix
    1 teaspoon ground red pepper
    5 pounds chicken wings (see Note)

Preheat the oven to 425°F. In a medium bowl, combine the butter, onion soup mix, and ground red pepper; mix well. Coat 2 large rimmed baking sheets with nonstick cooking spray. Place the chicken wings on the baking sheets and spoon the butter mixture evenly over them. Bake for 20 minutes, then turn the wings over and bake for 15 to 20 more minutes, or until no pink remains and the wings are crispy.

NOTE: Five-pound bags of split wings are usually available in the frozen meat section of your supermarket and they're perfect for this recipe. Just make sure they're thawed before using.

Bread Bowl Chili

8 servings

Don't worry about what to serve the chili in this year—simply serve it up in a bread bowl. And . . . the best part is we can eat up the sauce-soaked bowl when it's empty!

   2 pounds ground beef
   1 teaspoon minced garlic
   1 can (28 ounces) crushed tomatoes
   2 cans (15 ounces each) red kidney beans, undrained
   1 envelope (1 ounce) onion soup mix
   3 tablespoons chili powder
   8 kaiser rolls

In a soup pot, combine the ground beef and garlic over medium-high heat and brown for 10 minutes. Add the crushed tomatoes, kidney beans, onion soup mix, and chili powder; mix well and bring to a boil, stirring frequently. Reduce the heat to low and simmer for 30 minutes. Meanwhile, cut a 1½-inch circle off the top of each roll and remove. Hollow out the rolls, leaving ½ inch of bread around the sides, creating bowls; reserve the excess bread for dunking. Place the bread bowls on plates and spoon the chili into them, allowing the chili to over-flow.

NOTE: Make sure to have sour cream, chopped onions, and shredded cheese on hand to use as chili toppers.

Halftime Hoagies

4 to 8 servings

It's time for a change, so say good-bye to the same old deli sub and hello to a chicken breast hoagie. It's the best bet in the house!

> 1 cup salsa, divided
> 3 tablespoons honey
> 4 boneless, skinless chicken breast halves (1 to 1½ pounds total), each cut lengthwise into 3 strips
> ⅓ cup mayonnaise
> 4 hoagie rolls
> 2 cups shredded lettuce
> 1 large tomato, cut into 8 slices
> 4 slices (4 ounces) American cheese, each cut in half

Preheat the oven to 350°F. Coat a rimmed baking sheet with nonstick cooking spray. In a shallow dish, combine ½ cup salsa and the honey; mix well. Coat the chicken completely with the salsa mixture and place on the baking sheet. Spoon any remaining salsa mixture over the chicken and bake for 20 to 25 minutes, or until no pink remains. Meanwhile, in a small bowl, combine the mayonnaise and the remaining ½ cup salsa; spread over the hoagie rolls. Divide the lettuce, tomato, and cheese equally among the rolls and top with the chicken. Cut in half and serve immediately.

NOTE: If you prefer, you can cook the chicken ahead of time and serve these chilled. And why not serve a little extra salsa on the side for anybody who wants to add an extra kick!

Super Bowl Pennant Cakes

18 to 20 servings

Forget the pom-poms and marching band. All we'll need to cheer on our winning team is a slice of pennant cake and a tall glass of ice cold milk!

> 1 package (18.25 ounces) chocolate cake mix, batter
> prepared according to the package directions
> ½ gallon vanilla ice cream, softened
> 1 container (16 ounces) frozen whipped topping, thawed,
> divided
> Assorted food colors

Preheat the oven to 350°F. Line a 9" × 13" baking pan with aluminum foil and coat with nonstick cooking spray. Pour the cake batter into the pan. Bake for 30 to 35 minutes, or until a wooden toothpick inserted in the center comes out clean. Allow to cool completely in the pan. Spread the ice cream over the top, covering completely. Cover and freeze for at least 4 hours, or until firm. Uncover and invert the pan onto a cutting board, then remove the pan and aluminum foil. Slice the cake in half diagonally to form 2 pennant shapes. Place the cakes on 2 serving platters. Divide the whipped topping between 2 bowls and color each with food color to represent

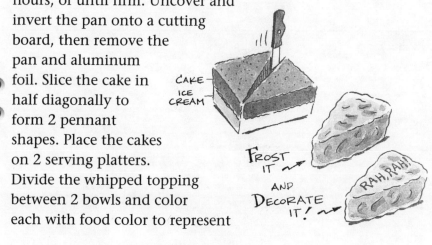

CAKE
ICE
CREAM

FROST IT
AND DECORATE IT!
RAH, RAH!

the two teams in the Super Bowl. Frost each pennant cake with a different-colored whipped topping. Freeze for at least 2 hours before serving. Once frozen, cover with plastic wrap.

NOTE: Use tubes of decorating gel to write the team names on the cakes. And while you're at it, why not sprinkle them with candies in the team colors?

Kickoff Punch

about 1 gallon, 12 to 16 servings

Looking for a change-of-pace adult drink to serve for kickoff? Look no more! Here's a punch that combines wine with fruit juice so we don't "feel the punch" quite so much.

2 bottles (48 ounces each) chilled cranberry juice cocktail
6 cups chilled Burgundy or other dry red wine
1 orange, sliced
1 lemon, sliced

Combine all the ingredients in a large punch bowl; mix well and serve.

NOTE: We can freeze half a bottle of the cranberry juice in a gelatin mold or small bowl for adding to the punch bowl right before serving. That way the punch stays cool without getting watered down.

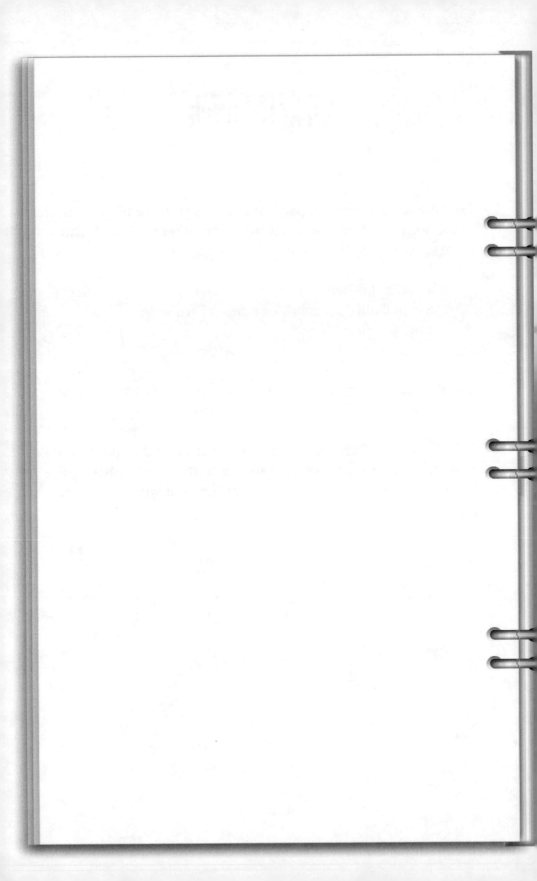

WEEK 5

Midwinter Picnic

By now, Old Man Winter has got you down. Wanna get rid of those winter blues? Well, just because it's chilly out, there's frost on the window, and your backyard is covered with snow, it doesn't mean you can't have a picnic! Yes—indoors! So crank up the thermostat, slip into shorts and T-shirts, spread out the blanket, and let the fun begin! Oh—I almost forgot! Know what the best part is? You don't have to worry about ants!

Barbecue-Style Chicken

Hot Bacon 'n' Potato Salad

Herbed Corn on the Cob

Caramel Ice Cream Balls

Minted Lemonade

Barbecue-Style Chicken

4 to 6 servings

Winter, spring, summer, or fall, any season will do for this out-door-barbecue-tasting, indoor-easy chicken.

> One 3- to 3½-pound chicken, cut into 8 pieces
> 1 cup ketchup
> ⅓ cup white vinegar
> ⅓ cup firmly packed light brown sugar
> ¼ cup lemon juice
> 1 teaspoon Worcestershire sauce
> 1 teaspoon black pepper

Preheat the oven to 425°F. Line a 9" × 13" baking pan with aluminum foil and coat with nonstick cooking spray. Place the chicken in the pan. In a large bowl, combine the remaining ingredients and pour over the chicken pieces. Bake for 60 to 65 minutes, or until no pink remains in the chicken, basting halfway through the cooking with the sauce from the pan. Serve the chicken with the sauce.

NOTE: If you want the chicken to have an extra-crispy coating, raise the oven temperature to 450°F. for the last 10 minutes of baking.

Hot Bacon 'n' Potato Salad

6 to 8 servings

Why in the world do we seem to make potato salad only in the summer? This one will surely make us want to have it as a year-round side dish from now on!

>5 pounds potatoes, washed and sliced ¼ inch thick
>1 teaspoon salt
>1 pound bacon
>2 cups mayonnaise
>½ cup sugar
>¼ cup white vinegar

Place the potatoes with the salt in a soup pot and add just enough water to cover them. Bring to a boil over high heat, then reduce the heat to medium and cook for 12 to 15 minutes, or until fork-tender; drain and place in a large bowl. Meanwhile, cook the bacon until crisp; let cool slightly, then crumble over the potatoes. Add the remaining ingredients; toss well. Serve hot.

NOTE: To give this a little more bacon flavor, add some of the bacon drippings along with the mayonnaise. And if you like your potato salad on the looser side, add up to an additional cup of mayonnaise. Don't worry if you can't make this right before serving; it tastes just as good chilled as it does hot.

Herbed Corn on the Cob

6 servings

No husking and no messy cleanup—just a rich, buttery herb taste for good old-fashioned eating.

> 3 tablespoons butter, softened
> 2 teaspoons finely chopped fresh dill
> 1 garlic clove, minced
> 1 package (6 small ears) frozen corn on the cob, cooked
>   according to the package directions

In a small bowl, combine the butter, dill, and garlic; mix well. Spread over the hot cooked corn and serve.

NOTE: Season with salt and pepper, if desired, and if you don't have any fresh dill on hand, don't worry—almost any fresh or dried herb can be used.

Caramel Ice Cream Balls

8 servings

Just because the temperature outside is chillier than our freezer, that's no reason not to make up a batch of novelty ice cream balls, is it? I don't think we can wait until spring for these!

    1 quart chocolate ice cream
    1½ cups crushed sugar wafer cookies
    1 cup caramel sauce, warmed

Line a rimmed baking sheet with waxed paper. Shape the ice cream into 8 equal rounded scoops and place on the baking sheet. Freeze for at least 1 hour, or until firm. Roll the ice cream balls in the crushed cookies, coating completely. Place in individual dessert bowls and drizzle with the caramel sauce. Serve immediately.

NOTE: If not serving immediately, after rolling the ice cream balls in the crushed cookies, return them to the baking sheet, cover, and freeze until ready to drizzle with caramel sauce and serve.

Minted Lemonade

about 2 quarts, 6 to 8 servings

All right, it's time to get out those oversized plastic picnic glasses and fill 'em with ice and some pure summer refreshment.

    8 cups (2 quarts) water
    1 cup sugar
    1 cup fresh mint leaves
    2 oranges, sliced
    1 cup fresh lemon juice

In a large saucepan, bring all the ingredients except the lemon juice to a rolling boil over high heat. Remove from the heat, cover, and allow to cool for 1 hour. Strain into a large pitcher, discarding the mint leaves. Add the lemon juice; mix well and serve over ice.

NOTE: For a true touch of summer, garnish each glass with a slice of lemon and a sprig of mint.

WEEK 6

Canned Food Creations

Wow! Time really flies—here it is February, and that means it's time to celebrate National Canned Food Month. So let's get right to it this week. Talk about quick and easy—we just have to take out the can opener and uncover all the goodies we've got right on hand in the pantry. Canned goods are great 'cause they keep for such a long time, they come in all sizes, and the processing methods are better than ever. Today's canned foods are chock-full of fresh taste and nutrition . . . and they're convenient, too, for all of us busy bees! (Sometimes I wonder why we don't celebrate canned food all year round!)

Marinated Salad

Cozy Beef Stew

Simple Peach Sorbet

Fruit Cocktail Cake

Marinated Salad

6 to 8 servings

This has got to be the simplest salad you can make! With all these yummy ingredients, it's gonna become a year-round winner at your house.

> 1 can (16 ounces) cut green beans, drained
> 1 can (15½ ounces) garbanzo beans (chick peas), drained
> 1 can (14 ounces) artichoke hearts, drained and quartered
> 1 can (5.75 ounces) large pitted black olives, drained
> 1 can (4 ounces) mushroom stems and pieces, drained
> 1 bottle (8 ounces) Italian dressing

In a large bowl, combine all the ingredients; mix well. Cover and chill for 1 hour; stir, then re-cover and chill for at least 1 more hour, or until completely chilled.

NOTE: Not only does this go together quickly, but it'll keep in the fridge for quite a few days.

Cozy Beef Stew

4 to 6 servings

This is the time of year when we want to come home to a hot and hearty meal. And after a busy day, the last thing we want to do is start chopping veggies for our stew. Who says we have to? We can use canned! They sure are a tasty, easy alternative!

> 2 tablespoons vegetable oil
> 2½ pounds beef stew meat, trimmed and cut into 1-inch chunks
> 1 medium onion, coarsely chopped
> 1 garlic clove, minced
> ½ teaspoon black pepper
> 2 cans (15 ounces each) mixed vegetables, undrained
> 1 can (15 ounces) whole potatoes, drained and quartered, with liquid reserved
> 1 can (14½ ounces) whole tomatoes, drained and quartered, with liquid reserved
> 1 can (10½ ounces) condensed beef broth

In a soup pot, heat the oil over high heat. Add the beef, onion, garlic, and pepper and cook for 10 minutes, or until the beef is browned, stirring frequently. Stir in the remaining ingredients, including the reserved liquids, and bring to a boil. Reduce the heat to medium and cook for 1 hour, or until the beef is tender and a thick gravy has formed, stirring occasionally.

NOTE: For a chunkier beef stew, use other types of canned vegetables—for instance, use a can of cut green beans and a can of sliced carrots instead of the 2 cans of mixed vegetables.

Simple Peach Sorbet

about 1 quart

Light and easy, this is a fruity treat that you can enjoy in a variety of flavors simply by changing the type of fruit you use. Pears and apricots work really great, too!

> 1 can (29 ounces) peaches in heavy syrup
> 1 tablespoon orange juice

Place the unopened can of peaches in the freezer until frozen solid, about 24 hours. Submerge the unopened can in very hot tap water for 1 minute. Open the can and pour any thawed syrup into the bowl of a food processor that has been fitted with its metal cutting blade. Remove the frozen fruit from the can and cut into large chunks; place in the food processor and add the orange juice. Process until smooth, scraping down the sides as needed. Serve immediately, or spoon into an airtight storage container; seal and keep frozen until ready to serve.

NOTE: For an even more heavenly flavor, substitute 1 tablespoon peach schnapps for the orange juice.

Fruit Cocktail Cake

12 to 15 servings

When I was coming up with recipes for this week, I thought, "What kind of cake uses canned food?" Then I remembered a cake I'd had years ago that was made with fruit cocktail . . . and I updated it to include lots of other goodies, too!

2¼ cups all-purpose flour
1 cup firmly packed light brown sugar
¼ cup (½ stick) butter, softened
1 can (17 ounces) fruit cocktail, undrained
2 eggs
2 teaspoons baking soda
1 teaspoon salt
½ cup semisweet chocolate chips
½ cup chopped pecans

Preheat the oven to 350°F. Coat a 9" × 13" baking pan with nonstick cooking spray. In a large bowl, with an electric beater on medium speed, beat the flour, brown sugar, butter, fruit cocktail, eggs, baking soda, and salt for 2 minutes, or until smooth. Pour into the baking pan and sprinkle the chocolate chips and pecans evenly over the top. Bake for 25 to 30 minutes, or until a wooden toothpick inserted in the center comes out clean. Allow to cool completely, then cut into squares and serve.

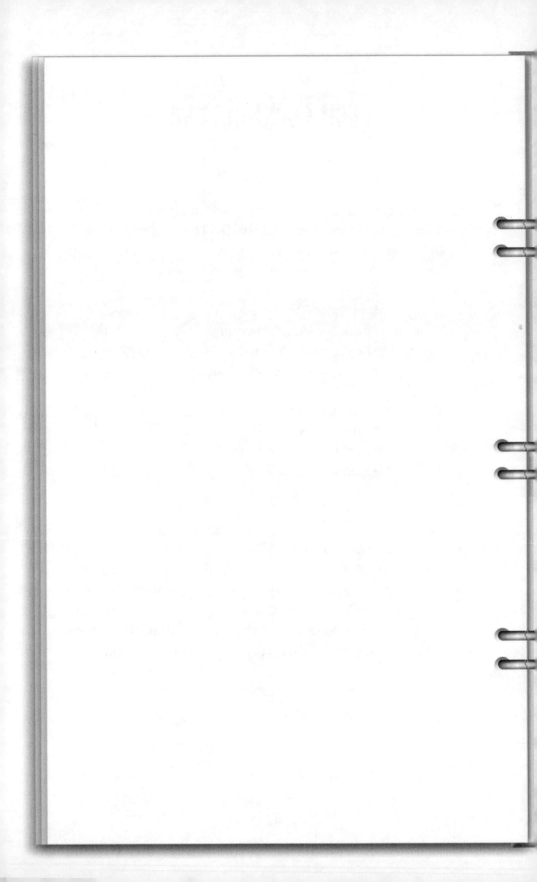

WEEK 7

Valentine's Day Dinner

Okay, all you romantics out there—get ready to dazzle that special someone! February 14 is Valentine's Day and, as the old saying goes, the way to someone's heart is through his or her stomach! And we're ready! Who needs Cupid when we have these delectable goodies—guaranteed to melt their hearts!

Two-Hearts Salad

Veal with Artichoke Hearts

Red Pepper Pilaf

Strawberry Sweetheart Cake

Two-Hearts Salad

2 servings

I've coupled hearts of palm and romaine to make this winning salad combo for two! Of course, it's so good that you may want to serve it to company sometime. (It's still easy—even when you're doubling the recipe.)

> 1 can (14 ounces) hearts of palm, drained and sliced ½ inch thick (see Note)
> 2 tablespoons mayonnaise
> 2 tablespoons sour cream
> 2 tablespoons fresh lemon juice
> ⅛ teaspoon minced garlic
> Heart of 1 head of romaine lettuce, cut lengthwise in half (see Note)
> 2 cherry tomatoes, cut in half

In a medium bowl, combine the hearts of palm, mayonnaise, sour cream, lemon juice, and garlic; mix well. Place each half of the romaine heart on an individual serving plate. Spoon the hearts of palm mixture over the romaine, dividing it evenly, and top with the cherry tomatoes. Serve, or chill until ready to serve.

NOTE: When you're chopping the hearts of palm, make sure to separate the rings after slicing and before combining with the other ingredients. What are hearts of romaine, you're wondering? They're the lighter green inside leaves that are the most tender and crisp. Many produce counters now sell them cleaned, packaged, and ready to go, but you can prepare them yourself by removing the dark green outside leaves from a whole head of romaine; reserve those for another use. After all, it's Valentine's Day and your sweetie deserves only the best!

Veal with Artichoke Hearts

2 servings

Get out your best china, fill your glasses with champagne, light the candles, and get ready to enjoy this elegant-easy main dish! It's just like restaurant-style veal française—without a lot of work . . . but with all the flavor!

   ¼ cup all-purpose flour
   ¼ teaspoon salt
   ¼ teaspoon black pepper
   ½ pound veal cutlets, pounded to ¼-inch thickness (see Note)
   ¼ cup (½ stick) butter
   1 can (14 ounces) artichoke hearts, drained and quartered
   1 tablespoon lemon juice
   ½ cup dry white wine

In a shallow dish, combine the flour, salt, and pepper; mix well. Coat the veal cutlets with the flour mixture. In a large skillet, melt the butter over medium heat. Add the coated veal cutlets and brown on both sides. Add the artichoke hearts, lemon juice, and wine; mix well. Cook for 2 to 3 minutes, or until heated through. Serve immediately.

NOTE: Depending on the size of the veal cutlets, they can be left whole or cut into smaller medallions before cooking.

Red Pepper Pilaf

When it comes to adding color to a recipe, red bell pepper is tops! And what better holiday than Valentine's Day to make good use of it—especially to brighten up our special rice!

    1 tablespoon butter
    1 cup long- or whole-grain rice, divided
    1 medium onion, finely chopped
    1 can (14½ ounces) ready-to-use-chicken broth
    ¼ cup water
    ½ of a medium red bell pepper, finely chopped

In a large skillet, melt the butter over high heat. Add ½ cup rice and brown, stirring constantly. Add the remaining rice, the onion, chicken broth, and water and bring to a boil. Reduce the heat to medium-low, cover, and simmer for 15 minutes. Stir in the red pepper and cook until heated through.

NOTE: I know this may make more rice than you need for two, but I think it's handy to have some left over for another meal.

Strawberry Sweetheart Cake

16 to 20 servings

Boy, oh boy—this one makes enough for all your loved ones! It's the cake I'm holding on the book cover. Just wait till they take a look and a taste of *yours!* This yummy confetti cake topped with whipped topping and brimming with ruby-red berries screams "I love you!" Why not make it for dessert for your romantic dinner . . . and the next day, share it with the kids!

> ¼ cup rainbow sprinkles
> 1 package (18.25 ounces) yellow cake mix, batter prepared according to the package directions (see Note)
> 1 container (8 ounces) frozen whipped topping, thawed
> 2 quarts fresh strawberries, washed and hulled

Preheat the oven according to the package directions. Stir the sprinkles into the cake batter; pour equal amounts into one 8-inch square pan and one 8-inch round pan. Bake according

to package directions. Let cool slightly, then remove to a wire rack to cool completely. Place the square cake on a large platter. Cut the round cake in half and place on the platter as shown in the illustration. Frost the top and sides with the whipped topping. Place the strawberries stem end down in the whipped topping, completely covering the top of the cake. Serve, or cover loosely and chill until ready to serve.

NOTE: Almost any flavor of cake mix can be used, including strawberry.

WEEK 8

Presidents' Day Salute

It's an American tradition to honor Presidents Washington and Lincoln at this time of year—and what better way than with classic foods that combine old-fashioned goodness with the easy methods and tastes of today? Now, when the third Monday of February gets here, be sure to have a few birthday candles on hand to help with the celebration!

Presidential Honey Walnut Salad

Shortnin' Bread

Colonial Spinach

Crusted Baked Salmon

Tart Cherry Pie

Presidential Honey Walnut Salad

4 to 6 servings

In honor of our very first president, let's make this super salad with sweet dark pitted cherries topping it. I cannot tell a lie—George would have loved it!

    ¼ cup chopped walnuts
    2 tablespoons peanut oil
    ½ cup Italian dressing
    ⅓ cup honey
    ¼ cup maple syrup
    1 head romaine lettuce, cut into bite-sized pieces
    1 can (17 ounces) sweet dark pitted cherries, drained

In a medium saucepan, brown the walnuts in the oil over medium heat for 3 to 5 minutes, stirring occasionally. Add the Italian dressing, honey, and maple syrup. Reduce the heat to low and simmer for 5 to 7 minutes, or until hot. Place the lettuce in a large bowl and toss with the dressing. Top with the cherries and serve warm.

NOTE: If you don't like cherries, you can use other types of canned fruit, like mandarin oranges, or even pineapple for a tropical-tasting salad.

Shortnin' Bread

3 dozen squares

Shortnin' bread is a southern classic. And by adding a bit of fresh dill to make it extra-special, I've brought this melt-in-your-mouth bread up to date. So give it a try, 'cause North or South, East or West, it's still a hit.

    3 cups all-purpose flour
    ⅓ cup sugar
    1 cup (2 sticks) butter, softened
    1 egg yolk
    1 tablespoon chopped fresh dill

Preheat the oven to 325°F. In a large bowl, with a pastry cutter or 2 knives, combine all the ingredients until crumbly. Using your hands, form into a smooth ball and pat evenly into an 8-inch square baking dish. Prick the top all over with a fork and bake for 30 to 35 minutes, or until golden. Allow to cool and cut into 36 squares.

NOTE: No dill? No problem! 'Cause without it, this is like a sweet shortbread-type biscuit.

Colonial Spinach

4 to 6 servings

The colonists may have had just as much trouble as we do getting the kids to eat spinach! So, how'd *they* do it? Probably with something like this.

    1 medium onion, grated
    ¼ cup (½ stick) butter
    2 packages (10 ounces each) fresh spinach, trimmed,
        washed, and dried
    1 teaspoon dried rosemary
    ½ teaspoon salt
    ¼ teaspoon black pepper

In a soup pot, brown the onion in the butter over medium heat. Add the remaining ingredients and cook for 3 to 5 minutes, or until the spinach wilts, stirring occasionally.

NOTE: Here's a tip for easier cooking: Add half the spinach at a time. When the first half cooks down a bit, add the remaining spinach.

Crusted Baked Salmon

4 servings

The abundance of salmon in the eastern waterways made it a favorite in colonial times. We're lucky that today's fish counters are brimming with fresh fillets, so we get to take advantage of this tasty recipe without having to take out our fishing rods!

> 4 salmon fillets (about 1½ pounds total)
> 1 teaspoon ground nutmeg
> ¼ teaspoon salt
> ¼ teaspoon black pepper
> ¼ cup (½ stick) butter
> ½ cup plain dry bread crumbs

Preheat the oven to 450°F. Coat a large rimmed baking sheet with nonstick cooking spray. Season the salmon with the nutmeg, salt, and pepper and place on the baking sheet. In a small saucepan, melt the butter over medium heat. Stir in the bread crumbs and cook until lightly browned. Spoon over the salmon, completely covering the tops of the fillets. Bake for 10 to 12 minutes, or until the salmon flakes easily with a fork. Serve immediately.

NOTE: The bread crumbs can be made from leftover bread that has been toasted and crumbled (that's the old-fashioned way to do it!). And remember—different types of bread will add different flavors to the salmon.

Tart Cherry Pie

6 to 8 servings

Okay, okay . . . we've all heard the old story about George Washington and the cherry tree. Well, whether it actually happened is something we'll never know for sure, but what we do know is that he's forever going to be linked to cherry trees—so let's celebrate old George as we sink our teeth into this scrumptious cherry pie.

> 1 package (15 ounces) folded refrigerated pie crusts
> 2 cans (16 ounces each) pitted tart red cherries in water, drained, with ½ cup liquid reserved
> 1½ cups sugar
> ¼ cup cornstarch
> ½ teaspoon lemon juice
> ¼ teaspoon red food color

Unfold 1 pie crust and place in a 9-inch pie plate, pressing it firmly against the plate; set aside. In a medium saucepan, cook the reserved ½ cup cherry liquid, the sugar, cornstarch, lemon juice, and red food color over medium heat for 5 to 6 minutes, or until thickened, stirring constantly. Stir in the cherries and pour into the pie crust. Unfold the second pie crust and place over the filling. Trim and pinch the edges together to seal, and flute, if desired. Using a sharp knife, cut four 1-inch slits in the top. Bake for 45 to 50 minutes, or until the crust is golden. Allow to cool slightly, then serve, or cover and chill until ready to serve.

NOTE: Nothing beats cherry pie à la mode, so you've gotta serve this with some vanilla ice cream for a dessert they won't soon forget.

WEEK 9

Homemade Takeout

Here comes the parade of colorful costumes, dragons, and, oh yes, lots of fireworks! Yup, the Chinese New Year begins sometime between mid-January and mid-February each year, and if you're lucky enough to be around when the celebration starts, you'll see it's the brightest party to hit the streets! So get ready for some Asian taste and excitement!

Easy Egg Rolls

Velvet Corn Soup

Pork Lo Mein

Kung Pao Beef

Almond Cookies

Easy Egg Rolls

1 dozen

Can't believe we can make our own egg rolls at home? It's a cinch—without a deep fryer! And for seafood lovers, these are filled with mini shrimp! But cooked shredded chicken or beef works great, too.

    1 can (14 ounces) bean sprouts, well drained
    1 can (6 ounces) shrimp, drained and chopped
    8 scallions, chopped
    2 celery stalks, chopped
    1 medium carrot, grated
    1 tablespoon soy sauce
    ½ teaspoon ground ginger
    12 egg roll skins (see Note)
    1 egg, beaten
    2 tablespoons vegetable oil

Preheat the oven to 450°F. Coat a rimmed baking sheet with nonstick cooking spray. In a large bowl, combine the bean sprouts, shrimp, scallions, celery, carrot, soy sauce, and ginger; mix well. Place an equal amount of the mixture in the center of each egg roll skin. Brush the edges of the skins with the beaten egg and fold as illustrated. Place on the baking sheet and brush

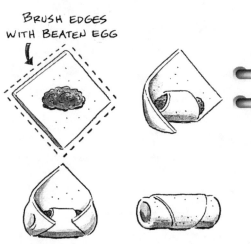

BRUSH EDGES
WITH BEATEN EGG

with the vegetable oil. Bake for 12 to 15 minutes, or until crisp and golden.

NOTE: Egg roll skins can usually be found in the supermarket produce or freezer section. All you have to do is ask for them! Be careful when serving these right out of the oven, 'cause the filling will still be very hot. Oh—don't forget the sweet-and-sour sauce and spicy mustard for dipping!

Velvet Corn Soup

6 to 8 servings

When it comes to Chinese soup, most Americans think of won-ton and egg drop first. We sure love those, but how 'bout adding another one to our list of favorites? This velvety soup is company-fancy, but so easy. They won't believe you made it yourself!

    4 cans (14½ ounces each) ready-to-use chicken broth
    2 cans (14¾ ounces each) cream-style corn
    2 tablespoons soy sauce
    2 tablespoons cold water
    2 tablespoons cornstarch
    2 eggs, slightly beaten
    2 scallions, thinly sliced

In a soup pot, bring the chicken broth and corn to a boil over high heat. In a small bowl, combine the soy sauce, water, and cornstarch until smooth. Add to the chicken broth mixture and boil for 2 to 4 minutes, or until slightly thickened. Remove from the heat and swirl the beaten eggs slowly into the soup, forming cooked egg strands. Top with the sliced scallions and serve.

NOTE: For a heartier soup, add an extra can of creamed corn or some cooked noodles or rice.

Pork Lo Mein

6 to 8 servings

Lo mein sounds fancy, but it's really just a Chinese version of spaghetti! And now that we know that it's something we can make at home, we can pass out the chopsticks and surprise the gang with this restaurant-style favorite!

> 1 pound spaghetti
> ¾ cup chicken broth
> ½ cup soy sauce
> 2 teaspoons sugar
> 2 tablespoons peanut oil
> 2 pork tenderloins (about 2 pounds total), thinly sliced
> 8 scallions, thinly sliced
> ½ pound fresh mushrooms, sliced
> ½ pound fresh snow peas, trimmed

Prepare the spaghetti according to the package directions; drain and keep warm in a large serving bowl. Meanwhile, in a small bowl, combine the chicken broth, soy sauce, and sugar; mix well and set aside. In a large skillet, heat the oil over high heat. Add the pork and cook until no longer pink, stirring constantly. Add the scallions, mushrooms, snow peas, and the chicken broth mixture. Stir-fry for 3 to 5 minutes, or until the vegetables are crisp-tender. Toss with the spaghetti and serve.

NOTE: This can also be made with beef or chicken—just slice it thin and stir-fry until no longer pink, then proceed as above.

Kung Pao Beef

6 to 8 servings

You might know this as "#42" or "#18," . . . or maybe you'll find it under "Column A" on your favorite Chinese restaurant menu. Now, you may have trouble pronouncing this, but you won't have any trouble preparing it! I found all the shortcuts, and I'm passing them on to you. One taste of this super beefy main dish will have you putting it on *your* menu again and again.

> ½ cup teriyaki sauce
> 2 tablespoons cornstarch
> 1 teaspoon crushed red pepper
> ½ teaspoon ground ginger
> 2 pounds flank steak, thinly sliced
> 1 tablespoon vegetable oil
> ⅔ cup salted peanuts
> 4 scallions, thinly sliced

In a large bowl, combine the teriyaki sauce, cornstarch, crushed red pepper, and ginger. Add the flank steak and toss to coat. In a large skillet, heat the oil over high heat. Add the steak mixture and cook for 5 to 7 minutes, or until the steak is cooked through, stirring constantly. Sprinkle with the peanuts and scallions and serve.

NOTE: Wanna be restaurant-authentic? Serve this over steamed white rice.

Almond Cookies

about 4 dozen

I have to admit that I was determined to make fortune cookies, but after four disastrous attempts, I gave up on all the rolling, folding, and baking and realized that it wasn't going to be a Mr. Food type of recipe! Instead, I found a Chinese cookie they'll be "nuts" about . . . and, yes, these are very easy to make!

1 cup (2 sticks) butter, softened
1 cup sugar
1 egg
4 teaspoons almond extract
2½ cups all-purpose flour
1½ teaspoons baking soda
½ teaspoon salt
About ⅓ cup blanched almonds

Preheat the oven to 350°F. Coat 2 large baking sheets with non-stick cooking spray. In a medium bowl, with an electric beater on medium speed, cream the butter and sugar. Add the egg and almond extract; mix well. Add the flour, baking soda, and salt; beat until well combined and the dough is stiff. Roll into 1-inch balls and place on the baking sheets. Flatten slightly and press an almond gently into the top of each cookie. Bake for 8 to 10 minutes, or until light golden. Remove to a wire rack to cool completely.

NOTE: You can add a little more or less almond extract, depending on how "almondy" you want the cookies to be.

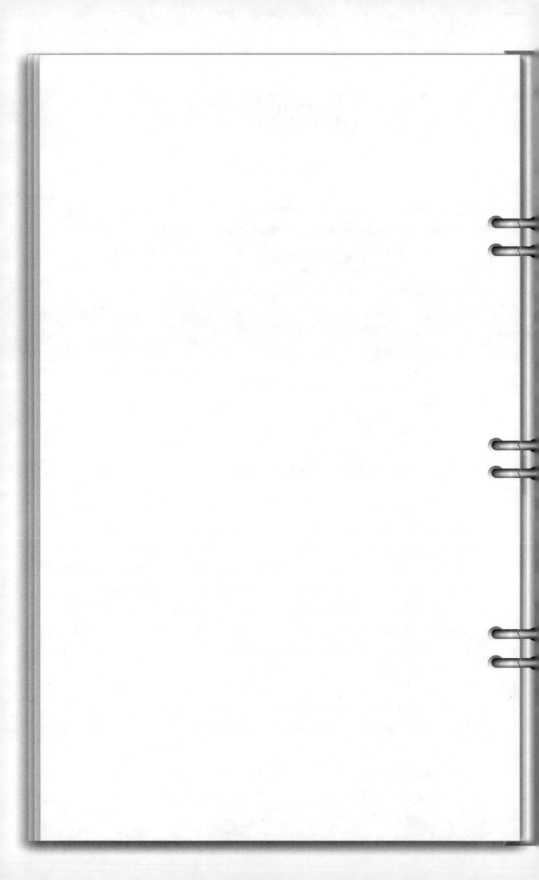

WEEK 10

Mardi Gras Feast

New Orleans sure is one city that knows how to throw a party! And since everybody loves a party, every year millions of people come from around the world to be part of the two-week-long celebration that ends on the Tuesday before Ash Wednesday, called Fat Tuesday (that's the translation of *Mardi Gras*). Mardi Gras is like a huge festival chock-full of great Cajun and Creole food, jazzy drinks, and super Dixieland and blues music! Sure, it's fun to experience it all firsthand, but if we can't be there in person, there are plenty of mouthwatering dishes we can concoct right at home to give us a taste of Bourbon Street and the famous French Quarter.

Eye of a Hurricane

"Jazzed-Up" Shrimp Étouffée

Festive Rice

Quick Beignets

Easy King Cake

Eye of a Hurricane

about 1½ quarts, 4 to 6 servings

It's the perfect time to throw a party and refresh the gang with a tropical-tasting "pick-me-up." This is a nonalcoholic spin-off of the popular drink traditionally enjoyed by Mardi Gras revelers!

    1 can (12 ounces) frozen tropical punch concentrate, thawed
    1 bottle (7 ounces) Roses® sweetened lime juice
    1 liter lemon-lime-flavored seltzer

Combine all the ingredients in a large pitcher; mix well. Serve in individual glasses over ice.

NOTE: For a real eye-popping Hurricane, garnish each glass with an orange slice and a cherry. And if you'd prefer a frosty Hurricane, put all the ingredients, plus a cup or so of ice, in a blender and give it a whirl. Wanna enjoy the real thing? Call Pat O'Brien's Bar at 1–800–597–4823. They're right in the heart of the French Quarter, and they'll ship the "have-fun" flavor of the original Hurricane right to your doorstep!

"Jazzed-Up" Shrimp Étouffée

6 to 8 servings

Boy, oh boy, it sure is simple to get everybody's attention! No, it doesn't take a fancy cooking course to turn out fancy-looking and -tasting Creole dishes. There's no big secret with this one— garlic and ground red pepper add all the pizzazz!

> 2 medium onions, chopped
> 1 medium green bell pepper, chopped
> 4 celery stalks, chopped
> 4 garlic cloves, minced
> 3 tablespoons all-purpose flour
> ½ cup (1 stick) butter
> 2 pounds shrimp, peeled and deveined, with tails left on
> ¾ teaspoon ground red pepper
> 1 teaspoon salt
> 1 cup chicken broth

In a medium bowl, combine the onions, bell pepper, celery, garlic, and flour; mix well. Melt the butter in a large skillet over medium heat. Add the onion mixture and cook for 5 minutes, stirring frequently. Season the shrimp with the ground red pepper and salt and add to the skillet. Add the broth and cook for 8 to 10 minutes, or until the shrimp turn pink and the vegetables are tender, stirring occasionally.

NOTE: Serve over Festive Rice (page 62) for a meal fit for a king.

Festive Rice

6 to 8 servings

If you've ever been to Mardi Gras, then you know that there are loads of parades during the two-week celebration . . . and you also know about all the streamers, beads, and confetti that get thrown around the parade routes! Well, with all the tiny flecks of fresh veggies sprinkled throughout, this rice reminds me of all the colorful Mardi Gras festivities!

> 2 cups parboiled rice (see Note)
> 1 can (14½ ounces) ready-to-use chicken broth
> ⅓ cup water
> 2 scallions, finely chopped
> ½ of a small red bell pepper, finely chopped
> ¼ cup chopped fresh parsley
> ¼ teaspoon garlic powder

In a medium saucepan, bring all the ingredients to a boil over medium-high heat, stirring occasionally. Reduce the heat to low, cover, and cook for 14 to 16 minutes, or until the water is absorbed and the rice is tender.

NOTE: Parboiled rice is the generic name for rice that has been partially cooked. It can be found along with the other rice products in the supermarket.

Quick Beignets

about 3½ dozen

When I go to New Orleans, I look forward to enjoying the fresh hot beignets. What are they? They're puffy pastries traditionally coated with confectioners' sugar. And now we can make them at home in no time, 'cause these start with store-bought bread dough.

> 1 loaf (16 ounces) frozen bread dough, thawed
> ¼ cup plus 1 tablespoon confectioners' sugar, divided
> 2 cups vegetable shortening

In a medium bowl, combine the bread dough and 1 tablespoon confectioners' sugar; mix well. Lightly flour a cutting board and, with a floured rolling pin, roll out the dough to an 8" × 20" rectangle. Cut into 2-inch squares. Heat the shortening in a large deep skillet over medium heat until hot. Add the dough squares a few at a time and cook in batches for about 1 minute, or until golden, turning halfway through the cooking. Drain on a paper towel–lined platter. Sprinkle the beignets with the remaining ¼ cup confectioners' sugar and serve warm.

NOTE: Served with chicory coffee or café au lait, which is simply a mix of half hot coffee and half hot milk, these are the perfect way to start any day.

Easy King Cake

Yup, it's the one and only tricolored Mardi Gras favorite dessert! The story goes like this: Traditionally, a little plastic toy king was baked right into the cake, and whoever was served the piece of cake containing the king had to throw the next party! Well, we've made it even easier—no need to search for tiny plastic kings—just place a gumdrop in the batter and bake. The finder hosts next year's bash! Oh—you'll often find this as a braided, more yeasty type of cake. This is a simplified version, so it's more cakey and it's not braided, but it does have the traditional colors decorating the top. And what do they signify? Purple stands for Justice, green is for Faith, and gold is for Power! So, you see, this is no ordinary cake!

> 1 tablespoon grated lemon peel
> 1½ teaspoons ground nutmeg
> 1 gumdrop
> 1 package (18.25 ounces) yellow cake mix, batter prepared
>   according to the package directions
> 1½ cups confectioners' sugar
> 1 tablespoon lemon juice
> 1 tablespoon water
> 3 tablespoons granulated sugar, divided
> Red, blue, yellow, and green food color

Preheat the oven to 350°F. Coat a 9" × 13" baking pan with non-stick cooking spray. Add the lemon peel, nutmeg, and gumdrop to the cake batter and bake in the prepared pan according to the package directions. Cool completely on a wire rack. In a small bowl, combine the confectioners' sugar, lemon juice, and water until the mixture forms a creamy glaze. Spread the glaze over the top of the cake. Place 1 tablespoon granulated sugar into each of 3 small resealable plastic storage bags. Add 1 drop of red and 1 drop of blue food color to one bag to create purple sugar; mix well. Add 2 drops of yellow food color to another bag; mix well. Add 2 drops of green food color to the remaining bag; mix well. Sprinkle the colored sugars over the glaze to decorate as desired.

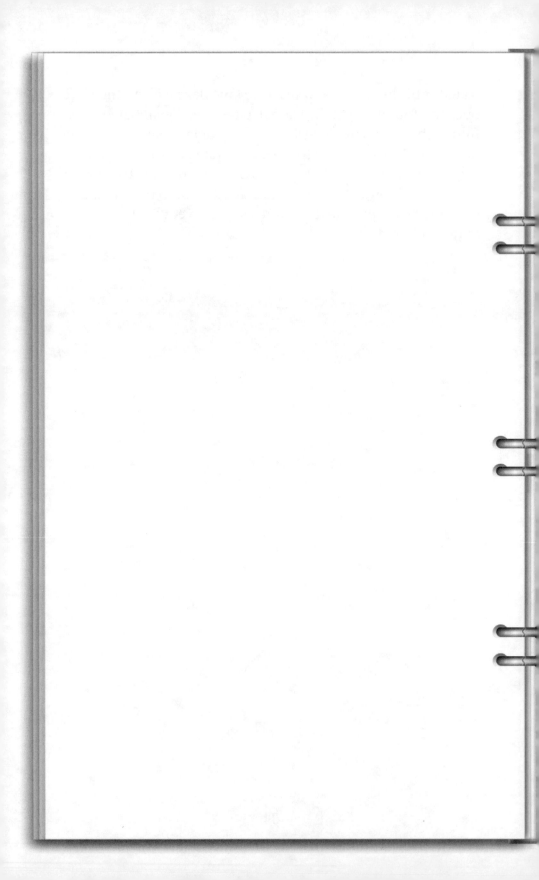

WEEK 11

March Madness Buffet

For all of us college basketball fans, the beginning of March means one thing—it's play-off time and we're gearing up to cheer for our favorite team! What better way than inviting the gang over to watch it all on television and enjoy some tasty treats at the same time! With all the excitement, the last thing we want is a lot of work or cleanup, so we're looking for easy, mouthwatering snacks that'll fill them up and keep us "cooks" out of the kitchen and in front of the TV . . . where all the action is!

Creamy Salsa Two-Step

"Timeout" Stuffed Spuds

Hot-Shot Meatball Hoagies

Nutty Caramel Corn

Peanut Butter Chippies

Creamy Salsa Two-Step

12 to 16 servings

Know what I like about this one? There are just two ingredients and two steps to a tongue-tingling spread that makes any party a slam-dunk success!

    2 packages (8 ounces each) reduced-fat cream cheese,
        softened
    1 cup salsa

Preheat the oven to 350°F. In a large bowl, with an electric beater on low speed, beat the cream cheese and salsa until well mixed. Spread in a 9-inch pie plate and bake for 20 to 25 minutes, or until heated through and the top is golden.

NOTE: Remember—this can be as spicy or as mild as you like, depending on the salsa you use. To add an extra touch of color, top it with chopped scallions or sliced olives before serving. And make sure to serve it with plenty of crackers.

"Timeout" Stuffed Spuds

1 dozen

When a timeout is called, it's a great time to take a break from the action and sink your teeth into everybody's favorite finger food—potato skins! This batch is stuffed with a delicious hot chicken salad that makes it as good as a three-point play!

6 large baking potatoes
¼ cup vegetable oil
½ teaspoon salt
¼ teaspoon black pepper
1 can (10 ounces) white chunk chicken, drained and flaked
2 cups (8 ounces) shredded pepper-Jack cheese, divided
3 scallions, chopped
¼ cup mayonnaise

Preheat the oven to 400°F. Scrub the potatoes and pierce the skins several times with a fork. Bake for 55 to 60 minutes (or microwave for 12 to 15 minutes), until tender. (Leave the oven on.) Allow to cool slightly, then cut each potato lengthwise in half. Using a spoon, scoop out the pulp, leaving a ¼-inch-thick shell; reserve the pulp for another use. In a medium bowl, combine the oil, salt, and pepper. Rub the potato shells inside and out with the oil mixture, coating completely, and place on a large rimmed baking sheet. In another medium bowl, combine the chicken, 1 cup cheese, the scallions, and mayonnaise; mix well and spoon equally into the potato shells. Sprinkle with the remaining 1 cup cheese. Bake for 30 to 40 minutes, or until the edges are crispy and brown.

NOTE: If you'd like, go ahead and load these up with additional toppings like sour cream or bacon bits just before serving.

Hot-Shot Meatball Hoagies

8 servings

It's easy to take the ho-hum out of the game-time menu. How? Serve up a batch of meatballs, fresh hoagie rolls, and this choice of Italian- and German-style sauces . . . and let 'em choose their favorite flavors.

> 4 pounds ground beef
> 2 cans (2.8 ounces each) French-fried onions, coarsely crushed
> 1 cup Italian-flavored bread crumbs
> 4 eggs
> 1 teaspoon salt
> 1 teaspoon black pepper
> 1 jar (18 ounces) beef gravy
> 1 tablespoon prepared white horseradish, drained
> 1 jar (26 ounces) spaghetti sauce
> ¼ cup grated Parmesan cheese
> 8 hoagie rolls, split

Preheat the oven to 350°F. In a large bowl, combine the ground beef, onions, bread crumbs, eggs, salt, and pepper; mix well. Shape into 24 meatballs and place on a large rimmed baking sheet. Bake for 18 to 20 minutes, or until cooked through and no pink remains. Meanwhile, in a medium saucepan, combine the gravy and horseradish over low heat. In another medium saucepan, combine the spaghetti sauce and Parmesan cheese over low heat. Simmer both sauces for 5 minutes, or until heated through, stirring occasionally. Place 3 meatballs on each hoagie roll and serve with bowls of each sauce for topping the sandwiches.

Nutty Caramel Corn

about 13 cups

When the ref makes a nutty call, you might be tempted to throw this crunchy treat at the TV . . . but don't do it! (He's not worth it!)

  1 cup firmly packed light brown sugar
  ½ cup (1 stick) butter
  ¼ cup honey
  1 teaspoon vanilla extract
  12 cups popped popcorn
  1 can (12 ounces) mixed nuts

Preheat the oven to 250°F. In a small saucepan, bring the brown sugar, butter, and honey to a boil over medium-high heat and cook for 5 minutes, stirring frequently. Remove from the heat and add the vanilla; mix well. In a large bowl, combine the popcorn and nuts. Pour the brown sugar mixture over the popcorn and nuts and stir until thoroughly coated. Spoon onto 2 ungreased large rimmed baking sheets and bake for 1 hour, stirring every 15 minutes. Let cool completely, until crispy. Serve, or store in an airtight container until ready to serve.

NOTE: Hey . . . March is National Peanut Month, so in celebration, why not make this caramel corn with only peanuts instead of mixed nuts?

Peanut Butter Chippies

about 4 dozen

When our team wins a play-off game, it's time to cheer. And these chippies are perfect for celebrating the sweet victory.

    1 package (18.25 ounces) chocolate cake mix
    2 eggs
    ½ cup water
    ⅓ cup creamy peanut butter
    3 tablespoons vegetable oil
    1½ cups coarsely crushed peanut butter sandwich cookies

Preheat the oven to 350°F. Coat 2 baking sheets with nonstick cooking spray. In a large bowl, with an electric beater on medium speed, beat all the ingredients except the crushed cookies until well mixed. Stir in the crushed cookies. Drop by rounded teaspoonfuls 2 inches apart onto the baking sheets. Bake for 8 to 10 minutes, or until light brown around the edges. Remove to wire racks to cool before serving.

NOTE: Sure, go ahead—use crunchy peanut butter to give your cookies an extra crunch.

WEEK 12

St. Patrick's Day Dinner

As the saying goes, "On St. Patrick's Day, every-body's Irish!" So let's all have a wee bit o' fun for the week of March 17 and cook up some tradi-tional goodies. Now it can't hurt to wear a little green for good luck—and you never know when we'll come across a four-leaf clover . . . or a lep-rechaun! But no matter—whether we're trying out some new tastes or enjoying an old favorite, these'll surely be hits with everyone! And it can be our secret that they're so versatile, we can enjoy them any time of year!

Cranberry Irish Soda Bread

Corned Beef and Carrots

Irish Potatoes

Minty Ice Cream Pie

Irish Coffee

Cranberry Irish Soda Bread

8 to 12 servings

This "berry easy" homemade bread is a cinch to make! And whether or not you're Irish, the fruity flavor of cranberries bursting from this bread will make it a favorite standard in your house. Oh—right after it cools, make sure to wrap and hide it well so a leprechaun won't eat it all up!

> 4 cups all-purpose flour
> 2 cups buttermilk
> 1 cup sweetened dried cranberries (see Note)
> ⅔ cup sugar
> ½ cup plus 1 tablespoon butter, melted, divided
> 2 eggs, beaten
> 2 teaspoons baking powder
> ¼ teaspoon baking soda
> ¼ teaspoon salt

Preheat the oven to 350°F. Coat a 9-inch round cake pan with nonstick cooking spray. In a large bowl, combine all the ingredients except 1 tablespoon melted butter; mix just until the dry ingredients are moistened. Pour into the cake pan and bake for 55 to 60 minutes, or until a wooden toothpick inserted in the center comes out clean. Brush the top with the remaining 1 tablespoon melted butter, then cut into wedges and serve warm.

NOTE: I know it's a little untraditional to use sweetened dried cranberries, but when I tried it, I loved it! If you don't have them, though, go ahead and use raisins.

74

Corned Beef and Carrots

6 to 8 servings

Nope, it's not a misprint—this tender corned beef is cooked up with sweet baby carrots, not cabbage. Wait'll you taste it! And if you think I've forgotten the cabbage . . . no way! Just check out the rest of this week's menu!

> One 3- to 3½-pound corned beef brisket with pickling spices
> 8 cups (2 quarts) water
> 1 tablespoon pickling spice
> 1 package (1 pound) peeled baby carrots (see Note)
> 3 medium onions, quartered

In a soup pot, bring the corned beef and its pickling spices, the water, and the additional 1 tablespoon pickling spice to a boil over high heat. Reduce the heat to low, cover, and simmer for 2 to 2½ hours, or until the meat is almost fork-tender. Add the carrots and onions and cook, covered, for 25 to 30 minutes, or until the vegetables and corned beef are fork-tender. Place the corned beef on a cutting board and slice across the grain. Drain the carrots and onions and serve with the sliced corned beef.

NOTE: It's so easy to use packaged peeled baby carrots, but sure, you can use regular carrots if you'd rather—just cut them into 1-inch chunks.

Irish Potatoes

6 to 8 servings

No self-respecting St. Patrick's Day corned beef would be complete without the crunch and taste of cabbage! Well, we've simply made it partners with our mashed potatoes to get an old favorite that's traditionally called colcannon.

> ¼ cup (½ stick) butter
> 1 small head cabbage, shredded (about 8 cups)
> ½ cup water
> ½ teaspoon salt
> ½ teaspoon black pepper
> 3 cups warm mashed potatoes (see Note)

Melt the butter in a large skillet over medium heat. Add the shredded cabbage, water, salt, and pepper; cover and cook for 15 minutes, stirring occasionally. Uncover and cook for 5 more minutes, or until the cabbage is wilted, stirring frequently. Add the potatoes and mix just until combined; serve.

NOTE: Season your potatoes with extra salt and pepper if desired, and don't worry about using instant mashed potatoes. (That's what I do!)

Minty Ice Cream Pie

8 servings

There's nothing more light and refreshing than the taste of mint after a big meal! And when we're celebrating by wearin' a bit o' the green, what better choice could we have than a slice of this creamy smooth pie?!

> 1 package (4.67 ounces) chocolate-covered thin mint candies
> 1 quart vanilla ice cream, softened
> 2 teaspoons crème de menthe liqueur, divided
> One 9-inch chocolate graham cracker pie crust

Reserve 8 thin mint candies, then chop the remaining candies and place in a large bowl. Add the ice cream and 1 teaspoon crème de menthe; mix well and spoon into the pie crust. Sprinkle with the remaining 1 teaspoon crème de menthe. Garnish with the reserved thin mint candies, pressing until the candies are halfway into the ice cream. Cover and freeze for at least 4 hours, or until firm. Slice and serve.

NOTE: If you don't have the crème de menthe liqueur, just mix in a few drops of green food color and 1 teaspoon mint extract to give it the holiday color and minty flavor.

Irish Coffee

6 servings

For many of us, St. Patrick's Day wouldn't be complete without a stemmed mug filled with steaming hot coffee, a splash of Irish whiskey, and a thick whipped cream topping! If your guests can't kiss the Blarney stone, they'll surely kiss the cook! (In case you couldn't guess, this one's for adults only.)

> 1 cup (½ pint) heavy cream
> 3 tablespoons sugar, divided
> 6 cups hot black coffee
> ¾ cup Irish whiskey

In a small bowl, with an electric beater on medium speed, beat the cream and 1 tablespoon sugar until stiff peaks form. Dissolve the remaining 2 tablespoons sugar in the coffee and pour it into 6 mugs. Stir an equal amount of whiskey into each mug and top with the whipped cream. Serve immediately.

NOTE: Guess what?! This tastes just as good without the whiskey—but then, what doesn't taste good with whipped cream on top?

WEEK 13

The Tastes of Spring

I love spring! Yup, it's one of my favorite times of the year—the cold weather is starting to fade, and the trees have buds again. It's time to enjoy the outdoors and the tastes of our early spring veggies and herbs. Now get ready for some super seasonal pick-me-ups that'll really shake off the winter doldrums!

Mint-Laced Popovers

Roasted Leg of Lamb

Spring Vegetable Couscous

Herb-Marinated Asparagus

Lemon Tart Cookies

Mint-Laced Popovers

6 popovers

If you've ever taken a bite of a popover, you'll still remember it. They're a real surprise—so light and airy—which is why they're perfect for a spring menu! And I bet you've never had any that have been laced with the fresh taste of mint! Wait till you try these puffy alternatives to ordinary biscuits!

   2 eggs
   1 cup milk
   2 tablespoons vegetable oil
   1 cup all-purpose flour
   2 tablespoons chopped fresh mint
   ½ teaspoon salt

Preheat the oven to 425°F. Coat 6 muffin cups with nonstick cooking spray. In a large bowl, combine all the ingredients, mixing with a spoon until just blended (a few lumps may remain). Immediately pour into the muffin cups and bake for 30 to 35 minutes, or until golden and puffy. Serve immediately.

NOTE: You may want to make more than one batch of these, 'cause, served hot with butter, they pop out of sight before you know it!

Roasted Leg of Lamb

6 to 8 servings

Lamb and springtime go together so well! If you've never tried it before, now's not the time to be sheepish. Lamb is mild and tender, and perfect for a special meal, particularly when it's flavored the traditional way—with fresh mint leaves. You're gonna love it!

> One 7- to 9-pound leg of lamb
> 12 garlic cloves
> 12 fresh mint leaves
> 1 teaspoon salt
> ½ teaspoon black pepper
> ¼ cup (½ stick) butter, melted

Preheat the oven to 325°F. Line a roasting pan with aluminum foil and coat the foil with nonstick cooking spray. Using a sharp paring knife, carefully pierce the surface of the lamb 12

"LET'S BUNDLE UP!"

times, spacing the slits evenly and making each about 1½ inches deep. Wrap each garlic clove with a mint leaf and stuff into the slits, making sure they are completely inside the meat. Rub the lamb with the salt and pepper and place in the roasting pan. Brush with the melted butter and roast for 3 to 3½ hours, or until a meat thermometer registers 160°F. for medium, or until desired doneness beyond that, basting with the pan juices every 30 minutes.

NOTE: If there's any lamb left over, just slice it up and make gyro sandwiches. Mmm, mmm!

Spring Vegetable Couscous

6 to 8 servings

Have you noticed boxes of the Middle Eastern bead-like pasta grain called couscous on the supermarket shelves lately? Want to know what to do with them? There are loads of varieties of couscous available these days, and they're a super alternative to rice. So with the abundance of fresh springtime veggies around now, let's dice up a bunch to mix into this great main-dish go-along!

　　¼ cup (½ stick) butter
　　1 medium zucchini, diced
　　1 large carrot, diced
　　1 medium yellow bell pepper, diced
　　1 small onion, diced
　　1 package (10 ounces) frozen peas, thawed
　　2¼ cups water
　　1¼ teaspoons salt
　　¼ teaspoon black pepper
　　1 package (10 ounces) couscous

Melt the butter in a large skillet over medium heat. Add the zucchini, carrot, bell pepper, and onion and sauté for 5 minutes, or until crisp-tender. Add the peas, water, salt, and black pepper and bring to a boil. Remove from the heat and add the couscous; mix well. Cover and allow to sit for 5 minutes, or until the liquid is absorbed. Fluff lightly with a fork and serve.

NOTE: I like to call this "leftover couscous," 'cause I dice and add whatever cooked vegetables I have on hand.

Herb-Marinated Asparagus

6 to 8 servings

Asparagus is in season right now—and since it's so abundant, now's the time to take advantage of its garden-fresh taste at very reasonable prices. You know, this version's so tasty, crisp, and appealing that even the kids are gonna want to dig in!

> 2 pounds fresh asparagus, trimmed (see Note)
> 1 cup Italian dressing
> ½ of a small red bell pepper, diced
> 2 tablespoons chopped fresh parsley
> ½ teaspoon dried chives
> 1 hard-boiled egg, finely chopped (optional)

Fill a soup pot with 1 inch of water and bring to a boil over high heat. Add the asparagus to the boiling water, cover, and steam for 6 to 8 minutes, or until fork-tender. Remove the asparagus and plunge it into a large bowl of ice water to stop the cooking process. In a 9" × 13" baking dish, combine the Italian dressing, bell pepper, parsley, and chives; mix well. Remove the asparagus from the water and add, making sure to coat completely with the dressing mixture. Cover and chill for at least 2 hours before serving. When ready to serve, sprinkle with the chopped egg, if desired.

NOTE: The easy way to trim asparagus is to hold the asparagus and break off the stem end. It'll separate where the tender part and the tough part meet.

Lemon Tart Cookies

about 1½ dozen

These cookies really scream springtime! Their sunny yellow appearance, tart lemony flavor, and creamy surprise are sure to please!

> 1 package (15 ounces) folded refrigerated pie crusts
>   (2 crusts)
> 1 package (8 ounces) cream cheese, softened
> ⅓ cup confectioners' sugar
> ⅓ cup lemon curd (see Note)

Preheat the oven to 450°F. Coat 2 baking sheets with nonstick cooking spray. Unfold the pie crusts onto a lightly floured surface. Using a 3-inch round cookie cutter, cut 9 to 10 circles from each crust. Place the dough circles on the baking sheets. Bake for 7 to 9 minutes, or until golden. Remove to a wire rack to cool completely. In a medium bowl, combine the cream cheese and confectioners' sugar; mix well. Spread evenly over the cookies, leaving a small border around the edges. Spread the lemon curd evenly over the cream cheese layer and serve, or cover and chill until ready to serve.

NOTE: Lemon curd can be found in the jam and jelly section of your local supermarket. It's a thick spread that's great served on everything from toast to desserts!

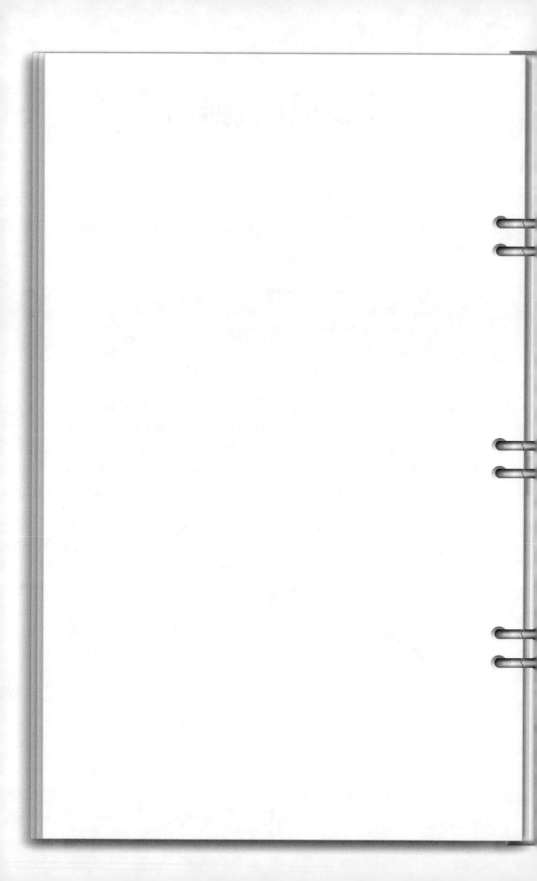

WEEK 14

April Foods That Fool 'Em

It's that time again—the stores are decorated, the malls are packed. . . . Can you believe that it's almost Christmas?! Gotcha—April Fool! And with April Fool's Day comes a whole menu that will fool 'em—and please 'em—over and over. There's a meat loaf decorated like a cake, lasagna for dessert, and more! It's all so tasty and so much fun, you're gonna wish May, June, and July had fool's days, too!

Pinecone Cheese Ball

Meat Loaf Cake

Spaghetti Squash Scampi

Cherry Lasagna

Pinecone Cheese Ball

10 to 12 servings

No, it's not a holiday decoration, and it didn't fall off the tree, but this pinecone appetizer is a great way to start off the month. Yup, it's a pinecone all right—a cheese ball that looks like a pinecone. It'll fool 'em, don't you worry!

> 2 cups (8 ounces) finely shredded sharp Cheddar cheese
> ½ cup crumbled blue cheese
> ½ cup heavy cream
> ½ teaspoon dry mustard
> 1 jar (6¾ ounces) whole roasted almonds
> 1 sprig fresh rosemary or parsley

In a medium bowl, combine the Cheddar cheese, blue cheese, heavy cream, and mustard; mix until well combined. Cover and chill for 2 hours. Spoon onto a serving dish and form into a pinecone shape. Place the almonds in the cheese mixture to make it look like a pinecone, as illustrated, covering the surface completely. Place the herb sprig at the wide end of the pinecone and serve, or cover and chill until ready to serve.

NOTE: Serve with your favorite crackers or thin slices of French bread.

Meat Loaf Cake

6 to 8 servings

Put away the birthday candles and the ice cream, 'cause this "cake" is a meaty main course "iced" with mashed potatoes!

    2 to 2½ pounds lean ground beef
    1 medium onion, finely chopped
    1 cup Italian-flavored bread crumbs
    1½ cups ketchup, divided
    2 eggs
    ½ teaspoon salt
    ½ teaspoon black pepper
    4 cups warm mashed potatoes
    8 cherry tomatoes, halved

Preheat the oven to 375°F. Coat a 10-inch Bundt or tube pan with nonstick cooking spray. In a large bowl, combine the ground beef, onion, bread crumbs, 1 cup ketchup, the eggs,

"Sweet cake? Ha! I'm meat loaf down here. Mashed potatoes up here!"

Cherry tomato garnish

89

salt, and pepper; mix well. Place in the prepared pan. Spread the remaining ½ cup ketchup over the top of the meat. Bake for 1 to 1¼ hours, or until the juices run clear; drain off any liquid. Allow to sit for 5 minutes, then remove to a serving platter. "Frost" the meat with the mashed potatoes and garnish the bottom edge with the cherry tomato halves, as illustrated.

NOTE: Feel free to decorate this "cake" any way you like. Sometimes I drizzle beef gravy over the mashed potato frosting to look like chocolate glaze. (Tee hee!)

Spaghetti Squash Scampi

6 to 8 servings

Bring out the pasta bowl full of this squash, and watch their expressions! They'll expect pasta, but boy, will they be (pleasantly) surprised with this spaghetti-like squash! Mmm, mmm! What a great way to get the kids to eat their veggies!

> 1 medium spaghetti squash
> ½ cup (1 stick) butter
> 4 garlic cloves, minced
> ¾ teaspoon salt
> ¾ teaspoon black pepper

Fill a soup pot with 1 inch of water. Add the whole squash and bring to a boil over medium-high heat. Cover and cook for 25 to 30 minutes, or until tender when pierced with a knife. Transfer to a cutting board and allow to cool slightly, about 15 minutes. Carefully cut the squash lengthwise in half, then use a soup spoon to remove and discard the seeds. Scrape the inside of the squash with a fork, separating it into noodle-like strands. Melt the butter in a large skillet over medium heat. Add the garlic and sauté for 1 minute, or until golden. Add the salt, pepper, and shredded squash and cook for 2 to 3 minutes, or until heated through, stirring constantly.

NOTE: If you prefer, you can make Spaghetti Squash Marinara by topping the cooked squash with spaghetti sauce instead of preparing it with garlic butter. Both ways will surprise your family or guests.

Cherry Lasagna

12 to 15 servings

Stop right there! You won't want to sprinkle *this* lasagna with grated Parmesan or crushed red pepper! Why? 'Cause it's full of sweetened cheese and ruby-red cherries, making it ideal for a dessert that'll really fool 'em.

> 2 cans (21 ounces each) cherry pie filling
>
> 8 lasagna noodles, cooked according to the package directions
>
> 1 container (15 ounces) ricotta cheese
>
> 3 eggs
>
> ½ cup granulated sugar
>
> ⅓ cup all-purpose flour
>
> ⅓ cup plus 3 tablespoons firmly packed light brown sugar, divided
>
> ¼ cup quick-cooking or old-fashioned rolled oats
>
> 3 tablespoons butter, softened
>
> ½ teaspoon ground cinnamon
>
> ½ cup sour cream

Preheat the oven to 350°F. Coat a 9" × 13" baking dish with nonstick cooking spray. Spread 1 can of cherry pie filling in the baking dish. Layer 4 noodles evenly over the pie filling. In a medium bowl, combine the ricotta cheese, eggs, and granulated sugar; mix well. Spread over the noodles and top with the remaining 4 noodles. Spoon the remaining can of pie filling over the noodles. In a small bowl, combine the flour, ⅓ cup brown sugar, the rolled oats, butter, and cinnamon until crumbly. Sprinkle over the pie filling and bake for 40 to 45 minutes, or until heated through. Allow to cool for 15 minutes. Meanwhile, in a medium bowl, combine the sour cream and the remaining 3 tablespoons brown sugar; mix well. Drizzle over the top of the lasagna and serve warm.

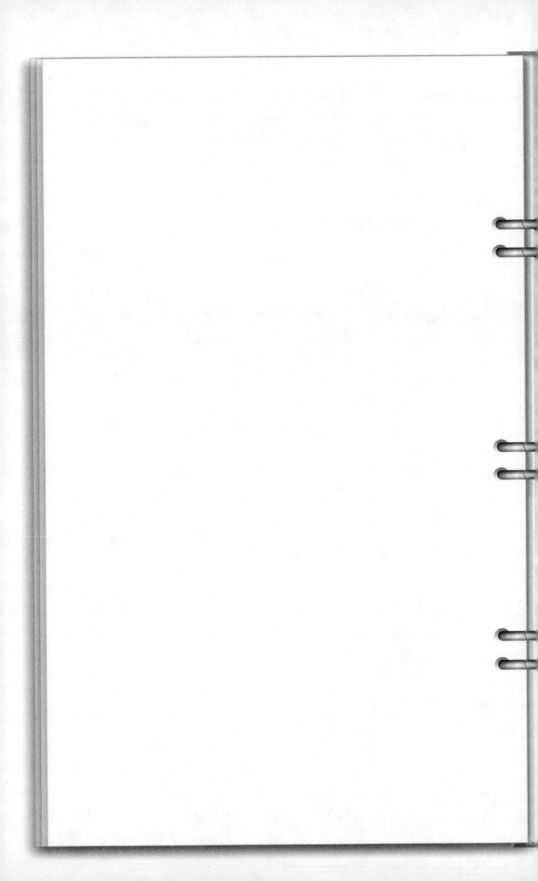

WEEK 15

Passover Seder

Passover is the springtime holiday when Jews around the world gather at their tables to celebrate freedom. The symbolism of various foods plays a major role in the seder, the traditional Passover service. So whether you're making your own seder for the first time, surprising your family with some new tastes, or salivating simply from the sound of these flavor-packed recipes, why not give them a try? And who knows . . . maybe it'll be the beginning of a whole new tradition at your house!

Passover Rolls

Homemade Chicken Soup

Aunt Sarah's Matzo Balls

Passover Brisket

Chocolate Raspberry Tarts

Passover Rolls

1 dozen

After a few days of eating matzo (the unleavened bread that's eaten during the eight days of Passover), we begin looking for another unleavened alternative. Well, look no more! Here's a roll that's so light and yummy you would never know it contains no flour, and it's great for filling with chicken, tuna, and egg salad, too!

>   2 cups matzo meal
>   1 tablespoon sugar
>   1 teaspoon salt
>   1 cup water
>   ½ cup peanut oil
>   5 eggs

Preheat the oven to 375°F. Coat a rimmed baking sheet with nonstick cooking spray. In a large bowl, combine the matzo meal, sugar, and salt; mix well. In a small saucepan, bring the water and oil to a boil over medium-high heat. Pour into the matzo meal mixture and beat with an electric beater on low speed until well combined. Add the eggs one at a time, beating thoroughly after each addition. Allow to sit for 15 minutes. With oiled hands, form the dough into 12 balls and place on the baking sheet. Bake for 40 to 45 minutes, or until golden. Serve warm.

NOTE: For crustier rolls, after baking, turn off the oven and allow the rolls to sit in the oven a bit.

Homemade Chicken Soup

6 to 8 servings

Almost all Jewish holiday meals seem to start off with a big steaming bowl of hot chicken soup. And whether or not you serve it with matzo balls, you're in for a real treat. Plus, it's a perfect way to soothe those springtime colds. That's why it's nicknamed Jewish Penicillin.

> One 3- to 3½-pound chicken, cut into 8 pieces
> 10 cups cold water
> 4 carrots, cut into 1-inch chunks
> 3 celery stalks, cut into 1-inch chunks
> 2 medium onions, cut into 1-inch chunks
> 1 tablespoon salt
> 1½ teaspoons black pepper

In a soup pot, bring all the ingredients to a boil over high heat. Reduce the heat to low and simmer for 2½ to 3 hours, or until the chicken is falling off the bones. Use tongs to remove the chicken from the soup and allow the chicken to cool slightly. Bone and skin the chicken, cut it into small pieces, and return the meat to the soup pot. Serve as is, or with matzo balls (see Note).

NOTE: For homemade matzo ball soup, prepare Aunt Sarah's Matzo Balls (page 98) and add them to this soup about 15 minutes before serving. And to lighten this soup a little, make it a day ahead and chill. Before reheating, remove and discard the fat that has hardened on top.

Aunt Sarah's Matzo Balls

about 1 dozen

It's too bad you couldn't have met my Aunt Sarah. What a cook she was! And when it came to matzo balls, she was a pro—they came out light and fluffy each and every time!

4 eggs
½ cup water
⅓ cup vegetable shortening, melted
1 teaspoon salt
1 cup matzo meal (see Note)

In a large bowl, combine the eggs, water, shortening, and salt; mix well. Add the matzo meal and stir until combined; *do not overmix*. Cover and chill for 30 minutes. Wet your hands slightly and form the mixture into 12 golf ball–size balls. Meanwhile, bring a soup pot of salted water to a rolling boil over medium-high heat. Carefully place the balls in the boiling water; cover and cook for 20 minutes, or until the matzo balls float to the top and are completely cooked inside. Remove the matzo balls with a slotted spoon and place in a shallow baking dish; let cool slightly, then cover and chill until ready to reheat in a pot of chicken soup. Or, to serve immediately, remove the matzo balls from the cooking pot and add to a pot of hot chicken soup.

NOTE: Matzo meal can be found in the ethnic foods aisle of the supermarket. And if you find packaged matzo ball mix there, you might want to give that a try, too. It's even easier than this and there's not a big difference in taste and texture!

Passover Brisket

The slow cooking really marries the flavors here, making it a top choice any time of the year—but especially at holiday times.

> One 4- to 5-pound beef brisket
> 1 teaspoon garlic powder
> 1 teaspoon paprika
> 1 teaspoon salt
> 1 teaspoon black pepper
> 3 medium onions, chopped
> 3 medium tomatoes, chopped
> ¼ cup water

Season the brisket with the garlic powder, paprika, salt, and pepper. In a soup pot, brown the brisket over medium-high heat for 5 to 6 minutes, turning once. Add the onions, tomatoes, and water. Reduce the heat to low, cover, and simmer for 3½ to 4 hours, or until fork-tender. Slice across the grain and serve with the sauce from the pot.

Chocolate Raspberry Tarts

3 dozen

What an awesome way to end a meal! Put out a platter of these extra-rich chocolate tarts, maybe alternated with coconut macaroons and/or meringue cookies. Add a nice cup of tea or coffee, then finish off the seder in song.

1 package (12 ounces) semisweet chocolate chips
½ cup (1 stick) margarine (see Note)
¼ cup sugar
¼ cup water
1 teaspoon instant coffee granules
3 eggs, beaten
½ pint fresh raspberries, washed

Preheat the oven to 425°F. Line 3 dozen mini muffin cups with miniature paper baking cups. In a medium saucepan, combine the chocolate chips, margarine, sugar, water, and coffee granules over medium heat for 2 to 3 minutes, or until the chocolate and margarine have melted, stirring constantly. Remove from the heat and add the eggs, stirring until smooth. Spoon equally into the paper baking cups. Bake for 5 to 6 minutes, or until the edges are firm; the centers will not be set. Allow to cool, cover loosely, and chill for 6 to 8 hours, or overnight. When ready to serve, top with the fresh raspberries.

NOTE: To keep a meal kosher, you wouldn't mix meat and dairy products, so be sure to use a nondairy margarine and nondairy semisweet chocolate chips if serving these after a meat meal. Other times, add whipped cream before topping these with the raspberries.

WEEK 16

Easter Traditions

It's time to go into the cellar or closet and pull out the box marked "Easter Decorations." You know, the one full of furry bunnies, pastel baskets, and fancy-looking holiday platters that help make our Easter goodies look as good as they taste! And wait until you see the extra surprises we can add to this year's baskets!

Colored Eggs

Hot Cross Buns

Maple-Glazed Ham and Sweet Potatoes

Fruity Egg Nests

Colored Eggs

1 dozen

Just mention the word *Easter* and watch the kids line up to color Easter eggs! What fun it is to see all those big eyes light up when they see their finished prizes.

> 2 cups water
> 4 teaspoons white vinegar
> 4 food colors
> 12 hard-boiled eggs

In each of 4 small bowls, combine ½ cup water and 1 teaspoon vinegar. Add ¼ teaspoon of a different food color to each bowl. Roll an egg in each bowl and allow to sit until the desired color is attained, turning occasionally. Drain on a rack over a paper towel–lined platter and allow to dry completely. Repeat until all the eggs are colored.

NOTE: Colored eggs can also be made with natural dyes. Try hard-boiling your eggs in water with blueberries to create blue-purple eggs. You can also try boiling them in water combined with seasonings, such as turmeric for yellow eggs. The options are endless. And once our eggs are colored, we can add additional decorations with stickers, rub-on transfers, and more. Have a ball!

Hot Cross Buns

2 dozen

No croissants or kaiser rolls will do on this holiday—no siree! We want the traditional icing-topped hot cross buns. And now that you know how easy they are to make, I bet you're going to start serving them more and more throughout the year!

    4 cups all-purpose flour, divided
    2 packages (¼ ounce each) active dry yeast
    ½ teaspoon ground cinnamon
    ¾ cup plus 2 tablespoons milk, divided
    ½ cup vegetable oil
    ⅓ cup granulated sugar
    ¾ teaspoon salt
    3 eggs
    ¼ cup raisins
    2 cups confectioners' sugar
    1 teaspoon vanilla extract

Coat a medium bowl and 2 baking sheets with nonstick cooking spray; set aside. In a large bowl, combine 2 cups flour, the yeast, and cinnamon; mix well. In a small saucepan, heat ¾ cup milk, the oil, granulated sugar, and salt just until warm. Add the milk mixture to the flour mixture. Add the eggs and beat with an electric beater on low speed for 30 seconds, scraping down the sides of the bowl as necessary. Increase the speed to high and beat for 3 more minutes. Stir in the raisins and the remaining 2 cups flour to form a soft dough. Shape into a ball and place in the coated medium bowl, turning to coat the dough on all sides. Cover and place in a warm place to rise for 30 minutes, or until doubled in size. Place the dough on a lightly floured surface, punch down, and divide into 24 equal pieces. Roll each piece into a small ball and place 1½ inches apart on the coated baking sheets. Cover and allow to rise in a warm place for 30 minutes, or until doubled in size. Preheat the oven to 375°F. Bake for 10 to 12 minutes, or until golden. Allow to cool. In a small bowl, combine the confectioners' sugar, vanilla, and the remaining 2 tablespoons milk; mix well. Spoon into a small resealable plastic storage bag. Cut a small corner off the bag and make a cross with the confectioners' sugar mixture on each bun. Serve, or cover until ready to serve.

Maple-Glazed Ham and Sweet Potatoes

8 to 10 servings

When oven space is at a premium, why not cook the ham and potatoes together in the same roasting pan? Not only do the flavors get to mingle, but we get the bonus of easier cleanup of our special holiday meal!

> One 5- to 6-pound fully cooked semi-boneless ham
> 1 cup maple syrup
> ¼ cup orange marmalade
> 1 tablespoon Dijon-style mustard
> 8 medium sweet potatoes, peeled and cut into 2-inch chunks

Preheat the oven to 350°F. Line a roasting pan with aluminum foil and coat the foil with nonstick cooking spray. Place the ham in the roasting pan. In a large bowl, combine the maple syrup, marmalade, and mustard; mix well. Add the potatoes and toss, coating completely. Place the potatoes around the ham and use the remaining maple syrup mixture to coat the ham on all sides. Bake for 1¾ to 2 hours, or until the ham is golden and the potatoes are fork-tender, basting with the pan juices every 30 minutes.

NOTE: Here's a shortcut: You can use canned sweet potatoes instead of fresh—it'll also cut down on the cooking time.

Fruity Egg Nests

about 3 dozen

Sweet and colorful, these are the perfect addition to any Easter basket—and soon to be everybody's new favorite!

> 5 cups fruit-flavored multigrain cereal rings (see Note)
> 2 cups colored miniature marshmallows
> 2 packages (6 ounces each) white baking bars
> 2 tablespoons vegetable shortening
> ¾ cup jelly beans

Line a large baking sheet with waxed paper. In a large bowl, toss together the cereal and marshmallows. Melt the baking bars and shortening in a small saucepan over low heat, stirring until smooth. Add to the cereal mixture, stirring until completely coated. Drop by rounded tablespoons onto the baking sheet. Press 2 to 3 jelly beans into the center of each nest and allow to cool until set. Serve, or place in an airtight container until ready to serve.

NOTE: I like to use Froot Loops® cereal, but any type of colorful sweetened cereal can be used.

WEEK 17

Two Tasty Tributes

Decisions, decisions . . . oh, what a dilemma! Should I choose this week's menu based on Earth Day or Secretaries Week? I mean, they're both important events that celebrate things we can't live without. So I decided to come up with recipes to salute both!

Chicken with Root Vegetables

Beet Mashed Potatoes

Mud Pie

Chocolate Almond Truffles

Quick Mini Éclairs

Chicken with Root Vegetables

4 to 6 servings

It's nice to see our kids and grandchildren becoming more ecology minded. And with that comes more attention to Earth Day. So, in honor of this special day, let's roast our chicken surrounded by all sorts of earthy root veggies for a change.

> One 3- to 3½-pound chicken
> 1¼ teaspoons salt, divided
> ¾ teaspoon black pepper, divided
> 2 medium onions, quartered
> 2 medium rutabagas (about 2 pounds), peeled and cut into
>   1-inch chunks
> 5 medium parsnips (about 1 pound), peeled and cut into
>   1-inch chunks
> ¼ cup (½ stick) butter, melted
> 3 tablespoons light brown sugar
> ¼ teaspoon ground cinnamon
> ⅛ teaspoon ground nutmeg

Preheat the oven to 350°F. Coat a roasting pan with nonstick cooking spray. Place the chicken in the roasting pan and season with ¼ teaspoon salt and ¼ teaspoon pepper. Place the onions around the chicken and roast for 1 hour. Meanwhile, place the rutabagas and parsnips in a large pot and add just enough water to cover them. Boil over high heat for 25 to 30 minutes, or until fork-tender; drain. Remove the chicken from the oven and place the rutabagas and parsnips around it. In a small bowl, combine the butter, brown sugar, cinnamon, nutmeg, and the remaining 1 teaspoon salt and ½ teaspoon pepper. Brush over the chicken and vegetables and roast for 30 minutes, or until no pink remains, basting every 10 minutes with the pan juices.

Beet Mashed Potatoes

4 to 6 servings

We all make mashed potatoes and, sure, they're a favorite. But to break up the old routine once in a while, let's add another vegetable and beat it into our cooked potatoes. We can use carrots or spinach—and here I use beets! It makes our finished dish very colorful, very different, and very down to earth.

> 6 medium potatoes (about 2 pounds), peeled and cut into chunks
> 1 can (15 ounces) beets, undrained
> ¼ cup (½ stick) butter, softened
> ¼ teaspoon onion powder
> ½ teaspoon salt
> ½ teaspoon black pepper

Place the potatoes in a soup pot and add just enough water to cover them. Add the beets and their liquid and bring to a boil over high heat. Reduce the heat to medium and cook for 12 to 15 minutes, or until the potatoes are fork-tender; drain and place in a large bowl. Add the remaining ingredients and beat with an electric beater on medium speed until well blended. Serve immediately.

NOTE: Yes, of course you can substitute an equal-sized can of carrots or spinach, if you prefer orange or green potatoes instead of red.

Mud Pie

6 to 8 servings

What kind of dessert is appropriate on Earth Day? Why, mud pie, of course! No, it's not really made with mud—it's ice cream, chocolate chips, and nuts in a graham cracker pie crust.

> 1 tablespoon instant coffee granules
> 3 tablespoons coffee-flavored liqueur (see Note)
> 1 quart chocolate ice cream, softened
> 1 container (8 ounces) frozen whipped topping, thawed, divided
> ½ cup plus 2 tablespoons chopped pecans, divided
> One 9-inch chocolate graham cracker pie crust
> ¼ cup semisweet chocolate chips, melted

In a large bowl, dissolve the coffee granules in the coffee liqueur. Add the ice cream, half of the whipped topping, and ½ cup pecans; mix well. Pour into the pie crust, cover, and freeze for at least 4 hours. Top with the remaining whipped topping and sprinkle with the remaining 2 tablespoons pecans. Drizzle with the melted chocolate and freeze for 4 more hours, or until firm. Serve, or cover and keep frozen until ready to serve.

NOTE: If you don't have coffee-flavored liqueur on hand, just dissolve the coffee granules in a tablespoon of hot water.

Chocolate Almond Truffles

about 1 dozen

Want to do something more creative than giving flowers (again!) for Secretaries Week? Bring a platter of homemade almond truffles to work and, boy, will your office staff feel special! Of course, then *you're* gonna be put to work . . . answering all the requests for the recipe!

> 1½ teaspoons instant coffee granules
> 1 tablespoon hot water
> 1½ cups confectioners' sugar
> 4 squares (4 ounces) unsweetened chocolate, melted
> 1 package (3 ounces) cream cheese, softened
> ½ cup sliced almonds, finely chopped

In a medium bowl, dissolve the coffee granules in the water. Add the remaining ingredients except the almonds. With an electric beater on medium speed, beat until smooth; cover and chill for 30 minutes. Roll into 1-inch balls, then roll in the chopped almonds, coating completely. Serve, or cover and chill until ready to serve.

NOTE: These truffles can also be coated in chocolate or colored sprinkles, confectioners' sugar, cocoa powder, or even other kinds of chopped nuts. What a pretty platter you could make with some of each!

Quick Mini Éclairs

1 dozen

When you bring that platter of truffles into the office, make sure you mix in some miniature éclairs. Wait until you hear all the comments like, "Are they ever cute!" and "They're so pretty I don't want to eat them!" Of course, seconds later, the whole crowd will be digging in to find their favorites.

> ½ cup frozen whipped topping, thawed
> 2 tablespoons seedless raspberry jam
> 1 package (3 ounces) ladyfingers
> ¼ cup semisweet chocolate chips
> 2 teaspoons vegetable shortening

In a small bowl, combine the whipped topping and jam; mix well. Split each ladyfinger and spread the raspberry mixture evenly between the halves. Replace the tops of the ladyfingers and place on a baking sheet. Melt the chocolate chips and shortening in a small saucepan over medium-low heat. Drizzle over the ladyfingers and chill for at least 1 hour, or until firm. Serve, or cover and chill until ready to serve.

NOTE: In a jam 'cause you have no raspberry jam? Strawberry or almost any flavor will work fine. I've made it a few times with orange marmalade and what a combo *that* is—tangy orange with a chocolate drizzle. . . . Mmm, mmm!

WEEK 18

Kentucky Derby Winners

It's time for the annual run for the roses! Yup, the first Saturday in May is traditionally Kentucky Derby day. This calls for some really special treats, so whether we're having a tailgate picnic at the track or a cold buffet in front of the TV at home, you know who's gonna be the big winner? All bets are on these super-easy treats. They come in first for flavor every time!

Derby Rolls

Winner's Circle Shrimp Pasta Salad

Kentucky Bourbon Parfaits

Mint Julep Iced Tea

Derby Rolls

I'm always looking for a reason to bake up homemade rolls 'cause, after all, there's nothing like the smell of fresh bread or rolls baking. And these couldn't be easier—so you'll be sure to have 'em out of the oven before the horses are out of the starting gate. I'm serious . . . no horsing around!

    2 tablespoons butter, softened
    1 tablespoon chopped fresh basil
    1 tablespoon grated Parmesan cheese
    1 package (8 ounces) refrigerated crescent rolls

Preheat the oven to 375°F. In a small bowl, combine the butter, basil, and Parmesan cheese; mix well. Unroll the crescent rolls and separate into 8 triangles. Spread the butter mixture evenly over the triangles. Roll up each triangle from the wide end to the point, and place seam side down on an ungreased baking sheet. Bake for 10 to 12 minutes, or until golden. Serve warm.

NOTE: I also like to make these with fresh dill or any other fresh herb that's available.

Winner's Circle Shrimp Pasta Salad

8 to 10 servings

Without a doubt, you'll be receiving raves for this super-looking shrimp and pasta salad brimming with in-season asparagus and tomatoes. So step up to the winner's circle to get your rewards!

> 1 pound penne pasta
> ¾ pound fresh asparagus, trimmed and cut into 1-inch pieces
> 1 package (12 ounces) frozen cooked shrimp, thawed
> 6 plum tomatoes, cut into ½-inch chunks
> 1 bottle (8 ounces) creamy Parmesan dressing
> ½ teaspoon garlic powder
> ½ teaspoon onion powder
> 1½ teaspoons salt

Cook the penne according to the package directions; drain, rinse, drain again, and set aside in a large bowl. Place the asparagus in a large saucepan and add just enough water to cover. Bring to a boil over medium-high heat and cook for 10 to 12 minutes, or until fork-tender. Drain and allow to cool. Add to the penne along with the remaining ingredients; mix well. Cover and chill for at least 2 hours before serving.

NOTE: I also like to add some chopped yellow bell pepper to make this a really colorful salad.

Kentucky Bourbon Parfaits

6 servings

What a day! And what a great ending—mounds of creamy pudding and whipped topping swirled together with a crunchy filling and a hint of Kentucky bourbon! This is a grown-ups–only treat, so if the little ones are home, be sure to make them a special kid-friendly batch without the bourbon so they can join in the day's celebration!

    1 package (4-serving size) instant chocolate pudding and
        pie filling
    1½ cups cold milk
    2 tablespoons Kentucky bourbon (see Note)
    1 container (8 ounces) frozen whipped topping, thawed
    ½ cup chopped pecans, toasted
    2½ cups coarsely crushed Pecan Sandies cookies
    1 tablespoon mini semisweet chocolate chips

In a large bowl, combine the pudding mix, milk, and bourbon; whisk until thickened and set aside. In a medium bowl, combine the whipped topping and pecans. Layer 6 parfait glasses or dessert dishes with half of the crushed cookies, half of the pudding mixture, and half of the whipped topping mixture. Repeat the layers, then sprinkle with the chocolate chips. Cover loosely and chill for at least 1 hour before serving.

NOTE: To make these without bourbon, just use 2 teaspoons of vanilla extract instead.

Mint Julep Iced Tea

about 2 quarts, 6 to 8 servings

When we take a big gulp of iced tea, we may take it for granted that tea bags were always available. But did you know that tea bags were invented in 1908 by Thomas Sullivan of New York City, when he decided to pack tea leaves in single-use silk bags? Today we use mostly filtered paper tea bags to make our icy thirst-quenchers. And now that we know a little tea history, let's toast the Derby winner with a tall glass of refreshing minty tea that we can make in a snap!

 8 cups (2 quarts) water, divided
 3 tea bags
 ¼ cup fresh mint leaves
 1 cup sugar

In a medium saucepan, combine 4 cups water, the tea bags, and mint leaves; bring to a boil over high heat. Reduce the heat to low, cover, and simmer for 10 minutes. Strain into a pitcher. Add the sugar and mix well. Stir in the remaining 4 cups water and serve over ice, or chill until ready to serve.

NOTE: This is nice garnished with sprigs of mint. If you'd like to give your Mint Julep Iced Tea an adults-only kick, add ¼ cup bourbon to the tea just before serving.

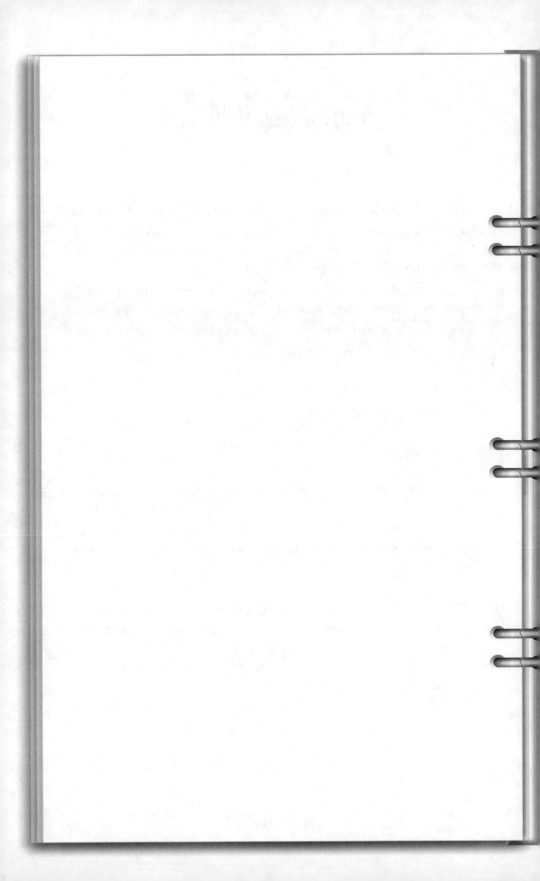

WEEK 19

Cinco de Mayo

It's time to celebrate Cinco de Mayo, which is Spanish for the Fifth of May. What is it? A Mexican holiday that we here in the United States can enjoy, too! And what better way to celebrate a holiday than with lots and lots of food. It's a fiesta, for sure—now filled with traditional favorites as well as some super new twists. And why not finish by lining up to take a swing at the *piñata*, followed by a well-deserved *siesta*? Okay, let's get going!

Chilled Shrimp with Lime

Steak Sandwiches with Black Bean Salsa

Spanish Flan

Frozen Virgin Margaritas

Chilled Shrimp with Lime

4 to 6 servings

The Spanish name for this dish is *ceviche de camarónes*. Sounds fancy, huh? Well, it's a bright and tasty seafood salad perked up with lively salsa and a super lime marinade. Call it what you like, but any way you say it, it's *muy bueno*—which means it's very good!

> 1 package (12 ounces) frozen cooked shrimp, thawed and
>   coarsely chopped
> 2 cups fresh lime juice
> 3 large tomatoes, seeded and chopped
> 1 medium onion, chopped
> ⅓ cup chopped fresh cilantro
> 3 garlic cloves, minced
> ½ cup salsa (see Note)
> ⅓ cup olive oil

In a medium bowl, combine the shrimp and lime juice. Cover and chill for 2 hours. Rinse the shrimp, drain, and return them to the bowl. Add the remaining ingredients and toss well. Cover and chill for at least 2 hours before serving.

NOTE: I like to use hot salsa to add a spicy twist, but any salsa will taste great. Serve this with your favorite crackers, thin slices of toasted French bread, or flour tortillas that have been cut into wedges and toasted.

Steak Sandwiches with Black Bean Salsa

4 sandwiches

The latest rage in so many restaurants today is zippy black beans or salsa served as a topper or go-along. They both add such great taste and texture that we've decided to mix the two together in this lively topper for tender slices of flank steak!

> 1 can (15½ ounces) black beans, drained
> 1 can (15¼ ounces) whole kernel corn, drained
> 1 cup salsa
> 2 tablespoons butter
> One 1-pound beef flank steak
> ½ teaspoon salt
> ½ teaspoon black pepper
> 1 loaf French bread, cut into 4 pieces and split

In a medium bowl, combine the black beans, corn, and salsa; mix well and set aside. In a large skillet, melt the butter over medium-high heat. Season the steak with the salt and pepper and add to the skillet. Cook for 2 to 3 minutes per side for medium-rare, or to desired doneness beyond that. Remove to a cutting board and thinly slice across the grain. Layer the steak evenly on the 4 sandwich bottoms and top with the black bean salsa and the sandwich tops.

NOTE: Serve with additional salsa on the side, if you'd like. Instead of making sandwiches, I also like to serve this steak and black bean salsa over chopped lettuce.

Spanish Flan

12 to 14 servings

If you've ever wondered how to make that delicate, sweet-tasting Spanish custard dessert, here's the answer. And this is one recipe that's best made a day in advance so that the flan is thoroughly chilled before serving.

1½ cups sugar, divided
8 eggs
2 teaspoons vanilla extract
4 cups whole milk

Preheat the oven to 350°F. In a small saucepan, cook ½ cup sugar over medium heat until completely melted, golden, and caramelized, stirring occasionally. Immediately pour into a 6-cup tube pan, coating the bottom of the pan. **Be careful when working with caramelized sugar: It is very hot!** In a large bowl, with an electric beater on medium speed, beat the eggs and vanilla for 1 minute. Add the remaining 1 cup sugar and beat until well combined. Add the milk and beat until completely mixed. Pour over the caramelized sugar in the tube pan. Place the tube pan in a large baking pan of hot water, with just enough water to come halfway up the sides of the tube pan. Bake for 70 to 75 minutes, or until a table knife inserted in the center comes out clean. Carefully remove from the hot water bath and allow to cool for 20 minutes. Cover and chill for at least 3 hours, or overnight. Just before serving, run a table knife around the edge of the pan to loosen the flan from the pan. Carefully invert the flan onto a 12-inch rimmed serving plate (so that the caramel sauce doesn't run off the plate). Serve each wedge with some of the caramel sauce.

Frozen Virgin Margaritas

4 servings

Get out the tall stemmed glasses and the salt, it's frozen margarita time! It's the one and only refreshing drink that can quench even the biggest thirsts! And these are perfect, 'cause they're nonalcoholic—so we can have as much as we want, and the kids can, too!

 2 tablespoons kosher (coarse) salt
 ½ of a lime, cut into 4 wedges
 1 can (6 ounces) frozen limeade concentrate, thawed
 ¼ cup orange juice
 4 cups ice cubes

Place the salt in a shallow dish. Rub the rim of each of 4 glasses with a lime wedge and dip the rims into the salt; set the lime wedges aside. In a blender, blend the limeade, orange juice, and ice cubes on high speed for 1 to 2 minutes, or until well blended and the ice cubes are crushed. Pour evenly into the glasses and garnish with the lime wedges. Serve immediately.

NOTE: I like these just the way they are, but if you prefer the original version, then add about ¾ cup tequila per batch and, of course, keep them for adults only.

WEEK 20

Mother's Day Brunch

Hooray for Mom! She's always there for us! And when it comes to cooking—whether she's the best on the block or not—she always serves up our favorite foods with love. We should celebrate her every day, but especially on the second Sunday in May. Yup, today's our day to salute Mom with a brunch fit for a queen, so let's be sure to show her *and* tell her how much she means to us!

Picture-Perfect Berries and Cream

Disappearing Stuffed French Toast

Sage Breakfast Sausage

Orange Smoothie

Picture-Perfect Berries and Cream

4 to 6 servings

These glasses of fresh berries are so pretty to look at, they almost don't look real! Mom sure won't be able to resist digging into the juicy fruit covered in a lightly sweetened coat!

    ¼ cup lemon-flavored yogurt
    1 tablespoon sour cream
    1 tablespoon light brown sugar
    1 teaspoon poppy seeds
    1 pint fresh strawberries, washed, hulled, and quartered
    1 pint fresh blueberries, washed
    ½ pint fresh raspberries, washed

In a large bowl, combine the yogurt, sour cream, brown sugar, and poppy seeds; mix well. Add the remaining ingredients and toss gently. Spoon into goblets and serve immediately.

NOTE: If other berries are available, sure, use them, too. Or if you'd rather, just use strawberries. Make it your own!

Disappearing Stuffed French Toast

4 servings

I'll tell you ahead of time that this is the creamiest, most tempting breakfast treat you'll ever sink your teeth into! Better make plenty, 'cause it'll be gone in an instant!

 1 package (3 ounces) cream cheese, softened
 2 tablespoons confectioners' sugar
 8 slices cinnamon-raisin bread
 2 eggs
 ½ cup half-and-half
 2 tablespoons granulated sugar
 4 tablespoons (½ stick) butter, divided

In a small bowl, combine the cream cheese and confectioners' sugar; mix well. Spread evenly over 4 bread slices. Top with the remaining bread slices, forming sandwiches. In a shallow bowl, whisk the eggs, half-and-half, and granulated sugar until well combined. Melt 2 tablespoons butter in a large skillet over medium heat. Dip 2 sandwiches into the egg mixture, completely coating both sides. Cook them for 1 to 2 minutes per side, or until golden. Coat the remaining 2 sandwiches; melt the remaining 2 tablespoons butter in the skillet and cook the sandwiches. Slice each sandwich diagonally in half and serve.

NOTE: Make this look and taste really fancy by serving it topped with additional confectioners' sugar and maple syrup, fresh fruit, or strawberry sauce.

Sage Breakfast Sausage

8 patties

This is the perfect go-along for our stuffed French toast, but don't forget about it anytime you make pancakes, waffles, or eggs! And when you tell Mom that you made it yourself . . . oh, will she be proud!

> 1 pound ground pork or veal
> 2 teaspoons ground sage
> ⅛ teaspoon ground nutmeg
> ¼ teaspoon salt
> ¾ teaspoon black pepper
> 2 tablespoons vegetable oil

In a medium bowl, combine all the ingredients except the oil; mix well. Form the mixture into 8 equal-sized patties. Heat the oil in a large skillet over medium-high heat and panfry the patties for 6 to 8 minutes, or until no pink remains, turning once.

NOTE: The great thing about making your own sausages is that you can shape them any way you like. Maybe roll some into links or, since it's a special day, get out the cookie cutters and shape this into hearts.

Orange Smoothie

4 to 5 servings

How 'bout making this ray of sunshine for Mom? It's a chilly, thick, and refreshing drink that can be made quicker than you can say "One-two-three." And won't Mom and the rest of the family be impressed!

2 cups milk
1 can (6 ounces) frozen orange juice concentrate, thawed
¼ cup sugar
1 teaspoon vanilla extract
2 cups ice cubes

In a blender, blend all the ingredients until the ice cubes are crushed and the mixture is well combined, thick, and frothy. Pour into glasses and serve immediately.

NOTE: Garnish each serving with a slice of orange. Oh—these can be made into orange smoothie shakes by using ice cream instead of ice cubes. Mmm, mmm!

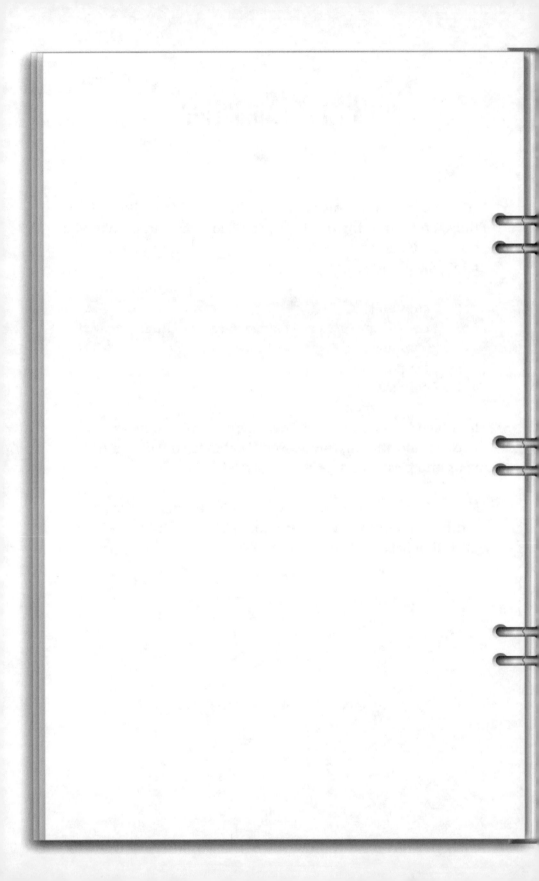

WEEK 21

College Graduation Party

It's time to party! Our graduates have made it all the way, so let's offer our congratulations with a big celebration. If you wanna make plenty of the stuff they love, here are some super ideas to help you flavor the festivities with just the right easy edibles!

Salad on a Stick

Fruity Chicken Salad

Super Stuffed Pizza

Graduation Cake

Cap-and-Gown Punch

Salad on a Stick

12 skewers

Anyone can toss a salad, but this one's just right for a buffet party 'cause everybody gets a whole serving of salad on a skewer. Finally—there's no more fishing in the salad bowl for a tomato or cucumber chunk!

½ of a medium head iceberg lettuce, cut into 12 chunks
1 small red onion, cut into 12 chunks
1 medium red bell pepper, cut into 12 chunks
1 small cucumber, cut into 12 chunks
12 cherry tomatoes
1 cup Italian dressing

Twelve 6-inch wooden skewers

Alternately thread a chunk of lettuce, onion, bell pepper, and cucumber and a tomato onto each skewer. Place on a serving tray and drizzle with the dressing. If not serving immediately, cover and chill, then drizzle with the dressing just before serving.

NOTE: Obviously, any of your favorite vegetables, including broccoli florets, cauliflower florets, radishes, carrots, or other bell peppers, can be included on these.

Fruity Chicken Salad

4 to 6 servings

I'm big on putting combos of flavors and textures together 'cause they add excitement to the "same old, same old." This sure is a super salad or even a yummy sandwich with those mini party rolls!

> 4 cups cooked chicken chunks
> 1 can (11 ounces) mandarin oranges, drained
> ½ cup seedless grapes, cut in half
> 2 celery stalks, coarsely chopped
> 1 cup coarsely chopped pecans
> 1 cup mayonnaise

Combine all the ingredients in a large bowl; mix well. Cover and chill for at least 2 hours, or until ready to serve.

NOTE: Serve on a lettuce-lined platter with toasted pita chips or, if you prefer, make sandwiches in pita halves or mini party rolls.

Super Stuffed Pizza

8 slices

Our college graduates have spent the last few years ordering pizza in their dorms, so what better way to celebrate than with the ultimate version of their all-time favorite food?! We'll all be able to sink our teeth into this one!

½ pound Italian sausage, casings removed (see Note)
½ pound fresh mushrooms, sliced
1 small onion, chopped
1 small green bell pepper, chopped
Two 17-ounce frozen thin-crust cheese pizzas, thawed
1 tablespoon olive oil
1 cup (4 ounces) shredded Italian cheese blend

Preheat the oven to 375°F. Place a 2½-foot-long sheet of aluminum foil on a 12- to 14-inch pizza pan. In a large skillet, cook the sausage, mushrooms, onion, and pepper over medium-high heat for 10 minutes, or until the sausage is browned and the vegetables are fork-tender, stirring occasionally; drain. Place 1 pizza cheese side up on the pan and spread the sausage mixture evenly over the pizza. Top with the remaining pizza cheese side down, pressing the pizzas together. Fold and seal the aluminum foil over the stuffed pizza. Bake for 20 to 25 minutes, or until heated through. Uncover the pizza; brush the top with the oil and sprinkle evenly with the cheese. Bake, uncovered, for 15 to 20 minutes, or until the cheese is golden.

NOTE: I like to use hot Italian sausage and make a spicy pizza, but use your favorite—or you can even make this with pepperoni instead.

Graduation Cake

28 to 32 servings

I think that every celebration deserves a special dessert, so it goes without saying that a momentous occasion like gradua- tion definitely deserves one like this. As you slice this sheet cake fit for a bunch, pass it around to wish your graduates sweet success. (You might want to think about topping it with scoops of ice cream—it'll be like serving it "with honors"!)

1 cup plus 6 tablespoons (2¾ sticks) butter, softened, divided

¼ cup unsweetened cocoa

1 cup water

2 cups all-purpose flour

2 cups granulated sugar

2 eggs

½ cup sour cream

1 teaspoon baking soda

½ teaspoon salt

1 cup chopped walnuts

4 cups confectioners' sugar

¼ cup milk

1 teaspoon vanilla extract

Preheat the oven to 350°F. Coat a 10" × 15" rimmed baking sheet with nonstick cooking spray. In a large bowl, combine 1 cup butter, the cocoa, and water; mix well. Add the flour, gran- ulated sugar, eggs, sour cream, baking soda, and salt. With an electric beater on medium speed, beat until well combined. Stir in the walnuts and pour onto the baking sheet. Bake for 20 to 25 minutes, or until a wooden toothpick inserted in the center comes out clean; set aside to cool. In a medium bowl, with an electric beater on low speed, beat the confectioners' sugar, milk, vanilla, and the remaining 6 tablespoons butter until smooth and creamy. Frost the cooled cake and serve.

NOTE: Decorate the cake for the special occasion by writing a graduation message with tubes of decorating gel and sprinkling it with candy in the school colors.

Cap-and-Gown Punch

about 1 gallon, 12 to 16 servings

Let's gather 'round the punch bowl and offer a toast to the graduates! This refreshing sparkling fruit drink will no doubt be a family favorite!

> 1 can (46 ounces) chilled white grape juice
> 1 quart apple cider, chilled
> 1 liter ginger ale, chilled
> 1 cup orange juice, chilled
> ½ cup lemon juice
> 1 lemon, sliced
> 1 lime, sliced

Combine all the ingredients in a punch bowl; mix well and serve.

NOTE: You can also combine additional grape juice or seltzer with some lemon and lime slices and freeze them in a gelatin mold to add to the punch just before serving. It'll look good and keep the punch cool without diluting it.

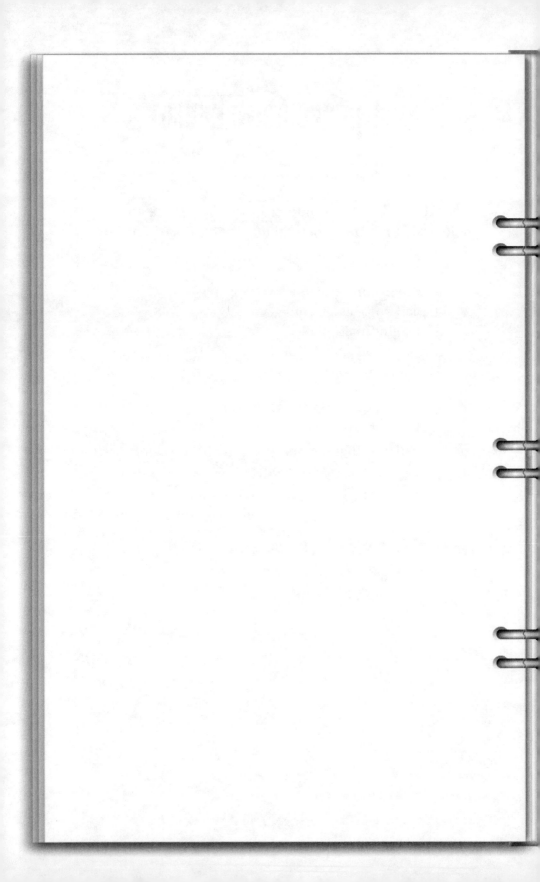

WEEK 22

Memorial Day

After attending the parades and memorial services to honor those who gave their lives in battle, most of us get together with family and friends to kick off the beginning of summer. So let's fire up the grill and enjoy!

Picnic-Time Deviled Eggs

Tangy Barbecued Spareribs

Veggie Cabbage Slaw

Grilled Veggie Kebabs

Limesicle Pie

Picnic-Time Deviled Eggs

1 dozen

We've been waiting for Memorial Day Weekend all winter! Well, it's here, and what better way to kick off our summer picnic season than with a platter of devilishly good eggs overflowing with a sharp Cheddar cheese stuffing!

6 eggs
¼ cup (1 ounce) finely shredded sharp Cheddar cheese
3 tablespoons butter, softened
1 tablespoon prepared yellow mustard
½ teaspoon black pepper

Place the eggs in a large saucepan and add just enough water to cover them. Bring to a boil over medium-high heat; remove the pan from the heat, cover, and let sit for 20 minutes. Drain off the water and run cold water over the eggs. Add some ice cubes and allow to cool for 5 to 10 minutes. Drain the eggs, carefully peel, and cut lengthwise in half. Remove the egg yolks and place in a small bowl. Place the egg whites on a serving platter. Add the remaining ingredients to the egg yolks; mix well. Fill each egg white half with an equal amount of the egg yolk mixture. Serve, or cover and chill until ready to serve.

NOTE: Sprinkle with chopped fresh parsley or paprika for that extra burst of color.

Tangy Barbecued Spareribs

4 to 5 servings

Everybody's makin' burgers and dogs, so let's make our cook-out stand out! Easy, tangy, restaurant-style barbecued ribs are perfect for an outdoor bash. Get ready to pass out the napkins and dig in!

> 5 pounds pork spareribs
> 1 teaspoon salt
> ¼ cup vegetable oil
> 1 small onion, chopped
> 1 garlic clove, minced
> 2 cups sweetened applesauce
> ½ cup ketchup
> 2 tablespoons lemon juice
> 1 tablespoon Worcestershire sauce
> 1 teaspoon prepared yellow mustard

Place the ribs in a soup pot and add just enough water to cover them. Add the salt and bring to a boil over medium-high heat. Partially cover and cook for 45 to 60 minutes, or until almost tender. Meanwhile, in a medium saucepan, heat the oil and sauté the onion and garlic over medium heat for 5 to 6 minutes, or until tender. Remove the saucepan from the heat and add the remaining ingredients (except the ribs); mix well. About 10 minutes before the ribs finish boiling, preheat the grill to medium-high heat. Drain the ribs, brush with the sauce, place on the grill, and close the grill cover. Grill the ribs, turning them over frequently and basting with the sauce each time you turn them, for about 12 to 15 minutes, or until they are browned and glazed.

(continued)

NOTE: If you prefer to bake instead of grill these, just preheat the oven to 400°F., place the boiled ribs on a rimmed baking sheet, and baste with the sauce. Bake for 30 minutes, or until browned and glazed, turning and basting halfway through the cooking. Serve with the remaining barbecue sauce.

Veggie Cabbage Slaw

8 to 10 servings

Sure, we could pick up some ready-made cold salads at the market, but when fresh is this easy, why not impress 'em with your own colorful, crunchy homemade slaw?!

> ½ of a medium head green cabbage, shredded
> ½ of a medium head red cabbage, shredded
> 2 large cucumbers, seeded and diced (see Note)
> 1 medium onion, finely chopped
> 1 can (15¼ ounces) whole kernel corn, drained
> ½ cup olive oil
> ½ cup apple cider vinegar
> ⅓ cup sugar
> 1½ teaspoons salt

In a large bowl, toss together the green and red cabbages, the cucumbers, onion, and corn. In a small bowl, combine the remaining ingredients; pour over the salad and toss well. Serve, or cover and chill until ready to serve.

NOTE: To seed the cucumbers, cut them lengthwise in half and use a spoon to scrape out the seeds.

Grilled Veggie Kebabs

10 skewers

If there's a choice between chips and veggies, you know which the kids are gonna pick. But kids and kebabs just seem to go together, so if you're expecting a big bunch for the holiday weekend, serve up your veggies this clever and colorful way, and the kids of all ages will be drawn to them, for sure!

Ten 10-inch metal or wooden skewers
½ cup olive oil
¼ cup balsamic vinegar
1 teaspoon garlic powder
1 teaspoon salt
½ teaspoon black pepper
1 medium yellow squash, cut into 20 chunks
1 red onion, cut into 20 chunks
1 medium zucchini, cut into 20 chunks

If using wooden skewers, soak them in water for 20 minutes. In a small bowl, combine the oil, vinegar, garlic powder, salt, and pepper; mix well. Alternately thread 2 chunks each of the yellow squash, onion, and zucchini onto each skewer. Place in a 9" × 13" baking dish and pour the marinade over the vegetables. Marinate for 30 minutes, turning halfway through the marinating. Preheat the grill to medium-high heat and grill the kebabs for 8 to 10 minutes, or until fork-tender, basting occasionally with the marinade.

NOTE: If you prefer to broil instead of grill, just preheat the broiler and broil the kebabs for 12 to 15 minutes, turning and basting halfway through the cooking.

Limesicle Pie

6 to 8 servings

When I was a kid, I used to love the taste and texture of orange Creamsicle® pops! They were a combo of vanilla ice cream and orange sherbet. So, with that thought in mind, I decided to make a similar creamy treat . . . but in a pie! And to make it even more refreshing, I've used lime sherbet! Wow—what a zippy way to start off the summer!

> 1 pint lime sherbet, softened
> One 9-inch graham cracker pie crust
> 1 pint vanilla ice cream, softened
> 1 teaspoon grated lime peel

Spread the lime sherbet in the pie crust, then spread the vanilla ice cream over the sherbet. Sprinkle with the grated lime peel, cover, and freeze for 3 hours, or until firm.

NOTE: To give this a fancy look, just before serving, top each piece with half a lime slice.

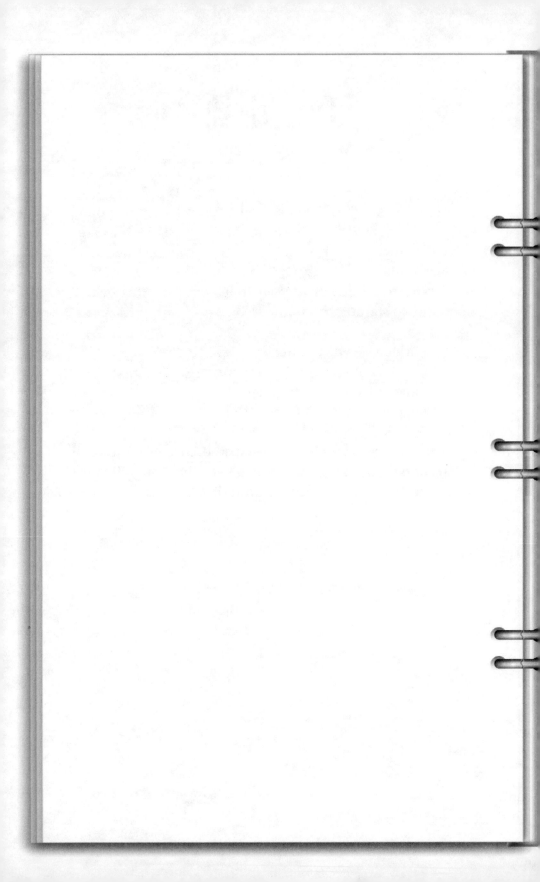

WEEK 23

Pre-Wedding Welcome

Where does the time go? Can you believe it's June already?! The weather is warming up and that means everything's blooming. Maybe that's why there are so many June weddings. And I have the perfect dinner for when the prospective bride and groom's families meet. Sure, you could get together at a restaurant, but nothing says "Welcome to the family!" like a home-cooked meal. And I promise, it's simple yet elegant enough to get you started off on the right foot with your new relations-to-be!

Strawberry Spinach Salad

Simple Chicken Cordon Bleu

Potato Roses

Wedding Basket Cake

Café Mochaccino

Strawberry Spinach Salad

This is a light salad that's fancy enough for your special dinner and easy enough to throw together any night of the week to make *that* a special dinner, too!

1 package (10 ounces) fresh spinach
1 pint fresh strawberries, washed, hulled, and sliced
½ of a small onion, finely chopped
3 tablespoons sugar
3 tablespoons water
2 tablespoons white vinegar
½ teaspoon dry mustard
¼ cup vegetable oil

Rinse the spinach leaves and remove the stems; dry well and tear into bite-sized pieces. Place the spinach in a large salad bowl and add the strawberries. In a small bowl, combine the remaining ingredients; whisk until well combined. Drizzle the dressing over the salad and toss to coat. Serve immediately.

NOTE: If you prefer, you can substitute a can of drained mandarin oranges for the fresh strawberries.

Simple Chicken Cordon Bleu

6 servings

You're not going to need a passport to visit the French cooking school that made *cordon bleu* famous. Only a few minutes of preparation and the oven does the rest!

> 6 boneless, skinless chicken breast halves (1½ to 2 pounds total)
> ½ teaspoon salt
> ⅛ teaspoon black pepper
> 6 slices (6 ounces) deli ham
> 6 slices (6 ounces) Swiss cheese
> ¾ cup plain dry bread crumbs
> 3 tablespoons butter, melted
> 1 tablespoon dried parsley
> 2 garlic cloves, minced

Preheat the oven to 425°F. Coat a 9" × 13" baking dish with nonstick cooking spray. Season the chicken breasts with the salt and pepper and place in the baking dish. Top each with a slice of ham, then a slice of cheese. In a small bowl, combine the remaining ingredients; mix well and spread over the cheese slices. Bake for 18 to 20 minutes, or until the topping is golden and no pink remains in the chicken.

NOTE: There are many varieties of deli and specialty hams available, and using a different one each time will give you different flavors.

Potato Roses

6 servings

June is the time for beautiful blooming rosebushes, so let's also make it the time for our dinner plates to be blooming with tasty and fancy-looking side dishes.

6 small potatoes (about 1 pound), washed and thinly sliced
¼ cup (½ stick) butter, melted
½ teaspoon dried thyme
¼ teaspoon salt
⅛ teaspoon black pepper

Preheat the oven to 425°F. Coat 6 muffin cups with nonstick cooking spray. In a large bowl, combine all the ingredients; mix well. Place 3 potato slices in the bottom of each muffin cup. Place additional potato slices around the insides of the muffin cups, overlapping them slightly to form rose petals. Continue adding potato slices to each cup until the center is filled and a rose has been formed. Bake for 30 to 35 minutes, or until golden. Using a serving spoon, carefully remove the potato roses to the dinner plates.

NOTE: Serve each potato on two basil leaves placed to look like flower leaves.

"A POTATO BY ANY OTHER NAME..."

Wedding Basket Cake

6 to 8 servings

Hmm . . . what should you serve for dessert? Ice cream? Not fancy enough. Fresh fruit? Too simple. But together . . . yup, that'll do the trick. It'll be perfect, so don't forget the camera!

> ½ pint fresh raspberries, washed
> ¼ cup sugar
> One 16-ounce chocolate pound cake
> 1 pint vanilla ice cream

In a small saucepan, cook the raspberries and sugar over medium heat for 5 minutes, or until the sugar has dissolved and the raspberries have formed a sauce, stirring occasionally. Remove from the heat and set aside. Without cutting through the bottom of the cake, make a vertical cut ¾ inch from the outside edge of the cake, going all the way around the cake.

(continued)

Gently remove the cake from inside the cut, leaving a basket with its bottom intact. (Save the cut-out cake for a snack.) Shape a basket handle with aluminum foil or pipe cleaners and decorate with ribbons, as illustrated; set aside. When ready to serve, fill the cake basket with small scoops of ice cream, piling the scoops so they overflow the top of the basket. Drizzle the ice cream with some of the raspberry sauce. Add the handle, as illustrated, and serve with the remaining raspberry sauce on the side.

NOTE: Of course, if you prefer a regular pound cake or choco-late ice cream (or another favorite flavor), that'll work, too. And to make this at any time of the year, you can even substi-tute a 16-ounce package of frozen raspberries for the fresh.

Café Mochaccino

6 servings

To finish off any special meal, we need a special coffee—sometimes cappuccino, other times espresso. But tonight I think mochaccino will do the trick!

1 tablespoon light brown sugar
6 cups chocolate milk
6 tablespoons instant coffee granules
½ cup whipped cream

Place the brown sugar in a shallow dish. Moisten the rims of 6 cups or coffee mugs with water and dip in the brown sugar; set aside. In a medium saucepan, combine the chocolate milk and coffee granules over medium heat until the coffee granules have dissolved and the milk is hot. Pour into the cups or mugs and top with the whipped cream. Serve immediately.

NOTE: Add some sugar to the saucepan if you prefer a sweeter mochaccino, or let people add their own, if desired.

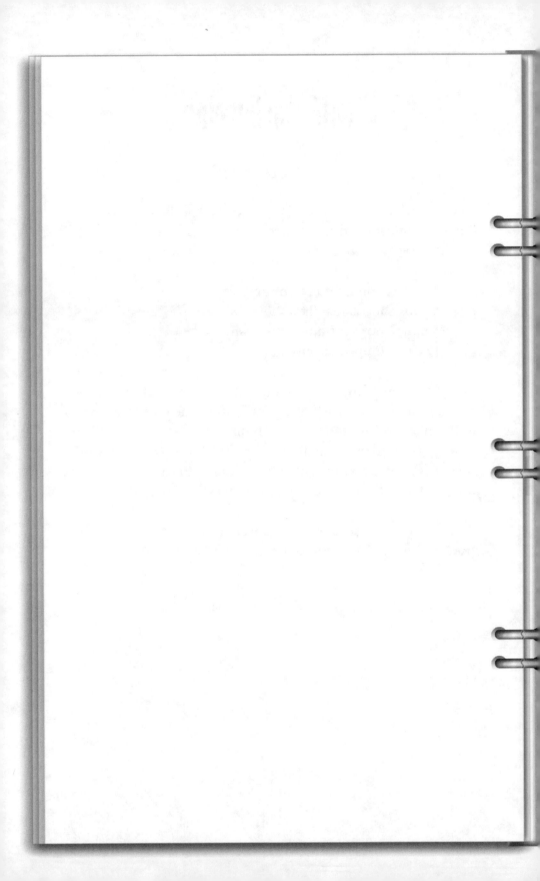

WEEK 24

Beefed-Up Dinners

Did you know that there's a National Beef Month? Well, we Americans sure do love our beef, and that's why I devoted this week to all sorts of favorites. Whether it's piled on a salad, sandwiched between hearty bread, roasted in the oven, or grilled on the barbecue, beef is a food we crave. And wait till you see what I've got for you here—an easy beef main course for every night of the work week.

Marinated Flank Steak Salad

Barbecue Joe

Tarragon Tenderloin

Skillet Round Steak

Diner-Style Salisbury Steak

Marinated Flank Steak Salad

4 to 6 servings

This is no ordinary salad! Topped with thinly sliced marinated beef, it's a perfect summertime main dish.

¼ cup olive oil
Juice of 1 lime
1 small onion, minced
1 tablespoon crushed red pepper
1 teaspoon salt
One 1½-pound beef flank steak
½ cup mayonnaise
½ cup chili sauce
1 head romaine lettuce, cut into bite-sized pieces
1 can (2.25 ounces) sliced olives, drained
1 package (4 ounces) crumbled feta cheese

In a 9" × 13" baking dish, combine the oil, lime juice, onion, red pepper, and salt; mix well. Add the steak and turn to coat. Cover and chill for 4 hours, turning halfway through the marinating time. In a small bowl, combine the mayonnaise and chili sauce; whisk until well combined, then cover and chill. Preheat the broiler. Place the lettuce on a serving platter; set aside. Remove the steak from the marinade, discarding any excess marinade, and place on a broiler pan or large rimmed baking sheet. Broil for 7 to 9 minutes per side for medium, or until desired doneness. Remove the steak to a cutting board and slice across the grain. Place the steak slices over the lettuce. Sprinkle with the olives and feta cheese and drizzle with the chilled mayonnaise mixture. Serve immediately.

NOTE: You can chill the steak before serving, if you'd prefer.

Barbecue Joe

This started out as a simple throw-together version of good ol'
Sloppy Joe—you know, ground beef in a flavorful tomato
sauce. But I decided to jazz it up a bit by replacing the tomato
sauce with barbecue sauce. And here we have it—Barbecue Joe!

1 pound ground beef
1 small onion, chopped
¾ cup barbecue sauce
1 teaspoon salt
½ teaspoon black pepper
4 hamburger buns, split

In a large saucepan, brown the ground beef and onion over
medium heat for 6 to 8 minutes; drain off any excess fat. Add
the barbecue sauce, salt, and pepper and cook for 3 to 4 minutes, or until heated through. Spoon over the buns and serve.

NOTE: I like to toast the hamburger buns so they hold up better with this hearty Barbecue Joe.

Tarragon Tenderloin

5 to 6 servings

Ever order filet mignon at a restaurant and wonder how they made it so tender and flavorful? There really is no secret—it's all in the cut of meat. With the tenderloin, we're guaranteed that every forkful will be restaurant-quality. And at home we don't have to tip the server!

> One 2- to 2½-pound beef tenderloin roast, trimmed
> 1 tablespoon vegetable oil
> ½ teaspoon onion powder
> ½ teaspoon garlic powder
> ½ teaspoon dried tarragon
> ¼ teaspoon black pepper

Preheat the oven to 350°F. Coat a large rimmed baking sheet with nonstick cooking spray. Place the tenderloin on the baking sheet. In a small bowl, combine the remaining ingredients and rub over the tenderloin. Cook for 35 to 40 minutes for medium-rare, or until desired doneness beyond that. Remove the tenderloin to a cutting board and slice across the grain into ½-inch slices.

NOTE: Serve with a quick béarnaise sauce made by combining 2 tablespoons white vinegar, 1½ teaspoons ground dried tarragon, ¼ teaspoon garlic powder, and ½ teaspoon chopped fresh parsley. Simmer in a small saucepan over medium heat for 2 minutes. Place in a small bowl and blend in 1 cup mayonnaise until smooth.

Skillet Round Steak

5 to 6 servings

Give me a hot skillet or wok, a thinly sliced steak, and a few veggies, and I'll give you dinner on the table in no time.

> 1½ pounds beef round steak, thinly sliced
> 1 medium onion, chopped
> ¼ cup (½ stick) butter
> 1 can (14½ ounces) ready-to-use beef broth
> ½ pound fresh mushrooms, sliced
> 1 large red bell pepper, cut into thin strips
> 2 tablespoons Worcestershire sauce
> ½ teaspoon salt
> ½ teaspoon black pepper
> ¼ cup water
> 2 tablespoons cornstarch

In a large skillet, brown the steak and onion in the butter over medium-high heat for 5 to 7 minutes. Add the beef broth, mushrooms, bell pepper, Worcestershire sauce, salt, and black pepper. Reduce the heat to medium-low, cover, and simmer for 30 minutes. In a small bowl, combine the water and cornstarch; mix well. Add to the skillet and cook for 1 to 2 minutes, or until the sauce has thickened.

NOTE: Serve over rice or noodles and add a tossed salad for a complete meal.

Diner-Style Salisbury Steak

Isn't it about time to take a trip down memory lane? Let's stay home and revisit the old diner that served up Salisbury steak and mashed potatoes smothered with mushroom gravy. Oh— we can't forget the green peas on the side!

  1½ pounds ground beef
  2 scallions, finely chopped
  ¼ cup seasoned bread crumbs
  1 egg
  1 tablespoon prepared yellow mustard
  1 container (12 ounces) beef gravy
  ½ cup water
  2 teaspoons prepared white horseradish
  ½ pound fresh mushrooms, sliced

Coat a large skillet with nonstick cooking spray. In a medium bowl, combine the ground beef, scallions, bread crumbs, egg, and mustard; mix well. Shape into four ½-inch-thick oval patties. Heat the skillet over medium-high heat and cook the patties for 3 to 4 minutes per side, or until no pink remains. Add the gravy, water, horseradish, and mushrooms and cook for 4 to 5 minutes, or until the mushrooms are tender, stirring occasionally.

NOTE: Each patty makes a hearty serving, so you can certainly make smaller portions—just form the mixture into 6 or 8 smaller patties.

WEEK 25

Fun Food

Three days, two days, one day . . . hurray! School's out! Can you believe it's summer vacation already? We still have a bit of time before camp starts, and we need help keeping everybody busy. So let's hit the kitchen and try a few fun recipes. They're good enough to enjoy until way past Labor Day!

Upside-down Chicken Pizza Muffins

Grilled Fluffwich

Taco Dogs

Peanut M&M® Bars

Cookies 'n' Ice Cream

Upside-down Chicken Pizza Muffins

1 dozen

Making pizza muffins is nothing new in our kitchen. And you know how the English muffins always seem to get soggy? Well, no more! Know why? Baking them upside down on the baking sheet gives them extra crunch. And the addition of chicken to this version makes it a real filler-upper.

> 6 English muffins, split
> ¾ cup spaghetti or pizza sauce
> 1 package (10½ ounces) breaded chicken nuggets, thawed
>   if frozen, chopped
> ¾ cup (3 ounces) shredded mozzarella cheese

Preheat the oven to 450°F. Coat a rimmed baking sheet with nonstick cooking spray. Place the muffin halves split side down on the baking sheet. Spread the sauce over the muffin halves. Top with the chopped chicken nuggets and sprinkle with the cheese. Bake for 8 to 10 minutes, or until heated through.

NOTE: For additional flavor, you may want to add seasonings like basil, oregano, or garlic powder, or use a different-flavored spaghetti sauce.

Grilled Fluffwich

4 sandwiches

This one's not too far from the old standby "fluffernutter" sandwiches that we grew up with—but this time it's grilled, which makes it even extra ooey-gooey!

¼ cup peanut butter
8 slices egg bread
½ cup marshmallow creme
2 tablespoons butter, softened, divided (see Note)

Spread the peanut butter evenly over 4 slices of bread. Spread the marshmallow creme over the remaining 4 slices of bread and place creme side down over the other slices to make sandwiches. Using 1 tablespoon butter, evenly coat the tops of the sandwiches. In a large skillet, melt the remaining 1 tablespoon butter over medium-high heat. Place the sandwiches buttered side up in the skillet and grill for about 1 minute. Turn the sandwiches over and grill for 1 more minute, or until golden. Serve immediately.

NOTE: Some people say these taste better with unsalted butter, but to me it doesn't matter—I like the slightly salty flavor of regular butter. If you want to get really adventurous, add some sliced bananas to the sandwiches; the kids'll love it!

Taco Dogs

8 servings

Isn't it time you invited the neighborhood kids over for lunch or dinner? And with little work, you can put out a grand help-yourself buffet in minutes!

    1 tablespoon butter
    8 chicken hot dogs (1 pound)
    1 can (15 ounces) chili without beans
    ¼ cup taco sauce
    8 taco shells
    1½ cups shredded iceberg lettuce
    ¾ cup (6 ounces) shredded Cheddar cheese
    1 medium tomato, chopped

Melt the butter in a large skillet over medium-high heat. Add the hot dogs and cook for 2 to 3 minutes, or until browned on all sides. Meanwhile, in a small saucepan, combine the chili and taco sauce over medium-high heat and cook for 2 to 3 minutes, or until heated through. Fill each taco shell with an equal amount of lettuce; place a hot dog in each, then fill equally with the chili mixture, cheese, and tomato. Serve, or place the ingredients in separate bowls and serve make-your-own tacos.

NOTE: You can also put out bowls of additional toppings like chopped onions or jalapeño peppers, sour cream, and/or hot pepper sauce.

Peanut M&M® Bars

9 to 12 bars

When the report cards come home, we're gonna want to make a little something special to reward the kids for all their hard work! They sure deserve it!

    1 cup sugar
    1 cup creamy peanut butter (see Note)
    1 egg
    1 teaspoon vanilla extract
    ¼ cup mini M&M's

Preheat the oven to 325°F. Coat an 8-inch square baking pan with nonstick cooking spray. In a medium bowl, combine the sugar, peanut butter, egg, and vanilla. Add the M&M's and mix well. Press evenly into the baking pan and bake for 25 to 30 minutes, or until a wooden toothpick inserted in the center comes out clean. Allow to cool, then cut into bars and serve.

NOTE: If you really like a peanutty flavor, use crunchy peanut butter.

Cookies 'n' Ice Cream

1 dozen

Make up a batch of these to keep in the freezer for an on-the-go treat that works perfectly for our busy lifestyles.

24 fudge-striped cookies
1 quart vanilla ice cream
⅔ cup chocolate sprinkles

Lay 12 of the cookies fudge side down on a cookie sheet and place a small scoop of ice cream on each cookie. Top with the remaining 12 cookies, forming sandwiches, and lightly press the cookies together. Roll the sides in the sprinkles, coating the ice cream completely. Freeze for 2 hours, or until firm. Serve, or wrap individually in plastic wrap and keep frozen until ready to serve.

NOTE: Using different types of cookies and flavors of ice cream makes the variations on this recipe virtually endless. And you can coat the edges in any type of sprinkles, too—or chopped nuts or even mini chocolate chips. Mmm!

WEEK 26

Father's Day Barbecue

Happy Father's Day! What a great idea it is to have a special day to salute all us dads. Now that doesn't mean we shouldn't honor our dads all year long, but on the third Sunday in June every year, we have to have a barbecue! Yup, you know where to find all of us dads—showing off at the grill and sharing good times with our families!

Bacon 'n' Blue-Cheese Burger

Sweet-Pickle Potato Salad

Grilled Corn on the Cob

Grilled Caramelized Onions

Layered Watermelon Cake

Bacon 'n' Blue-Cheese Burger

8 servings

On the Fourth of July we'll be celebrating the red, white, and blue, but today let's salute the beef, bacon, and blue . . . blue cheese, that is!

    2 pounds ground beef
    1 package (4 ounces) crumbled blue cheese
    ¼ cup real bacon bits
    ½ teaspoon black pepper

Preheat the grill to medium-high heat. In a large bowl, combine all the ingredients; mix well. Shape the mixture into 8 equal-sized patties. Grill for 8 to 12 minutes, or until cooked to medium-well or well-done, turning halfway through the grilling.

NOTE: Serve these on hamburger buns with romaine lettuce and some creamy blue cheese dressing.

Sweet-Pickle Potato Salad

8 to 12 servings

We all have our favorite variation of potato salad, but you've gotta try this southern-style one that I got from a viewer who said she got it from her dad. That makes it extra appropriate for Father's Day!

> 5 pounds red potatoes, washed and cut into 1-inch chunks
> 2 cups mayonnaise
> 1 jar (12 ounces) super-sweet dill pickles, drained and
>   chopped, with juice reserved
> 8 hard-boiled eggs, chopped
> 4 celery stalks, chopped
> 1 tablespoon salt
> 1 teaspoon black pepper

Place the potatoes in a soup pot and add just enough water to cover them. Bring to a boil over high heat, then reduce the heat to medium and cook for 12 to 15 minutes, or until fork-tender; drain. Allow to cool slightly, then place in a large bowl. Add the remaining ingredients, including the reserved pickle juice; mix well. Cover and chill for at least 2 hours before serving.

NOTE: If you like extra-moist potato salad, then add an extra cup of mayonnaise before serving.

Grilled Corn on the Cob

8 servings

Put away the pot for the boiling water, 'cause we're cooking *this* corn on the grill. Oh, do these seasonings give it an extra-special kick!

> ½ cup (1 stick) butter, softened
> 1 tablespoon chili powder
> 1 teaspoon salt
> ¼ teaspoon black pepper (see Note)
> 8 ears fresh corn, husked

Preheat the grill to medium-high heat. In a small bowl, combine the butter, chili powder, salt, and pepper; mix well. Brush the corn with the butter mixture, coating completely. Wrap each ear in a piece of heavy-duty aluminum foil. Place the wrapped corn on the grill rack and cook for 10 to 12 minutes, or until the kernels are tender, turning halfway through the cooking. Carefully open the foil, remove the corn, and serve hot.

NOTE: For even more flavor kick, use ground red pepper instead of black pepper.

Grilled Caramelized Onions

8 servings

If Dad makes these onions for you while wearing his "Kiss the Cook" apron, don't worry! They get perfectly caramelized and beautifully mellow from cooking for a while in honey.

¼ cup (½ stick) butter, melted
2 tablespoons honey
¼ teaspoon salt
4 medium onions, cut in half

Preheat the grill to medium-high heat. In a large bowl, combine the butter, honey, and salt; mix well. Add the onions and mix well, then place on a large piece of heavy-duty aluminum foil and seal tightly. Place seam side up on the grill rack and cook for 20 to 22 minutes, or until tender and caramelized, carefully turning halfway through the cooking. Carefully open the foil, remove the caramelized onions, and serve hot.

Layered Watermelon Cake

12 to 16 servings

It's green on the outside, pink on the inside, and it has edible seeds. . . . Yup, it's watermelon . . . watermelon *cake!*

> 1 package (7 ounces) chocolate-covered raisins
> 20 drops red food color, divided
> 1 package (18.25 ounces) white cake mix, batter prepared according to the package directions
> 1 container (16 ounces) vanilla frosting (see Note)
> 8 drops green food color

Reserve 2 tablespoons of the chocolate-covered raisins. Add the remaining chocolate-covered raisins and 12 drops red food color to the cake batter; mix well. Bake according to the package directions in two 8-inch round cake pans that have been coated with nonstick cooking spray, lined with waxed paper, and coated again with nonstick cooking spray. Let cool for 10 minutes, then invert onto wire racks to cool completely. Place the frosting in 2 medium bowls, dividing it equally. Add the green food color to one bowl; mix well. Add the remaining 8 drops red food color to the second bowl; mix well. Place 1 cake layer upside down on a serving plate and frost the top with half of the red frosting. Place the second layer on the first and frost the top with the remaining red frosting. Frost the sides with the green frosting. Sprinkle the reserved 2 tablespoons chocolate-covered raisins over the top to look like seeds. Serve, or cover loosely until ready to serve.

NOTE: Instead of frosting, you can use low-fat frozen whipped topping that has been thawed—just color it as above and frost the cake, but be sure to keep it chilled.

WEEK 27

Red, White, and Blue Birthday Bash

Get out the candles and party hats. We're celebrating BIG, really BIG, with fireworks and lots of food in honor of our nation's birthday. So sport that red, white, and blue and let the party begin.

Mixed Berry Salad

New England Lobster Boil

Red, White, and Blue Ribbon Cookies

Patriotic Milk Shakes

Mixed Berry Salad

4 to 6 servings

No ordinary salad will work for this special event. Oh, no! We're bringing out those red and blue berries to add a bit of patriotism to every bite.

    1 medium head iceberg lettuce, washed and cut into bite-
        sized pieces
    1 quart fresh strawberries, washed, hulled, and sliced
    ½ pint fresh blueberries, washed
    1 bottle (8 ounces) Italian dressing
    ½ of a small onion, finely chopped
    ⅓ cup sugar

In a large salad bowl, combine the lettuce, strawberries, and blueberries. In a small bowl, combine the remaining ingredients; mix well and add to the lettuce mixture. Toss and serve.

NOTE: If you prefer to make this in advance, chill the salad and the dressing mixtures separately; then just toss and serve.

New England Lobster Boil

4 servings

Doesn't the gang celebrating the Declaration of Independence deserve more than the standard grilled hamburgers and hot dogs? You betcha! So let's have a big ol' lobster boil, with everything made in one pot!

> 4 medium potatoes, washed and quartered
> 2 tablespoons salt
> 4 ears fresh corn, husked
> 4 live Maine lobsters (1 to 1½ pounds each)

Fill a 12-quart stockpot with 2 inches of water; add the potatoes and salt and bring to a rapid boil over high heat; continue boiling for 10 minutes. Add the corn and lobsters, then cover and steam for 10 to 15 minutes, or until the lobsters are bright red and the corn and potatoes are tender. Remove from the pot and serve.

NOTE: If you don't have an extra-large stockpot, then you can split up the ingredients and cook 1 or 2 servings at a time in a regular soup pot. Oh—make sure to have lobster crackers on hand (the kitchen gadgets, I mean—not crackers that you eat!) for cracking open the shells, and serve it all with lemon wedges and plenty of melted butter.

Red, White, and Blue Ribbon Cookies

about 3 dozen

Why not show your patriotism and take these along when you go to watch the Fourth of July parade or fireworks?

> 2 packages (18 ounces each) refrigerated sugar cookie dough
> ¼ teaspoon red food color
> ¼ teaspoon blue food color

Line an empty waxed paper (or other food wrap) box with waxed paper. In a large bowl, combine the 2 packages of cookie dough, then divide the dough into 3 equal parts. In a medium bowl, combine 1 piece of dough and the red food color. Using your hands, work the food color into the dough until it is evenly colored; place in the bottom of the waxed paper box. Using a spatula, smooth the dough down into an even layer. Place the second piece of dough over the red layer and level it with the spatula. In the same bowl, combine the remaining dough and the blue food color. Using your hands, work the food color into the dough until evenly colored. Place it over the uncolored dough and level it with the spatula. Cover with waxed paper and close the box. Freeze for at least 1 hour, or until the dough is firm. Preheat the oven to 350°F. Coat 2 large baking sheets with nonstick cooking spray. Remove the dough from the box and cut into ¼-inch slices, making sure that the dough is still firm and retains its square shape; rechill if necessary. Place 2 inches apart on the baking sheets and bake for 9 to 10 minutes, or until golden around the edges.

NOTE: If you prefer, you can freeze the dough longer—until it is almost solid—then use a sharp knife to slice or cut just the amount you need from the block; wrap and return the remaining cookie dough to the freezer for later use.

Patriotic Milk Shakes

4 servings

To top off our Fourth of July celebration, many of us stop by the local ice cream store for a refreshing cone. But for a change, why not go home for a strawberry milk shake topped with whipped cream and fresh blueberries? How could anybody resist?!

1 quart strawberry ice cream
1 cup milk
½ cup strawberry preserves
¼ cup frozen whipped topping, thawed
¼ cup fresh blueberries, washed

In a blender, combine the ice cream, milk, and strawberry preserves. Blend for 1 to 2 minutes, or until well combined. Pour into 4 glasses and top each with a dollop of whipped topping. Top with the blueberries and serve immediately.

NOTE: You can make a light version by using nonfat strawberry frozen yogurt, low-fat milk, and light whipped topping. I'd say that calls for a real celebration!

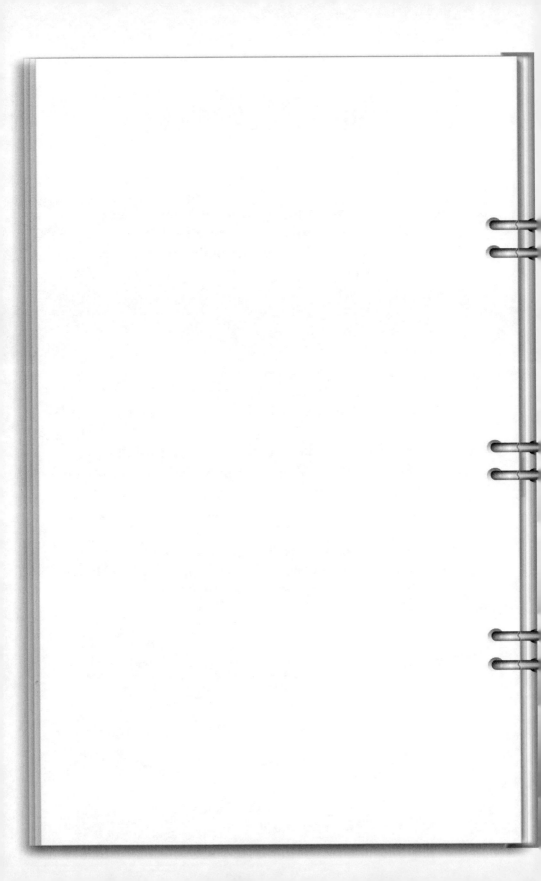

WEEK 28

Campfire Cookin'

When July rolls around, it means the mercury is rising and many of us are heading for our long-awaited summer vacations. Camping is still one of the most popular choices. And there's one thing we all have in common, whether we camp in a camper, a cabin, a tent, or out under the stars: camping food. It has a special taste, whether it's cooked on a griddle, on a propane stove, or over an open fire. So git along to the wilderness . . . and when you're lingering over the roasting marshmallows, don't forget the ghost stories!

Toss-Together Corn Salad

Hot Potato Packets

Campfire Hot Diggity Dogs

S'more Brownie Pie

Hot Chocolate Mix

Toss-Together Corn Salad

6 to 8 servings

The fun part of this salad is that you change it every time, depending on what you bring along or can get at the campground's produce stand. Add peppers one time, cucumbers another, and sugar snap peas the next. Before you know it, you'll be going camping just so you can make this salad!

    2 cans (15¼ ounces each) whole kernel corn, drained
    ¼ cup Italian dressing
    1 small green bell pepper, finely chopped
    1 small red bell pepper, finely chopped

In a medium bowl, combine all the ingredients; mix well. Cover and chill for at least 1 hour before serving.

NOTE: You can make this in advance, but if you plan to make it on the camping trip, be sure to bring a good old-fashioned hand-operated can opener with you.

Hot Potato Packets

6 servings

There's nothing wrong with eating a baked potato that you've cooked in foil over an open fire, but after a few nights of that you're going to be ready for an alternative. And here it is! After a quick mix, simply wrap these up and onto the heat they go! It couldn't be easier or tastier! (Of course, when we want that campfire taste at home, we can make these in the oven.)

    6 medium potatoes, washed and thinly sliced
    1 medium onion, thinly sliced
    ½ cup (1 stick) butter, melted
    2 cups (8 ounces) shredded Cheddar cheese
    ⅓ cup real bacon bits
    1 teaspoon salt
    ½ teaspoon black pepper

Prepare a barbecue fire with a grill rack (or preheat the oven to 375°F.). Coat six 12" × 24" pieces of aluminum foil with non-stick cooking spray. In a large bowl, combine all the ingredients; mix well. Place an equal amount of the potato mixture on each piece of foil. Seal each packet and place on the grill rack over medium-high heat (or on a large baking sheet in the oven). Cook for 55 to 60 minutes, or until the potatoes are tender.

NOTE: These packets can be prepared ahead of time and brought along in a cooler. Then all you have to do is place the packets on the grill or on a rack over a campfire until the potatoes are tender.

Campfire Hot Diggity Dogs

8 servings

It's said that we eat with our eyes, so why not turn ho-hum franks and beans into this great-looking supper the whole gang will be chatting about? Hot diggity dog!

    8 hot dogs (1 pound)
    1 can (16 ounces) baked beans
    8 hamburger buns, split

Cut crosswise slits in each hot dog at ½-inch intervals, cutting to within ¼ inch of the other side. Carefully bend each hot dog into a circle (cut side out) and fasten with a toothpick, as illustrated. In a medium skillet, cook the hot dogs over medium heat or on a grill until lightly browned, turning once. Meanwhile, warm the baked beans in a heat-proof saucepan over medium heat or the fire until heated through. Let the hot dogs cool slightly, then place each hot dog on a hamburger bun and **carefully remove the toothpicks**. Spoon some baked beans into the center of the circles formed by the hot dogs and serve with the remaining baked beans on the side.

NOTE: To give the baked beans additional flavor, add 2 tablespoons light brown sugar, 1 tablespoon ketchup, and 2 tablespoons real bacon bits, and cook until well combined and heated through.

CUT AT ½-INCH INTERVALS

BEND INTO A CIRCLE

TOOTHPICK

GRILL, THEN REMOVE TOOTHPICK AND ADD BAKED BEANS

S'more Brownie Pie

6 to 8 servings

This is our way to make and bake s'mores ahead of time for bringing along to the campsite (or to almost any get-together)! Now, if you want to serve it extra gooey, go ahead and warm it up over the campfire just before serving.

    1 package (20 ounces) brownie mix, batter prepared
        according to the package directions
    ½ cup (3 ounces) semisweet chocolate chips
    ½ cup marshmallow creme, melted
    ½ cup coarsely crushed graham crackers

Coat a 9-inch deep-dish pie plate with nonstick cooking spray and spread the brownie batter in it; bake for 35 to 40 minutes, or until a wooden toothpick inserted in the center comes out clean. Remove from the oven and immediately sprinkle the chocolate chips over the top; using a knife, spread the melting chips over the top of the brownies like frosting. Drizzle with the marshmallow creme and sprinkle with the crushed graham crackers. Allow to cool slightly; serve, or wrap well. Just before serving, unwrap and reheat, if desired, then cut into wedges.

NOTE: If enjoying this campfire goodie at home, why not serve each portion with a scoop of vanilla ice cream and a glass of milk? That'll guarantee that they ask for s'more!

Hot Chocolate Mix

3¾ cups mix; 15 servings

As nighttime falls, we're surrounded by darkness and silence, except for the glowing moon and the sounds of nature. That's when we know it's time for some bone-chilling ghost stories and a mug full of steamin' hot chocolate. Aah, yes, that's what camping is all about.

    2 cups nonfat dry milk
    ¾ cup sugar
    ½ cup unsweetened cocoa
    ½ cup powdered nondairy creamer
    ⅛ teaspoon salt

In a large bowl, combine all the ingredients; mix well. Store in an airtight container. To make a mug of hot chocolate, simply place ¼ cup of the mix in a mug and add ¾ cup boiling water; stir to blend.

NOTE: This is perfect for taking along on a camping trip, 'cause whenever you need to warm up, you can just boil water over the campfire and enjoy a cup of hot chocolate in the chilly night air. And for a Mocha Joe, stir 2 tablespoons of this mix into a cup of coffee.

WEEK 29

Le French Buffet

Bonjour, mes amis, and welcome to a very special day—Bastille Day. What is it, you ask? It all began on July 14, 1789, when French citizens stormed the Bastille, a state prison, in Paris, in an uprising against their unjust rulers. The Bastille has become a symbol of liberty and democracy for people around the world, so you can bet it's a national holiday in France and Canada and in French-influenced areas through-out the world. In our year of celebrations, here's our occasion to enjoy a French buffet. *Oui?* Of course, *oui!*

Hazelnut-Crusted Brie

Vichyssoise

Beef Bourguignon

Mixed-up Roasted Vegetables

Light and Easy Crepes Suzette

Hazelnut-Crusted Brie

2 Bries

If you look over this recipe quickly, you might ask, "Why make *two* Brie rounds?" Easy—if you make just one, you're likely to miss out 'cause it's so rich and creamy that it won't last long.

> 2 Brie cheese rounds (8 ounces each)
> 1 package (17¼ ounces) frozen puff pastry (2 sheets), thawed
> 1 egg, beaten
> ½ cup chopped hazelnuts

Preheat the oven to 350°F. Coat a large rimmed baking sheet with nonstick cooking spray. Place 1 Brie round in the center of each sheet of puff pastry and bring the edges up to the center, completely covering the Brie; pinch the dough firmly to seal. Trim and discard any excess dough and place seam side down on the baking sheet. Brush the tops of the puff pastry with the beaten egg and sprinkle with the hazelnuts. Bake for 25 to 30 minutes, or until the pastry is golden and the Brie is melted. Allow to cool slightly before serving.

NOTE: It adds a nice touch to serve this with baguette chips that you make by thinly slicing a long thin baguette (French bread) and toasting until golden.

Vichyssoise

6 to 8 servings

Ready for a little French cuisine trivia? Vichyssoise, a chilled potato soup, was created at New York's Ritz-Carlton Hotel by chef Louis Diat in 1910. He adapted it from a hot French soup that was made with potatoes and leeks. Well, you know me, I've simplified the now-famous cold version, made it with potatoes and onions, and topped it with lots of colorful scallion ringlets.

2 tablespoons butter
2 large onions, diced
⅛ teaspoon black pepper
2 cans (14½ ounces each) ready-to-use chicken broth
4 large potatoes, peeled and diced
¼ teaspoon ground nutmeg
2 cups (1 pint) half-and-half
3 scallions, sliced into ringlets

Melt the butter in a soup pot over medium-high heat. Add the onions and black pepper and sauté for 5 to 6 minutes, or until the onions are tender. Add the chicken broth, potatoes, and nutmeg. Bring to a boil and cook for 10 minutes, or until the potatoes are tender. Remove from the heat and stir in the half-and-half. Chill for at least 4 hours, or until well chilled. In a blender, purée the chilled soup on high speed until smooth. Pour into individual bowls and top with the scallions.

NOTE: If you can, plan to make this soup a day in advance. That way it will have plenty of time to chill before serving.

Beef Bourguignon

6 to 8 servings

Don't let the name scare you! If you like beef and mushrooms, boy, are you in for a treat! *Bon appétit!*

¼ cup (½ stick) butter
1 medium onion, chopped
½ cup all-purpose flour
1 teaspoon salt
¾ teaspoon black pepper
2 pounds beef round steak, cut into 1-inch chunks
½ pound fresh mushrooms, sliced
1 cup dry red wine
1 cup beef broth
1 bay leaf
1 pound wide egg noodles, cooked according to the package directions

Melt the butter in a soup pot over medium-high heat and sauté the onion for 3 to 5 minutes. Meanwhile, in a medium bowl, combine the flour, salt, and pepper; mix well. Add the beef and toss to coat evenly. Add the coated beef to the pot and brown for 6 to 8 minutes. Stir in the mushrooms and cook for 2 to 3 minutes. Add the red wine, beef broth, and bay leaf. Reduce the heat to low, cover, and simmer for 1½ hours. Uncover and cook for 15 to 20 more minutes, or until the beef is tender and the sauce has thickened. **Remove and discard the bay leaf.** Serve over the noodles.

NOTE: Thyme—fresh or dried—can be added along with the red wine for additional French flavor.

Mixed-up Roasted Vegetables

There's no need to wonder what kind of veggies we're going to serve with our beef bourguignon. . . . Why, this colorful medley of vegetables is just the dish!

> 4 medium yellow squash, cut into ½-inch slices
> 3 medium zucchini, cut into ½-inch slices
> 3 medium onions, quartered
> 4 medium bell peppers (any combination of red, yellow, and/or green), cut into 1½-inch chunks
> 2 tablespoons vegetable oil
> 1 teaspoon garlic powder
> 1 teaspoon salt
> ½ teaspoon black pepper

Preheat the oven to 450°F. Coat 2 large rimmed baking sheets with nonstick cooking spray. Combine all the vegetables in a large bowl; toss to combine. In a small bowl, combine the remaining ingredients; mix well. Drizzle over the vegetables and toss until well coated. Lay the vegetables in a single layer on the baking sheets. Roast for 20 minutes, or until tender, turning the vegetables halfway through the cooking.

NOTE: Sometimes I like to add chunks of red onion and peeled eggplant. The great thing about this recipe is that whatever vegetables you have on hand will work—so clean out that veggie bin!

Light and Easy Crepes Suzette

10 crepes

I used to make crepes suzette that were really rich and heavy. Sure, they were good, but I guess after a big meal that isn't really the most satisfying type of dessert. So I came up with this light and easy version. They have got the same big taste, but without that heavy "fill-you-up, weigh-you-down" feeling.

    1 cup all-purpose flour
    1 cup low-fat milk
    ¼ cup egg substitute
    1 tablespoon vegetable oil, plus extra for cooking
    1 tablespoon granulated sugar
    ¼ teaspoon salt
    Juice of 2 oranges
    ½ cup firmly packed light brown sugar
    1 tablespoon butter, melted
    1 tablespoon cornstarch

In a medium bowl, with an electric beater on medium speed, beat the flour, milk, egg substitute, 1 tablespoon oil, the granulated sugar, and salt until smooth. Lightly brush a small skillet with oil, then heat over medium-low heat. Pour ¼ cup of the batter into the skillet, tilting the skillet to coat the bottom evenly with the batter; cook for 1 minute per side, or until the edges are brown. Remove to a baking sheet, cover loosely with aluminum foil, and keep warm in a 200°F. oven until ready to serve. Continue with the remaining batter, brushing the skillet with oil as needed. Reserve 2 tablespoons of the orange juice. In a small saucepan, combine the remaining orange juice, the brown sugar, and butter over low heat. Cook for 5 minutes, stirring frequently. In a small bowl, combine the reserved 2 tablespoons orange juice and the cornstarch; mix well. Stir into the sauce and cook until thickened. Fold each crepe in half, then in half again; place on a serving platter and spoon the orange sauce over the top. Serve immediately.

NOTE: Now, for anybody who's not concerned with lightening up, here's where the light part goes out the window: If you want, you can top each crepe with a scoop of vanilla ice cream or frozen yogurt, and then spoon the orange sauce over that. Or you can even place a scoop of ice cream on each flat crepe and roll it up, then top with the sauce.

WEEK 30

Ice Cream Sampler

It's July, one of the most important months of the year. Why? It's none other than National Ice Cream Month. What a great reason to eat ice cream . . . not that we need one!

Pistachio Ice Cream

Frozen Peanut Butter Cups

Coconut Cream Pie Ice Cream

Spumoni

Frozen Mochaccino

Pistachio Ice Cream

about 2 quarts

Many years ago, when our kids were little, we frequented a little ice cream stand called Moxie's outside of Troy, New York—where we're from. They had incredible, luscious flavors. Unfortunately, we haven't gotten back there in years, and finding really flavorful pistachio ice cream is a rarity, so I figured it was time to make a homemade version. You know, it's as tasty as I remember it, but now I get to wipe it off my *grand*children's faces!

> 6 cups half-and-half
> 1 cup sugar
> 4 eggs
> 1 package (4-serving size) instant pistachio pudding and
>   pie filling
> 1 cup pistachios, coarsely chopped
> 1½ teaspoons vanilla extract

In a soup pot, combine the half-and-half, sugar, and eggs; mix well. Cook over medium-high heat for 20 minutes, or until thickened, stirring constantly; the mixture will boil. Remove from the heat and stir in the pudding mix, pistachios, and vanilla; allow to cool completely. Pour into an airtight container and freeze for at least 8 hours, or until firm.

NOTE: For a creamier ice cream, once the mixture is frozen, cut it into chunks and process in a food processor until creamy. Serve, or refreeze until ready to serve.

Frozen Peanut Butter Cups

1 dozen

If you can make only one recipe from this book, let this be the one! It's truly unbelievable!

    1 package (12 ounces) semisweet chocolate chips
    2 tablespoons vegetable shortening
    1 quart vanilla ice cream, softened
    1 cup creamy peanut butter
    4 Butterfinger® candy bars (2.1 ounces each), coarsely
        crushed

Place 12 paper baking cups into muffin cups. In a small saucepan, heat the chocolate and shortening over low heat for 1 to 2 minutes, stirring just until the chocolate melts and the mixture is smooth. Allow to cool slightly; the mixture should still be pourable. Starting at the top edge of each paper cup, spoon the chocolate over the insides of the cups, completely covering the inside of each cup with about 4 teaspoons of the mixture. Chill the cups until firm, about 30 minutes. In a large bowl, combine the ice cream, peanut butter, and crushed candy bars; mix well. Spoon evenly into the chocolate cups. Cover and freeze for at least 2 hours, or until firm.

" Peanut Butter
    Ice cream in
    Chocolate cups!
    Yummy! "

(continued)

NOTE: In a hurry for peanut butter cup ice cream? Skip the part where you make the chocolate cups and, instead, just stir 1 cup of chocolate chips into the other ingredients. It's not as fancy as the cups, but it tastes just as good.

Coconut Cream Pie Ice Cream

about 1½ quarts

Remember that classic coconut cream pie piled high and bursting with coconut that we used to get at our favorite diner? Well, here are those tasty memories served up ice cream style. Just wait till you try it! Wanna mix in some broken graham crackers to stand in for the crust? Go for it!

½ cup sweetened flaked coconut
2 cups (1 pint) heavy cream
1 can (15 ounces) cream of coconut

Preheat the oven to 350°F. Place the coconut on a large rimmed baking sheet and bake for 4 to 5 minutes, or until golden, stirring once; allow to cool. In a large bowl, with an electric beater on medium speed, beat the heavy cream until stiff peaks form. Slowly beat in the cream of coconut until well combined. Add the toasted coconut and mix well. Cover and freeze for at least 8 hours, or until firm.

NOTE: Scoop into bowls and top with chocolate-flavored hard-shell topping for a homemade version of a frozen Mounds® candy bar.

Spumoni

9 to 12 servings

In our test kitchen, we rate all of our recipes for taste, consistency, and looks on a scale from 1 to 5, with 5 being super. Well, this colorful dessert rated 5+ for taste, 5+ for consistency, and 10 for looks!

>   2 cups (1 pint) heavy cream
>   1 can (14 ounces) sweetened condensed milk
>   ½ cup (3 ounces) semisweet chocolate chips
>   2 tablespoons sliced almonds
>   2 drops green food color
>   ¼ cup maraschino cherries, drained and halved
>   2 drops red food color
>   ½ cup raisins
>   ⅛ teaspoon rum extract

In a medium bowl, with an electric beater on medium speed, beat the cream until stiff peaks form. Slowly beat in the sweetened condensed milk until well combined. Spoon the mixture into 3 bowls, dividing it equally. Add the chocolate chips, almonds, and green food color to the first bowl; mix well and spoon evenly into an 8-inch square baking dish that has been lined with aluminum foil. Add the cherries and red food color to the second bowl; mix well and spoon evenly over the green layer. Add the raisins and rum extract to the third bowl; mix well and spoon evenly over the red layer. Cover and freeze for at least 4 hours, or until firm. Cut into squares and serve.

NOTE: This can also be made in a gelatin mold and cut into wedges, or as individual spumoni in a muffin tin lined with paper baking cups.

Frozen Mochaccino

6 servings

What better way to celebrate National Ice Cream Month than with a frozen version of trendy cappuccino? And with a bit of chocolate mixed in we have a heavenly mocha delight without all the loud hissing and bubbling (and mess!) of the cappuccino machine!

> 1 cup (½ pint) heavy cream
> ¼ cup confectioners' sugar
> 2 tablespoons instant coffee granules
> 1 teaspoon hot water
> 1 quart chocolate ice cream, softened
> Ground cinnamon for topping

In a medium bowl, with an electric beater on medium speed, beat the cream and confectioners' sugar until stiff peaks form. In a large bowl, dissolve the instant coffee granules in the water. Add the ice cream and 1 cup of the whipped cream mixture; mix well. Spoon equal amounts of the ice cream mixture into 6 small clear plastic cups and spread the remaining whipped cream mixture over the top. Sprinkle with the cinnamon, cover, and freeze for at least 4 hours, or until firm.

NOTE: I try to use clear plastic cups or, when I can find them, clear plastic coffee cups with handles, so that we can see the different layers of the frozen cappuccino.

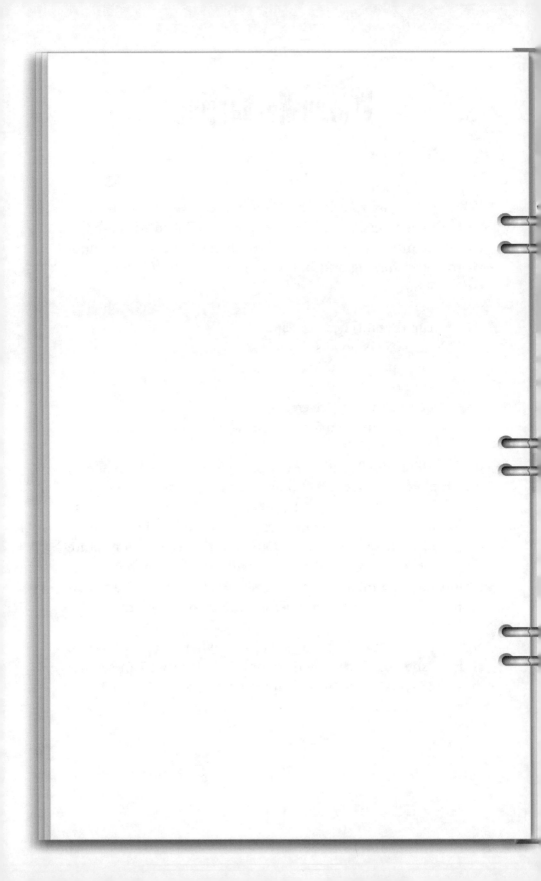

WEEK 31

Rhode Island Sensations

In the '70s, while Barry Manilow was singing his hit "Weekend in New England," our family was experiencing "one week a year in Rhode Island." Ethel ("Mrs. Food") and I still try to get there for a week or so every summer. We love the people and the incredible restaurants! We make sure we get our share of fish and seafood in one form or another, and lots of fabulous Italian food, too, since there are so many terrific Italian restaurants in our littlest state.

Parmesan-Garlic Oil

Creamy Clam Chowder

Easy Caesar Salad

Linguine and Clams in Red Sauce

Dreamy Orange Swirl Cheesecake

Parmesan-Garlic Oil

about 1¼ cups

Mamma mia! This is no ordinary dipping sauce that we're gonna be serving with our Italian bread! I've talked about it so much that maybe that's why my grandson asked me if this was the "Big Dipper thing" he's heard about!

        1 cup olive oil
        ½ cup grated Parmesan cheese
        1½ teaspoons chopped fresh parsley
        ½ teaspoon garlic powder
        ½ teaspoon black pepper

In a small bowl, whisk all the ingredients until well combined. Spoon onto individual bread and butter plates and serve with thick slices of Italian bread for dunking.

NOTE: If you have some fresh basil on hand—or any of your other favorite fresh herbs—go ahead and use that instead of the parsley.

Creamy Clam Chowder

8 to 10 servings

This is for those times when we want fresh-from-the-shore clam chowder but can't quite get to the shore. Simply toss together a pot of this and you'll think you're there!

6 large potatoes, peeled and diced
2 large onions, finely chopped
4 celery stalks, finely chopped
4 cans (6½ ounces each) chopped clams, undrained
2 bottles (8 ounces each) clam juice
1½ teaspoons dried thyme
½ teaspoon black pepper
¼ cup (½ stick) butter
2 cups (1 pint) heavy cream (see Note)

In a soup pot, bring the potatoes, onions, celery, clams, clam juice, thyme, and pepper to a boil over medium-high heat. Cover and cook for 10 to 12 minutes, or until the potatoes are tender. Add the butter, reduce the heat to low, and simmer uncovered for 15 to 20 minutes, or until thickened. Stir in the cream until well combined and the soup is heated through.

NOTE: To lighten this up a bit, just use half-and-half or milk in place of the heavy cream.

Easy Caesar Salad

6 to 8 servings

To me, Rhode Island means lots of great seafood and Italian food. But one of the best Caesar salads I ever had was tossed there, too, so now's the time for me to share it with you.

   1 cup mayonnaise
   ¼ cup grated Parmesan cheese
   4 anchovies
   Juice of 1 lemon
   1 teaspoon Worcestershire sauce
   1 garlic clove
   ¼ teaspoon black pepper
   1 large head romaine lettuce, torn into bite-sized pieces

In a blender, blend all the ingredients except the lettuce for 1 to 2 minutes, or until smooth and creamy. Place the lettuce in a large bowl and toss with the dressing. Serve immediately.

NOTE: If you want, toss this with croutons and sprinkle with additional Parmesan cheese. And for easy-to-make croutons, cube a few slices of Italian bread and toast in a skillet with 1 to 2 tablespoons of butter and ½ teaspoon garlic powder. If you use a smaller head of lettuce, or would rather use less dressing on your salad, store the leftover dressing in an airtight container in the refrigerator.

Linguine and Clams in Red Sauce

6 to 8 servings

No need to stick your neck out on this recipe, 'cause it has only six ingredients and is packed with hearty flavor. It's kind of an Italian clambake all in one dish. Ooh, I like this one!

1 jar (28 ounces) spaghetti sauce
1 can (5.5 ounces) vegetable juice
4 dozen littleneck clams, scrubbed
1 teaspoon crushed red pepper
1 pound linguine
¼ cup grated Parmesan cheese

In a soup pot, bring the spaghetti sauce and vegetable juice to a boil over high heat, stirring frequently. Add the clams, cover, and cook for 10 minutes, or until the clams open; **discard any clams that do not open.** Stir in the crushed red pepper. Meanwhile, cook the linguine according to the package directions; drain and place in a large bowl. Top with the clam sauce. Sprinkle with the cheese and serve immediately.

NOTE: The taste of this dish depends on the type of spaghetti sauce you use, so use your favorite and go ahead and add extra seasonings to your own liking.

Dreamy Orange Swirl Cheesecake

6 to 8 servings

Here's the perfect meal topper to help us say good-bye to "I can't eat another bite" and hello to "rich and creamy!" It's perfect after a meal like this big Rhode Island one!

> 2 packages (8 ounces each) cream cheese, softened
> ½ cup sugar
> 2 eggs
> ¾ cup sour cream
> 1 teaspoon vanilla extract
> 1 teaspoon orange extract
> 2 drops yellow food color
> 1 drop red food color
> One 9-inch graham cracker pie crust

Preheat the oven to 350°F. In a large bowl, with an electric beater on medium speed, beat the cream cheese and sugar until light and fluffy. Add the eggs and beat well. Add the sour cream and vanilla; mix well. Place 1 cup of the cream cheese mixture in a small bowl and stir in the orange extract and the yellow and red food color. Pour the remaining cream cheese mixture into the pie crust. Drop the orange cream cheese mixture by spoonfuls onto the cream cheese mixture in the crust and swirl with a knife to create a marbled effect. Bake for 30 to 35 minutes, until firm around the edges; the center will be slightly loose. Allow to cool for 1 hour, then cover and chill for at least 8 hours before serving.

NOTE: Why not dollop each slice with whipped topping and half an orange slice?

WEEK 32

Magic with Mustard

Yes, it's true—mustard lovers from across the country unite in Wisconsin on the first Saturday in August to celebrate the flavorful golden condiment. Mustard is a favorite, for sure, and it's come a long way from just plain ol' bright yellow mustard. There are almost endless varieties, from sweet or spicy to creamy smooth or grainy. So let's get ready to celebrate National Mustard Day by adding a little mustard magic to everything from soup to nuts . . . okay, *almost* everything.

Honey-Mustard-Swirl Bread

Maple Mustard Dressing

Parsley Buttered Potatoes

Orange Mustard Pork Tenderloin

Honey-Mustard-Swirl Bread

1 loaf

It'll look as if we spent the day in the kitchen, but this recipe is ready to go in about an hour, including baking time. And this easy homemade bread gives everything a really zippy taste. Go ahead, give it a swirl!

> 1 loaf (16 ounces) frozen bread dough, thawed
> 3 tablespoons spicy brown mustard
> 2 tablespoons honey

Coat a 9" × 5" loaf pan with nonstick cooking spray. Place the dough on a piece of plastic wrap and, using your fingers, spread it out to a 9" × 12" rectangle. In a small bowl, combine the mustard and honey; mix well. Spread over the dough, leaving a ½-inch border around the edges. Pulling the dough up with the plastic wrap, roll up the dough jelly-roll style from a shorter side. Discard the plastic wrap and place the roll seam side down in the loaf pan. Cover with plastic wrap and allow to rise for 30 minutes, or until doubled in size. Preheat the oven to 375°F. Uncover the dough and bake for 30 to 35 minutes, or until a wooden toothpick inserted in the center comes out clean.

Maple Mustard Dressing

about 2½ cups

Kind of a spin-off of an old favorite, this dressing creates a whole new taste as it teams the richness of maple syrup with the very popular honey-mustard dressing.

1¼ cups mayonnaise
⅔ cup vegetable oil
⅓ cup real maple syrup
2 tablespoons prepared yellow mustard
1 tablespoon white vinegar
2 tablespoons chopped fresh parsley
1 teaspoon minced onion flakes

In a medium bowl, whisk together all the ingredients until smooth and creamy. Serve immediately, or cover and chill; whisk again just before serving.

NOTE: This is perfect tossed with fresh spinach or mixed salad greens and topped with shredded carrots.

Parsley Buttered Potatoes

6 to 8 servings

Not the same old boiled potatoes again . . . ?! Nope! This time they're glazed with a tangy mustard butter. And when they're teamed with our favorite main dish, are we ever in for some "fancy, schmancy" eating!

> 5 pounds small red potatoes, washed and quartered (see Note)
> 1 cup (2 sticks) butter, melted
> ⅓ cup chopped fresh parsley
> 1 tablespoon dry mustard
> 2 teaspoons salt
> 1 teaspoon black pepper

Place the potatoes in a soup pot and add just enough water to cover them. Bring to a boil over high heat, then reduce the heat to medium and cook for 12 to 15 minutes, or until fork-tender; drain and place in a large bowl. In a small bowl, combine the remaining ingredients; mix well and pour over the warm potatoes. Toss until well coated and serve immediately.

NOTE: I like to use the smallest potatoes I can find, but if your potatoes are a little larger, cut them into 1½-inch chunks.

Orange Mustard Pork Tenderloin

6 to 8 servings

What happens when we team light pork tenderloin with the fresh taste of oranges and the sophisticated taste of mustard? Easy—we get an elegant meal in minutes.

2 pork tenderloins (about 2 pounds total)
¼ teaspoon salt
⅓ cup orange marmalade
1 tablespoon spicy brown mustard

Preheat the oven to 350°F. Coat a 9" × 13" baking dish with nonstick cooking spray. Place the tenderloins in the baking dish and season with the salt. In a small bowl, combine the marmalade and mustard; mix well and brush over the tenderloins. Bake for 35 to 40 minutes, or until no longer pink, basting occasionally with the pan juices. Slice and serve.

NOTE: In addition to the Parsley Buttered Potatoes, serve this with an easy stir-fry of carrots, broccoli, and cauliflower.

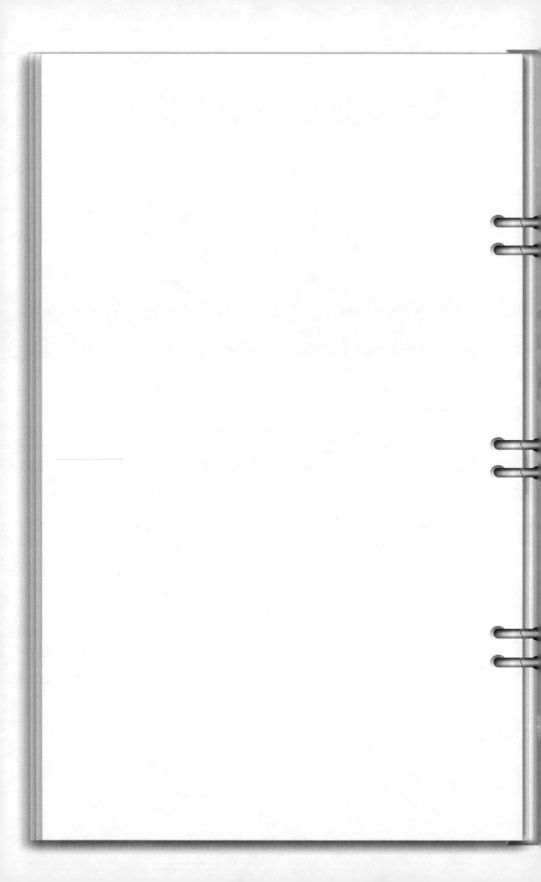

WEEK 33

Blueberry Bonanza

Summertime means that our fruits and vegetables are at their best—especially those berries bursting with flavor. Over the years, I've really stretched the season by mixing the blue bundles of joy into every recipe imaginable. Enjoy a blueberry bonanza this week by mixing them into all these homemade goodies!

Blueberry Muffins

Blueberry Cobbler

Awesome Blueberry Pie

Toasted Blueberry Shortcake

Blueberry Custard Pie

Blueberry Muffins

1 dozen

What a delicious smell to wake up to! Fresh, hot blueberry muffins are a winner every time. A cup of java and a muffin or two will surely clear the cobwebs out of our eyes!

1¼ cups plus 2 tablespoons sugar, divided
½ cup (1 stick) butter, softened
2 eggs
2 cups all-purpose flour
2 teaspoons baking powder
½ teaspoon salt
½ cup milk
1 teaspoon vanilla extract
1 pint fresh blueberries, washed

Preheat the oven to 375°F. Line 12 muffin cups with paper baking cups and coat with nonstick cooking spray. In a large bowl, with an electric beater on medium speed, beat 1¼ cups sugar and the butter until creamy. Add the eggs one at a time, beating well after each addition. Add the flour, baking powder, and salt; beat well. Add the milk and vanilla and beat until thoroughly combined. Mash ½ cup blueberries and stir into the batter. Stir in the remaining whole blueberries and spoon into the baking cups, distributing the batter evenly. Sprinkle the tops with the remaining 2 tablespoons sugar and bake for 25 to 30 minutes, or until a wooden toothpick inserted in the center comes out clean. Remove to a wire rack to cool completely.

NOTE: I use this recipe to make chocolate chip muffins, too—I just replace the blueberries with a cup of chocolate chips.

Blueberry Cobbler

A seasonal alternative to traditional apple cobbler, this works really well with blueberries under the crispy sugary topping. Aah—what a perfect ending to a summer barbecue.

    1 pint fresh blueberries, washed
    1 cup plus 2 tablespoons sugar, divided
    6 tablespoons (¾ stick) butter, softened, divided
    1 teaspoon vanilla extract
    1 cup all-purpose flour
    1 egg
    ¼ teaspoon salt

Preheat the oven to 400°F. Coat an 8-inch square baking dish with nonstick cooking spray. In a medium bowl, combine the blueberries, 1 cup sugar, 2 tablespoons butter, and the vanilla; mix well, then pour into the baking dish. In another medium bowl, combine the flour, egg, salt, and the remaining 2 tablespoons sugar and 4 tablespoons butter; mix until crumbly and spoon over the blueberry mixture. Bake for 20 to 25 minutes, or until bubbly and the topping is golden. Serve warm.

NOTE: My favorite way to eat any type of cobbler is topped with vanilla ice cream.

Awesome Blueberry Pie

6 to 8 servings

Every summer when my young family spent time in Rhode Island, we would be sure to visit the Red Rooster Tavern in North Kingstown. We had to—their dinners were fabulous—but we all couldn't wait to get to dessert, because they served the most incredible blueberry pie. It was just bursting with crunchy, sweet fresh blueberries! I never did get their recipe, so I had to figure out how to make my own version of this special pie. And I must have succeeded (or at least come pretty close), 'cause my family is thrilled with this fruit pie that's nothing less than awesome! Give it a try.

> One 9-inch frozen ready-to-bake pie shell, thawed
> 1 package (4-serving size) lemon gelatin
> ½ cup sugar
> ¼ cup cornstarch
> ¾ cup ginger ale
> 3 pints fresh blueberries, washed

Bake the pie shell according to the package directions; set aside to cool. In a medium saucepan, combine all the remaining ingredients except 2 pints blueberries over medium heat. Cook for 5 to 7 minutes, or until the gelatin mix has dissolved and the blueberries have popped and colored the mixture blue, stirring frequently. Remove from the heat and let cool for about 5 minutes. Stir in the remaining 2 pints blueberries and spoon into the baked pie shell, mounding up the center for a nice high pie. Chill for at least 4 hours, or until set. Serve, or cover and keep chilled until ready to serve.

NOTE: Before serving, top each slice with a dollop of fresh whipped cream and additional fresh blueberries.

Toasted Blueberry Shortcake

6 to 8 servings

Stack 'em up—the higher the better!—'cause you're gonna want as many blueberries as you can get in every bite. And don't forget an extra-large dollop of whipped cream to add just the perfect shortcake touch.

> One 16-ounce pound cake
> 1 tablespoon butter, melted
> 3 tablespoons sugar, divided
> 1 teaspoon ground cinnamon
> 1 cup (½ pint) heavy cream
> ½ pint fresh blueberries, washed

Preheat the broiler. Slice the pound cake horizontally into 3 layers and lay out separately on a baking sheet; brush the tops with the melted butter. In a small bowl, combine 2 tablespoons sugar and the cinnamon; mix well and sprinkle evenly over the buttered cake layers. Broil for 3 to 5 minutes, or until lightly toasted, watching carefully so that the cake doesn't burn; allow to cool. In a medium bowl, beat the cream and the remaining 1 tablespoon sugar with an electric beater on medium speed until stiff peaks form. Place the bottom cake layer toasted side up on a serving platter; spread with one third of the whipped cream and sprinkle with one third of the blueberries. Repeat the layers twice more and serve, or cover and chill until ready to serve.

NOTE: If the pound cake has a large curved dome in the center, slice it off (and eat it later!) so that you have 3 even slices of pound cake to make this. You want the whipped cream and berries to sit evenly on the cake without falling off!

Blueberry Custard Pie

6 to 8 servings

In honor of my son Steve, a "blueberry-holic," I've added berries to my traditional custard pie. He likes this so much, he never wants to share!

1 cup sour cream
¾ cup sugar
1 egg
2 tablespoons all-purpose flour
½ teaspoon lemon juice
¼ teaspoon salt
1 pint fresh blueberries, washed
One 9-inch frozen ready-to-bake pie shell, thawed

Preheat the oven to 400°F. In a medium bowl, combine the sour cream, sugar, egg, flour, lemon juice, and salt; mix well. Stir in the blueberries and pour into the pie shell. Bake for 30 to 35 minutes, or until light golden and set in the center. Allow to cool slightly, then cover and chill for at least 4 hours, or until firm.

WEEK 34

Light 'n' Healthy Summer Celebration

During the hot summer months, the last thing we want to eat is a big steaming pot of stew. Instead, we enjoy lighter meals at this time of year—especially cold salads. We also want to take advantage of the late-summer fruits and vegetables, 'cause they won't be around much longer at our local farm stands. So let's get ready to enjoy this light 'n' luscious summer feast.

Light 'n' Flaky Biscuits

Lemonade-Poached Salmon

Pineapple-Carrot Slaw

Citrus Twist Pasta

Upside-down Pineapple Muffins

Light 'n' Flaky Biscuits

about 1 dozen

Who wants biscuits that taste like hockey pucks? We sure don't, so don't worry—these little ones are guaranteed to come out light and flaky every time. And yes, they taste as good as they smell!

     2 cups all-purpose flour
     1 tablespoon baking powder
     ½ teaspoon salt
     ⅔ cup skim milk
     ¼ cup canola or vegetable oil

Preheat the oven to 450°F. Coat a large baking sheet with non-stick cooking spray. In a large bowl, combine the flour, baking powder, and salt; mix well. Add the milk and oil and stir just until a soft dough forms. Lightly flour a work surface and use a rolling pin to roll out the dough to a ½-inch thickness. Using a 2½-inch round biscuit or cookie cutter, cut into biscuits and place on the baking sheet. Bake for 8 to 10 minutes, or until light golden. Serve warm.

NOTE: To keep the biscuits light and fluffy, do not overmix the dough or overhandle it when rolling it out.

Lemonade-Poached Salmon

4 servings

What a great alternative to ordinary baked salmon! This recipe has been a big hit at many a summer get-together.

>   1 cup mayonnaise
>   1 can (12 ounces) frozen lemonade concentrate, thawed,
>   divided
>   ¼ teaspoon black pepper
>   ¼ cup water
>   4 salmon fillets (about 1½ pounds total)

In a medium bowl, combine the mayonnaise, 3 tablespoons lemonade concentrate, and the pepper; mix well, then cover and chill. In a large skillet, bring the remaining lemonade concentrate and the water to a boil over medium-low heat. Add the salmon and reduce the heat to low; cover and cook for 8 to 10 minutes, or until the fish flakes easily with a fork. Allow to cool to room temperature and serve with the chilled lemonade sauce.

NOTE: This salmon can also be made ahead and served well chilled for a refreshing light lunch.

Pineapple-Carrot Slaw

6 to 8 servings

This chilly salad is sure to beat the summer heat. Its mix of fruit and carrots is a little different, but one taste and you'll be convinced that it's a match made in heaven.

6 cups shredded carrots (about 1½ pounds)
1 can (8 ounces) crushed pineapple, drained
1 container (8 ounces) lemon-flavored yogurt
1 tablespoon honey

In a large bowl, combine all the ingredients; mix well. Cover and chill for at least 1 hour before serving.

NOTE: This also makes a great lunchtime treat for packing in the kids' lunch boxes.

Citrus Twist Pasta

6 to 8 servings

Serve this up with Lemonade-Poached Salmon (page 221) for a real citrus delight. There won't be any rising temperatures after *this* meal!

1 pound tricolored twist pasta
1 container (8 ounces) lemon-flavored yogurt
1 container (8 ounces) orange-flavored yogurt
1 teaspoon salt
½ teaspoon black pepper
5 ounces fresh spinach, trimmed, washed, and torn
2 cans (11 ounces each) mandarin oranges, drained

Cook the pasta according to the package directions; drain, rinse, drain again, and allow to cool slightly. In a large bowl, combine the lemon and orange yogurts, salt, and pepper; mix well. Add the pasta and mix well, then add the spinach and oranges, mixing until thoroughly combined. Cover and chill for at least 1 hour before serving.

Upside-down Pineapple Muffins

2 dozen

Remember how popular pineapple upside-down cake used to be? Well, here's a twist on that old favorite . . . yup, muffin-style! Upside down or right side up, they're delicious every time.

  2 cans (20 ounces each) sliced pineapple, drained
  1 can (8¼ ounces) sliced pineapple, drained
  24 maraschino cherries
  ½ cup firmly packed light brown sugar
  1 package (18.25 ounces) white cake mix
  ¼ cup vegetable oil
  3 egg whites
  1 can (20 ounces) crushed pineapple, drained, with juice
     reserved

Preheat the oven to 350°F. Coat 24 muffin cups with nonstick cooking spray. Place a pineapple ring in the bottom of each cup. Place a cherry in the center of each pineapple ring and sprinkle each with an equal amount of brown sugar; set aside. In a large bowl, with an electric beater on medium speed, beat the cake mix, oil, egg whites, and the reserved pineapple juice until well combined. Stir in the crushed pineapple and divide the mixture among the muffin cups. Bake for 20 to 25 minutes, or until golden. Allow to cool for 15 minutes, then invert the muffins onto a cookie sheet. Allow to cool and serve, or cover until ready to serve.

NOTE: Make sure to invert the muffins while still warm so that they'll easily pop out of the muffin cups.

WEEK 35

An English Tea

While I was working on this cookbook, England and the world lost beloved Princess Diana. The reaction to the untimely, senseless death of this compassionate, generous person showed us how quickly people all around the world can come together. Sharing an English tea is just one of my ways to remember this true princess.

Teatime Scones

English Rose Jelly

Watercress-Salmon Tea Sandwiches

Cucumber Tea Sandwiches

Snowflake Tea Cookies

Teatime Scones

about 1 dozen

This longtime English favorite is truly the perfect mate for a cup of tea. And don't forget to drink your tea English-style: with sugar and just a little cream.

    2 cups all-purpose flour
    ¼ cup plus 1 teaspoon sugar, divided
    1 tablespoon baking powder
    ¼ teaspoon salt
    ¼ cup (½ stick) butter, softened
    1 can (5 ounces) evaporated milk
    1 egg

Preheat the oven to 400°F. In a medium bowl, combine the flour, ¼ cup sugar, the baking powder, and salt; mix well. Cut in the butter until crumbly. In a small bowl, combine the evaporated milk and egg; whisk until combined. Add to the flour mixture and stir just until blended. On a floured surface, knead the dough 5 to 6 times. Lightly pat to a ½-inch thickness and, using a 2-inch round biscuit cutter or a drinking glass, cut into rounds. Place on an ungreased baking sheet and sprinkle with the remaining 1 teaspoon sugar. Bake for 11 to 15 minutes, or until light golden.

NOTE: Add some chopped pecans or walnuts and/or raisins or sweetened dried cranberries to the scones, if you'd like. Serve them warm with butter and lemon curd or English Rose Jelly (page 227) on the side.

English Rose Jelly

about 1 quart

This traditional jelly is a sweet and pretty go-along for teatime scones or even plain old American toast.

> 2¼ cups water
> 2 cups packed fresh organically grown rose petals, thoroughly washed and dried (see Note)
> 1¾ cups sugar
> 1 package (3 ounces) liquid fruit pectin
> ½ teaspoon vanilla extract
> 2 drops red food color

In a large saucepan, combine the water, rose petals, and sugar. Bring to a boil over medium-high heat and cook for 1 minute, stirring constantly. Stir in the pectin, then return to a boil and cook for 1 minute, stirring constantly. Remove from the heat and stir in the vanilla and food color. Quickly spoon into jars and seal, or pour into a decorative mold and cover. Allow to cool to room temperature, then chill until ready to serve.

NOTE: Be sure to check with your florist to make sure that your roses are pesticide-free; then wash them well. For 2 cups of rose petals, you'll need about 1 dozen large roses. The more fragrant the roses, the more flavorful the jelly. I like to enjoy the roses for a couple of days in a vase, then remove the petals and wash them well under cold running water so I can make this and enjoy the roses even longer!

Watercress-Salmon Tea Sandwiches

What these sandwiches lack in size, they make up for in taste. You see, the watercress adds a peppery zip to each bite. Better make a lot, 'cause they sure do go fast!

> 8 slices pumpernickel bread
> 2 tablespoons butter, softened
> 1 bunch watercress, washed and stems removed
> 1 can (7 ounces) skinless, boneless salmon, drained and
>   flaked
> 2 tablespoons malt vinegar

Trim the crusts from the bread and cut each slice in half. Spread the butter evenly over the 16 pieces. Distribute the watercress leaves evenly over the buttered bread. In a small bowl, combine the salmon and vinegar; mix well. Spoon equally over the watercress leaves and serve, or cover (see Note) and keep chilled until ready to serve.

NOTE: To keep these sandwiches fresh while chilled, place on a tray, cover with a damp paper towel, and wrap with plastic wrap.

Cucumber Tea Sandwiches

16 sandwiches

Another classic English favorite, these are usually served with watercress tea sandwiches. Take a tip from my old catering days and garnish the tray with radish rosebuds and bunches of parsley!

16 slices white bread
¼ cup heavy cream
¼ cup (1 ounce) shredded sharp Cheddar cheese
2 ounces cream cheese, softened
1 teaspoon prepared yellow mustard (optional)
½ of a medium cucumber, peeled and cut into 16 thin
   slices

Using a 2-inch round biscuit or cookie cutter, cut 2 bread rounds from each slice of bread; discard the scraps. In a medium bowl, with an electric beater on medium speed, beat the heavy cream, Cheddar cheese, cream cheese, and mustard (if desired) for 1 to 2 minutes, or until well blended and smooth. Spread evenly over 16 bread rounds. Place a cucumber slice over the cheese mixture on each and top with the remaining bread rounds. Serve, or cover and keep chilled until ready to serve.

Snowflake Tea Cookies

about 4 dozen

A traditional English tea just isn't complete without crisp but-tery cookies (they call them biscuits). And the great thing about these is that you can easily change the flavor each time by using a different flavored jam. Of course, with each different flavor we get a whole new treat.

> 1½ cups (3 sticks) butter, softened
> 1 cup sugar
> 1 egg
> 2 teaspoons vanilla extract
> ¼ teaspoon salt
> 4½ cups all-purpose flour
> ¾ cup jam or preserves (see Note)
> Confectioners' sugar for sprinkling

In a large bowl, with an electric beater on medium speed, beat the butter, sugar, egg, vanilla, and salt until creamy. Gradually add the flour, beating until well mixed. Cover and chill for 1 hour. Preheat the oven to 375°F. Divide the dough into 4 pieces. On a lightly floured surface, roll out each piece to a ⅛-inch thickness. Using a 2-inch round cookie cutter, cut into circles. Using a plastic drinking straw, randomly cut out circles of dough from half of the cookies. Place 1 inch apart on ungreased cookie sheets and bake for 10 to 12 minutes, or until light golden. Remove to wire racks to cool completely. Spread the jam evenly over the solid cookies. Sprinkle the remaining cookies with confectioners' sugar. Assemble the tea cookies by placing the cookies with the holes over the jam-topped cook-ies. Serve, or store in an airtight container until ready to serve.

NOTE: Any flavor of jam can be used, but I like to use an assortment so there will be different colors peeking through the holes in the cookies.

WEEK 36

Labor Day Get-Together

To most people, Labor Day means the end of summer—and that's the way it's been celebrated since 1893! It's time for the change of seasons and school is starting again, but we all want to enjoy that last summer weekend by relaxing, spending time with family and friends, *not* worrying about work, and, most of all, EATING! Who could ask for a better holiday?!

Orange-Grilled Strip Steaks

Apple Baked Beans

Onion Straws

Chocolate Chip Bars

Pineapple Cran-Orange Refresher

Orange-Grilled Strip Steaks

4 servings

For an untraditional turn on a traditional favorite, serve this at your Labor Day barbecue. My mouth is watering just thinking about these zesty orange-flavored steaks!

½ cup olive oil
½ cup orange juice
¼ cup soy sauce
Grated peel of 1 orange
1 garlic clove, minced
1 tablespoon sugar
½ teaspoon crushed red pepper
Four 8-ounce boneless beef loin strip steaks

In a large resealable plastic storage bag, combine all the ingredients except the steaks; mix well. Add the steaks and seal the bag. Marinate in the refrigerator for at least 3 hours, turning occasionally. Preheat the grill to medium-high heat. Remove the steaks from the marinade and discard the marinade; grill the steaks for 5 to 6 minutes per side for medium-rare, or until desired doneness beyond that. Serve immediately.

NOTE: These can also be broiled for about the same time if the weather keeps you from enjoying an outdoor barbecue.

Apple Baked Beans

4 to 6 servings

Here's the perfect summer/fall combination—a delicious ripe apple paired with tangy baked beans for a side dish I promise will make you the "apple of their eyes"!

2 cans (16 ounces each) navy beans, undrained
¾ cup molasses
¼ cup firmly packed dark brown sugar
1 large apple, cored and diced (see Note)
1 medium onion, chopped
2 garlic cloves, minced
1 tablespoon prepared yellow mustard
½ teaspoon ground ginger

Preheat the oven to 425°F. Coat a 2-quart baking dish with nonstick cooking spray. In a large bowl, combine all the ingredients; mix well. Pour into the baking dish and bake for 1¼ to 1½ hours, or until thick and bubbly, stirring occasionally.

NOTE: Use your favorite type of apple, peeled or not—the choice is yours.

Onion Straws

4 to 6 servings

Savor the sweet taste of the last of the Vidalia onion growing season with my version of the all-American favorite—onion rings.

2 cups vegetable oil
¾ cup all-purpose flour
⅔ cup cold water
½ teaspoon baking soda
¾ teaspoon ground red pepper
1 teaspoon salt
3 large Vidalia or other sweet onions, cut in half and thinly sliced

Heat the oil in a large skillet over medium heat until hot but not smoking. In a medium bowl, combine the flour, water, baking soda, pepper, and salt until a batter forms. Add the onions and stir to coat. Drop in small batches into the oil and fry for 1 to 2 minutes, or until golden, allowing the oil to heat back up between batches. Drain on a paper towel–lined platter and serve hot.

NOTE: If making these ahead of time, place on a baking sheet, cover, and refrigerate until ready to heat; then reheat in a hot oven until hot and crispy.

Chocolate Chip Bars

15 to 18 bars

Think we're cheating a little bit by using a cake mix? After they try this scrumptious dessert, they'll be begging for the recipe. Don't tell . . . it's our secret!

> 1 cup (6 ounces) semisweet chocolate chips
> 1 cup chopped pecans
> 3 tablespoons light brown sugar
> 1 package (18.25 ounces) yellow cake mix
> ½ cup (1 stick) butter, softened
> 2 eggs

Preheat the oven to 350°F. Coat a 9" × 13" baking dish with nonstick cooking spray. In a small bowl, combine the chocolate chips, pecans, and brown sugar; mix well and set aside. In a large bowl, with an electric beater on medium speed, beat the cake mix, butter, and eggs until thoroughly combined (the mixture will be stiff). Stir half of the nut mixture into the batter and spread over the bottom of the baking dish. Sprinkle the remaining nut mixture over the batter and bake for 30 to 35 minutes, or until a wooden toothpick inserted in the center comes out clean. Allow to cool completely, then cut into bars and serve.

NOTE: Individually wrapped, these bars make the perfect lunch box treat.

Pineapple Cran-Orange Refresher

about 1 gallon, 12 to 16 servings

Relive those tropical summer memories with this fruity punch. Close your eyes and you'll practically feel the summer sun on your face!

> 1 can (46 ounces) pineapple juice, chilled
> 1 can (12 ounces) frozen cranberry juice concentrate, thawed
> 1 can (12 ounces) frozen orange juice concentrate, thawed
> 1 liter chilled ginger ale
> 1 orange, thinly sliced
> 4 cups ice cubes

In a large punch bowl, combine all the ingredients; mix well and serve immediately.

NOTE: This is also the perfect take-along for a picnic or back-yard barbecue; just store it in an insulated plastic jug.

WEEK 37

Back-to-School Favorites

Back to school doesn't have to mean the end of fun! These recipes practically guarantee that our little ones will look forward to heading off to school each day. Who wouldn't, with lunches and snacks like these to daydream about all morning?! Trust me, with three children and six grandchildren of my own, I know what works . . . and these definitely do!

Macaroni and Cheese Soup

Ham and Nacho Cheese Roll-ups

Cheese Pretzel Sandwiches

Peanut Butter and Jelly Bars

Strawberry-Banana Smoothie

Macaroni and Cheese Soup

6 to 8 servings

On those cold winter mornings, thoughts of this soup kept my kids warm all day. Wherever you live, this hearty dish is sure to be a favorite at your house, too!

  2½ cups water
  1 package (10 ounces) frozen peas and carrots, thawed
  1 package (7.25 ounces) macaroni and cheese mix
  4 cups (1 quart) milk
  1 cup (4 ounces) shredded sharp Cheddar cheese
  1½ teaspoons salt
  ½ teaspoon black pepper

In a soup pot, bring the water to a boil over high heat. Stir in the peas and carrots and the macaroni, reserving the cheese packet. Cover and boil for 5 minutes; do not drain. Add the remaining ingredients, including the reserved cheese packet. Reduce the heat to medium, cover, and simmer for 10 minutes, or until hot and creamy, stirring occasionally.

NOTE: Pack this to go in a lunch box thermos for a hot meal the kids can't wait to gobble up!

Ham and Nacho Cheese Roll-ups

4 servings

Olé! This south-of-the-border lunch is a tasty alternative to that old standby, PB&J.

Four 6- or 8-inch flour tortillas
½ cup nacho cheese spread
1 cup crushed tortilla chips
4 slices (4 ounces) deli ham

Place the tortillas on a work surface and spread evenly with the cheese spread. Sprinkle with the crushed tortilla chips and top each with a slice of ham. Roll up tightly jelly-roll style and wrap individually in waxed paper or plastic wrap. Chill until ready to serve.

NOTE: The perfect make-ahead lunch box meal, these roll-ups are actually better when chilled overnight—it helps them hold together better. Serve whole or sliced to look like colorful pinwheels.

Cheese Pretzel Sandwiches

6 servings

Looking for an after-school snack that's easy to make and filling, too? Let me introduce you to the pretzel sandwich—a variation on those fresh pretzels sold on the streets of New York, but better—'cause these have melted cheese!

>   1 package (13 ounces) frozen baked soft pretzels
>   (6 pretzels), thawed
>   6 slices (6 ounces) American cheese

Preheat the oven to 400°F. Using a serrated knife, cut each pretzel horizontally in half. Place the halves back together and place on a large baking sheet. Bake for 1 to 2 minutes, until warmed through. Remove from the oven and immediately place a slice of cheese between each pair of pretzel halves. The warmth of the pretzel will melt the cheese and hold the pretzel together. Serve, or wrap individually and chill, then serve as is or rewarmed.

NOTE: For kids who like mustard on their pretzels, squeeze some yellow mustard onto the bottom pretzel halves before adding the cheese. And the beauty about using frozen pretzels is that you don't need to make them all at once—if you need only two, take two out of the freezer and just make those!

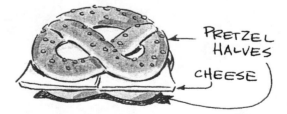

PRETZEL HALVES

CHEESE

Peanut Butter and Jelly Bars

15 to 18 bars

Peanut butter and jelly is a classic combination, so these bars are sure to have your whole gang jumping for joy!

2¼ cups all-purpose flour
½ cup (1 stick) butter, melted
½ cup creamy peanut butter
½ cup firmly packed light brown sugar
¼ cup granulated sugar
1 egg
1 cup strawberry jelly (see Note)

Preheat the oven to 350°F. Coat a 9" × 13" baking dish with nonstick cooking spray. In a large bowl, combine all the ingredients except the jelly. Beat with an electric beater on medium speed for 2 minutes, or until blended and crumbly. Reserve 1 cup of the peanut butter mixture. Spread the remaining mixture over the bottom of the baking dish. Spread the jelly evenly over the mixture and crumble the reserved peanut butter mixture over the top. Bake for 40 to 45 minutes, or until the topping is golden. Allow to cool completely, then cut into bars and serve.

NOTE: Sure, you can use your favorite flavor of jam or preserves in place of the strawberry jelly.

Strawberry-Banana Smoothie

4 servings

What a perfect way to get the kids started in the morning! A glassful of this has lots of goodness, so they're on their way to getting their five servings of fruits and vegetables for the day.

2 packages (10 ounces each) frozen sliced strawberries in syrup
2 containers (8 ounces each) strawberry yogurt
1 ripe banana, peeled
1 cup milk

In a blender, blend all the ingredients for 1 to 2 minutes, or until smooth and creamy. Pour into glasses and serve immediately.

NOTE: For that last taste of summer, you can't beat a smoothie made with frozen peach slices and peach yogurt, but almost any frozen fruit and matching flavor yogurt can be made into your own special fruit smoothie.

WEEK 38

Grandparents' Day Dinner

If you're anything like me, which I know you are, family is very important to you. And grandparents hold a really special place in our lives. I mean, who doesn't remember Grandma baking our favorite treats or Grandpa taking us out for a big ice cream sundae and always sharing a story or two? Well, here's our opportunity to show them how much we love and appreciate them. Let's make them a meal of can't-miss favorites!

Glazed Grapefruit

Saucy Chicken

Buttery Squash

Baked Mashed Potatoes

Fruit Pinwheels

Glazed Grapefruit

This easy but tasty treat is a perfect way to start dinner. It'll get Grandma and Grandpa ready for the yummy meal to follow!

> 3 grapefruits, cut in half crosswise
> 6 tablespoons light brown sugar
> 6 maraschino cherries

Preheat the broiler. Using a grapefruit or other serrated knife, separate the grapefruit sections from the membranes and the peel and place the grapefruit halves cut side up on a large rimmed baking sheet. Sprinkle 1 tablespoon brown sugar over each grapefruit half and broil for 3 to 4 minutes, or until the sugar melts and is bubbly. Remove from the oven and place a cherry in the center of each grapefruit half. Serve immediately.

Saucy Chicken

6 servings

Grandma used to spend all day in the kitchen preparing this savory dish. With a few shortcuts, we can have the same taste with a lot less work.

> 2 tablespoons butter
> 2 tablespoons vegetable oil
> 1 small onion, finely chopped
> 6 boneless, skinless chicken breast halves (1½ to 2 pounds total)
> ¼ cup white vinegar
> ¼ cup ketchup
> 3 tablespoons sugar
> ¼ teaspoon hot pepper sauce
> ½ teaspoon salt
> ¼ teaspoon black pepper

Melt the butter with the oil in a large skillet over medium heat. Add the onion and chicken and brown the chicken for 3 to 4 minutes per side. In a small bowl, combine the remaining ingredients; mix well and add to the skillet. Reduce the heat to low, cover, and simmer for 20 minutes. Uncover and cook for 5 to 10 more minutes, or until the sauce has thickened and the chicken is no longer pink.

NOTE: If your barbecue grill is available, you may want to cook this outside—just make the sauce as above and marinate the chicken in the sauce mixture, then discard the marinade and grill the chicken for 6 to 7 minutes per side, or until no pink remains.

Buttery Squash

4 to 6 servings

Remember how Grandma made us eat all our vegetables and clean our plates? Here's our way of showing her what a good job she did in teaching us to like veggies. (It's not only good for us, it's tasty, too!)

> ¼ cup (½ stick) butter
> 8 medium yellow squash (about 2 pounds), sliced into ½-inch rounds
> 1 medium onion, finely chopped
> ½ teaspoon salt
> ½ teaspoon black pepper

Melt the butter in a large skillet over high heat. Add the remaining ingredients and cook for 18 to 20 minutes, or until the vegetables are tender and the squash is beginning to brown, stirring frequently.

NOTE: You can also make this simple vegetable side dish by using half zucchini and half yellow squash for a more colorful mix.

Baked Mashed Potatoes

6 servings

This hearty dish is the perfect side for any Sunday dinner. When you're expecting a big bunch, you'd better make an extra batch, 'cause it goes quickly!

6 medium potatoes, peeled and cut into ¼-inch slices
½ cup Italian-flavored bread crumbs
½ cup (1 stick) butter, softened
¼ cup sour cream
2 eggs, beaten
2 tablespoons chopped fresh parsley
1¼ teaspoons salt
½ teaspoon black pepper

Preheat the oven to 450°F. Coat a large baking sheet with non-stick cooking spray. Place the potatoes in a soup pot and add just enough water to cover them. Bring to a boil over high heat and boil for 12 to 15 minutes, or until fork-tender; drain and place in a large bowl. Mash the potatoes slightly and add the remaining ingredients; mix well. Shape into 12 balls and place on the baking sheet. Bake for 15 to 18 minutes, or until light golden.

NOTE: Make these your own by mixing finely chopped onions, garlic, or even shredded cheese into the potato mixture before baking.

Fruit Pinwheels

1 dozen

We used to visit my grandparents' favorite bakery for these old-time fruit roll-ups. Now I know how easy they are to make at home—with fresh ingredients and for less than the cost of today's packaged ones!

    1 cup golden raisins
    ¼ cup orange juice
    4 tablespoons (½ stick) butter, melted, divided
    1 cup chopped prunes
    ½ cup chopped walnuts
    2 tablespoons light corn syrup
    One 10-ounce refrigerated pizza crust

Preheat the oven to 425°F. In a small saucepan, combine the raisins, orange juice, and 2 tablespoons butter over medium heat and cook for 5 to 8 minutes, or until the raisins are plumped. Remove from the heat and stir in the prunes and walnuts. In a small bowl, combine the remaining 2 tablespoons melted butter and the corn syrup; mix well and pour into 12 muffin cups, dividing it evenly. Spread the pizza crust on a work surface to form an 8" × 12" rectangle. Spread the fruit mixture evenly over the crust. Starting from a long side, roll up jelly-roll style. Cut into 12 slices and place cut side down in the muffin cups. Bake for 10 to 12 minutes, or until golden. Serve warm.

NOTE: Feel free to experiment with other dried fruit like apricots or sweetened dried cranberries.

WEEK 39

State Fair Fare

State fairs have always been a favorite of mine, no matter where I've lived. And now I love to take my grandchildren and watch them marvel at the many novelties there while waiting in line for a Ferris wheel ride or strolling down the midway. Did you know that we can easily prepare some of our fair favorites at home? Then we get to enjoy them all year round, not just during the summer. This week, to celebrate the anniversary of the first state fair, maybe you'll even feel like creating some of your own carnival games to go along with these goodies and really bring back the flavors and fun of the fair!

Walkaway Turkey Drumsticks

Sausage, Pepper, and Onion Sandwich

Seasoned Fries

Old-fashioned Candy Apples

Black-and-White Soda

Walkaway Turkey Drumsticks

6 servings

This finger-licking walkaway meal is a long-time favorite of fairgoers. Every year after the fair, I found myself dreaming of these juicy turkey legs, so I created a recipe that'll help us enjoy them all year. Oh—don't forget to be ready with lots and lots of napkins!

> 3 tablespoons vegetable oil
> 2 teaspoons Worcestershire sauce
> ½ teaspoon garlic powder
> ¼ teaspoon paprika
> 1 teaspoon salt
> ½ teaspoon black pepper
> 6 turkey legs (about 6 pounds total)

Preheat the oven to 400°F. In a small bowl, combine all the ingredients except the turkey legs; mix well. Place the turkey legs on a rack in a roasting pan and brush evenly with the oil mixture. Bake for 1¼ to 1½ hours, or until the skin is golden brown and no pink remains, basting occasionally.

NOTE: There's no knife and fork needed for these—just grab hold and enjoy . . . well, that's how it's done at the fair!

Sausage, Pepper, and Onion Sandwich

4 sandwiches

This sandwich is perfect any time of the year, whether we grill or panfry it. Close your eyes, wash it down with your favorite bubbly beverage, and you'll be back at the state fair all over again. And this time you won't have to pay for parking!

> ¼ cup vegetable oil
> 1 pound hot Italian rope sausage, cut into 2-inch lengths
> 3 large green bell peppers, cut into ½-inch strips
> 1 large onion, cut into ¼-inch slices
> 4 hoagie rolls, split

Heat the oil in a large skillet over medium-high heat until hot but not smoking. Add the sausage, peppers, and onion and cook for 25 to 30 minutes, or until the sausage is cooked through and the peppers and onions are tender, stirring occasionally. Place the mixture on the hoagie rolls and serve.

NOTE: To make this even more special and colorful, use a combination of red and green bell peppers.

Seasoned Fries

4 to 6 servings

We perfected this recipe in our test kitchen to re-create the fries we get at carnival booths. Now all we need to do is buy a small pushcart, don red-and-white-striped shirts, and go into business for ourselves . . . or just enjoy the fries at home with the family. That's a lot easier!

> ¾ cup seasoned bread crumbs
> ¼ cup grated Parmesan cheese
> ¼ teaspoon salt
> ¼ teaspoon black pepper
> 6 medium potatoes, peeled and cut lengthwise into ½-inch strips
> ⅓ cup butter, melted

Preheat the oven to 450°F. Coat a large rimmed baking sheet with nonstick cooking spray. In a shallow dish, combine the bread crumbs, Parmesan cheese, salt, and pepper; mix well. Dip the potato strips in the melted butter and then in the bread crumb mixture, coating completely. Place on the baking sheet and bake for 20 to 25 minutes, or until golden and crispy, turning halfway through the cooking.

NOTE: These can be prepared ahead of time and baked for 10 minutes or so. Then, just before you're ready to serve the fries, finish the baking.

Old-fashioned Candy Apples

8 apple treats

These sweet cinnamon snacks (not to be eaten by anybody with braces or false teeth!) are loved by kids of all ages, including me. You know what they say—"An apple a day keeps the doctor away," but with *these* apples, I'm not sure that applies to the dentist!

8 medium Red Delicious apples, washed and dried
3 cups sugar
¾ cup water
1 teaspoon lemon juice
12 whole cloves
¼ teaspoon cream of tartar
⅛ teaspoon red food color

8 wooden craft sticks

Remove the stems from the apples and insert a craft stick securely into the stem end of each. Coat a baking sheet with nonstick cooking spray. In a medium saucepan, combine the remaining ingredients and cook over low heat for about 5 minutes, or until the sugar has dissolved, stirring constantly. Increase the heat to medium, cover, and cook for 5 more minutes. Uncover and cook for 25 to 30 minutes, or until the mixture reaches the hard crack stage (300°F.—see Note). Remove the cloves with a slotted spoon; **be careful—the mixture is very hot.** Quickly dip each apple into the syrup mixture, coating completely. Place on the baking sheet and allow to cool. Serve, or wrap individually in plastic wrap until ready to serve.

(continued)

NOTE: To determine when the mixture has reached the hard crack stage, drop a bit of the mixture from a teaspoon into a glass of cold water. If it hardens and forms strands in the water, it has reached the hard crack stage; if not, continue to cook the mixture, then test it again after a bit.

Black-and-White Soda

1 serving

Some people call these black-and-whites, others call 'em ice cream sodas, and still others call them egg creams topped with ice cream. The name doesn't really matter, 'cause to me, they're simply a state fair favorite!

 ¼ cup milk
 3 tablespoons chocolate flavor syrup
 1 cup cold seltzer
 2 scoops vanilla ice cream
 1 tablespoon whipped cream (optional)

In a tall glass, combine the milk and chocolate syrup; mix well. Add the seltzer; stir until well combined. Add the ice cream and top with the whipped cream, if desired.

NOTE: Sprinkle the whipped cream with some chocolate sprinkles and serve with a long-handled spoon and a straw for that authentic soda fountain look.

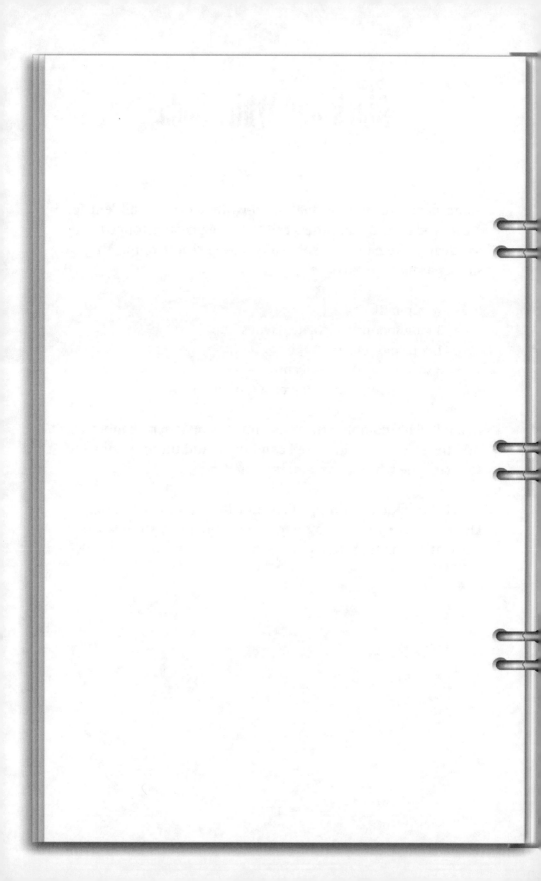

WEEK 40

Oktoberfest

Guten Tag! That's the German greeting "Good day!"—and it *will* be a good day when you try these flavorful German dishes. With its variety of spices and textures, German food has always been among my favorites. And in honor of the annual Oktoberfest celebration, let's prepare some of these classics that are, of course, now easier than ever!

Traditional German Braten Stew

Apple Sauerkraut

Autumn Creamed Spinach

"Sweet Potato" Dumplings

Black Forest Cake Roll

Traditional German Braten Stew

German-style marinated pot roast is called *braten*. Now let's take this traditional dish one step further by adding some more ingredients and turning it into our own braten stew.

3 pounds beef short ribs
2 tablespoons vegetable oil
1 can (10¾ ounces) condensed onion soup
1 cup water
1 tablespoon lemon juice
1 bay leaf
¼ teaspoon ground cloves
½ teaspoon black pepper
1 slice pumpernickel bread, crumbled

In a soup pot, brown the short ribs in the oil over medium-high heat for 6 to 8 minutes; drain. Add the remaining ingredients except the crumbled bread and bring to a boil. Reduce the heat to medium-low, cover, and cook for 1½ to 2 hours, or until desired tenderness, stirring occasionally. **Remove and discard the bay leaf.** Stir in the crumbled bread and serve.

NOTE: I like to serve this with some additional pumpernickel bread.

Apple Sauerkraut

4 to 6 servings

I thought this would be a sweet twist on the traditional savory dish . . . and I know you won't miss the sausage!

1 can (27 ounces) sauerkraut, rinsed and drained
2 cups apple juice
1 large Red Delicious apple, coarsely chopped
¼ cup sugar
½ teaspoon ground cloves

In a soup pot, bring all the ingredients to a boil over medium-high heat and cook for 25 to 30 minutes, or until the apple is tender, stirring occasionally.

Autumn Creamed Spinach

4 to 6 servings

This rich and creamy dish is so tasty that it turns spinach haters into spinach lovers. Trust me . . . I've seen it happen right in front of my eyes!

    2 tablespoons butter
    2 tablespoons all-purpose flour
    2 packages (10 ounces each) frozen chopped spinach,
        thawed and well drained (see Note)
    1 cup (½ pint) heavy cream
    ½ teaspoon ground nutmeg
    ½ teaspoon salt

Melt the butter in a large skillet over medium heat; stir in the flour until combined and golden. Add the remaining ingredients; mix well and cook for 3 to 5 minutes, or until heated through.

NOTE: Two 10-ounce packages of fresh spinach can also be used; just chop it and boil until tender, then drain well and proceed as above.

"Sweet Potato" Dumplings

about 1 dozen

Kartoffel means potato in German, and, let me tell you, are these ever sweet potato dumplings. . . . Well, they're not made with sweet potatoes, but they're dumplings made with potatoes, and they're sweet. Get it? (Now you've *gotta* try it, right?!)

> 6 cups water
> 2 cans (10¾ ounces each) condensed chicken broth
> 2 cups warm mashed potatoes
> 1¼ cups all-purpose flour
> 2 eggs
> 1½ teaspoons cornstarch
> ½ teaspoon baking powder
> ½ teaspoon sugar
> ⅛ teaspoon ground nutmeg
> ⅛ teaspoon ground cinnamon
> ½ teaspoon salt

In a soup pot, bring the water and broth to a rolling boil over high heat. Meanwhile, in a large bowl, combine the remaining ingredients; mix well. Carefully drop the batter by ¼-cup measures into the soup pot to form dumplings and boil for 5 to 7 minutes, or until firm. Remove with a slotted spoon and serve.

NOTE: Wanna know an easy way to make the dumplings? Use an ice cream scoop to drop the batter into the boiling liquid.

Black Forest Cake Roll

10 to 12 servings

Who wants plain old chocolate cake when we can have a Bavarian-style fruit-filled cake roll with the same amount of work? We'll serve this and the whole table will be chanting *"Ach Das Schmeckt!"* which, of course, means "OOH IT'S SO GOOD!!®"

    ¾ cup all-purpose flour
    ¼ cup unsweetened cocoa
    1 teaspoon baking powder
    ¼ teaspoon salt
    3 eggs
    1 cup granulated sugar
    ⅓ cup water
    1 teaspoon vanilla extract
    Confectioners' sugar for sprinkling
    1 can (21 ounces) cherry pie filling
    2 cups frozen whipped topping, thawed
    2 tablespoons mini semisweet chocolate chips

Preheat the oven to 375°F. Line a 10" × 15" rimmed baking sheet or jelly-roll pan with aluminum foil and coat with nonstick cooking spray. In a small bowl, combine the flour, cocoa, baking powder, and salt; set aside. In a large bowl, with an electric beater on high speed, beat the eggs until soft peaks form. Gradually beat in the granulated sugar, then beat in the water and vanilla until well blended. Reduce the speed to low and beat in the flour mixture just until smooth. Pour onto the baking sheet. Bake for 10 to 12 minutes, or until a wooden toothpick inserted in the center comes out clean. Sprinkle a clean kitchen towel with the confectioners' sugar and invert the cake onto the towel. While still hot, peel off the aluminum foil and roll up the cake and towel jelly-roll style, starting from a narrow end. Allow to cool on a wire rack. Unroll the cake and remove the towel. Spread the cherry pie filling over the top of the cake, leaving a 1-inch border all around, and roll up. Place on a serving platter, frost with the whipped topping, and sprinkle with the chocolate chips. Cover loosely and chill for at least 1 hour, or until ready to serve.

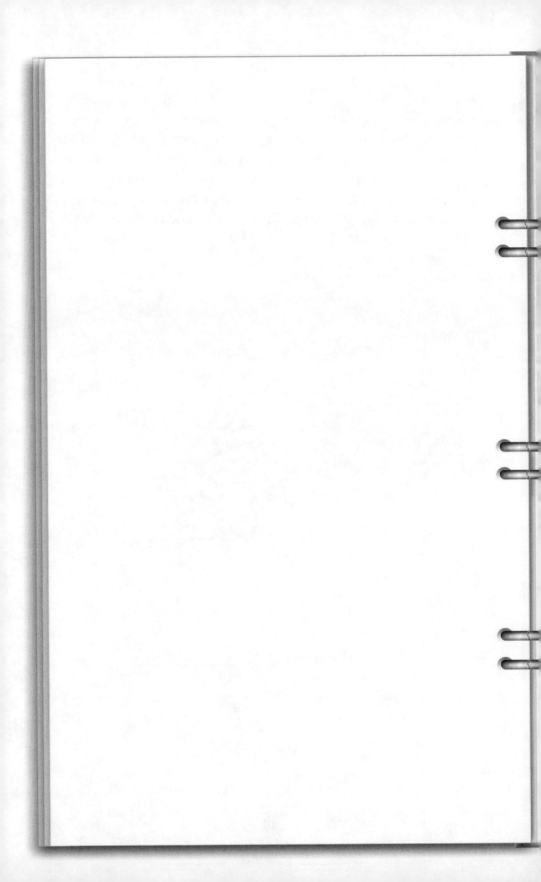

WEEK 41

Orchard Goodies

Throughout the Northeast, autumn traditionally means apple season, which to us means classic pies bursting with flavor, fresh-baked pastries . . . the dessert list goes on and on. But let's not forget about the loads of other ways to use apples. Here are some great recipes and ideas to get you started.

Apple Chart

Apple-Glazed Chicken

Orchard Sweet Potato Bake

Upside-down Apple Pie

Simmering Cider

Apple Chart

Here's a quick guide that tells you the best apples for snacking, baking, and making candy or caramel apples. Of course, you can use your favorites, but this helps when you want to make the most of whichever fresh ones are available. For example, the apples suggested for applesauce are those that stay the most flavorful when cooked. For baked apples, you should choose ones that hold their shape and get sweeter when baked. For breads, cakes, and muffins, you do best with apples that keep their shape and have both tart and sweet flavor; for pies, cobblers, and crisps, the best are the ones that retain their texture and flavor through long baking; and for candy and caramel apples, the best are those that stay crunchy under sweet coatings. For eating raw, well . . . the ones I suggest are sweet, crisp, and juicy—but go with what you and your family like the best.

Apple	Best Use(s)
Braeburn	Eating raw, and for salads, baked apples, and applesauce
Cortland	Eating raw, and for salads and garnishes, baked apples, pies, cobblers, and crisps
Crispin	Eating raw, and for applesauce, breads, cakes, muffins, and pastries
Empire	Eating raw, and for salads, pies, and applesauce
Fuji	Eating raw, and for salads and applesauce
Gala	Eating raw, and for salads
Golden Delicious	Baked apples, pies, cobblers, crisps, breads, cakes, muffins, and pastries

Apple	Best Use(s)
Granny Smith	Eating raw, and for breads, cakes, muffins, pastries, baked apples, pies, cobblers, and crisps
Jonathan	Applesauce
Macoun	Eating raw, and for salads, applesauce, and candy and caramel apples
McIntosh	Eating raw, and for pies, applesauce, and candy and caramel apples
Newtown Pippin	Applesauce, pies, cobblers, and crisps
Red Delicious	Eating raw, and for salads
Rome	Applesauce, baked apples, breads, cakes, muffins, pastries, and pies
Winesap	Eating raw, and for applesauce, breads, cakes, muffins, and pastries

Apple-Glazed Chicken

4 to 6 servings

Johnny Appleseed never ate chicken this good. With each mouthwatering bite, you'll be thanking him for planting those orchards many years ago—and you might even think about planting a few trees of your own.

⅓ cup all-purpose flour
¼ teaspoon salt
½ teaspoon black pepper
One 3- to 3½-pound chicken, cut into 8 pieces
2 tablespoons vegetable oil
1 cup apple jelly
1 teaspoon lemon juice
¼ teaspoon ground cinnamon
3 red apples, cored and cut into ½-inch wedges (see Note)

In a shallow dish, combine the flour, salt, and pepper. Dip the chicken into the flour mixture, coating completely. Heat the oil in a large skillet over medium heat. Brown the chicken in batches for 5 to 7 minutes per side. Meanwhile, in a medium bowl, combine the apple jelly, lemon juice, and cinnamon; mix well and stir in the apples. Add to the skillet and reduce the heat to medium-low. Simmer for 25 to 30 minutes, or until no pink remains in the chicken and the sauce has glazed the chicken, turning halfway through cooking. Serve the chicken with the apples and any glaze remaining in the skillet.

NOTE: I like to use Cortland apples for their particular color and taste, but any apple you have on hand can be used. And if you prefer, you can peel them.

Orchard Sweet Potato Bake

6 to 8 servings

This is no ordinary sweet potato casserole. The addition of some Granny Smiths or Cortlands changes this everyday taste into something "apple-luscious"!

¾ cup orange juice
¾ cup honey
¼ cup (½ stick) butter, melted
1 teaspoon salt
2 cans (29 ounces each) sweet potatoes or yams, drained
2 cans (14½ ounces each) sliced carrots, drained
3 Golden Delicious apples, peeled, cored, and cut into
   1-inch chunks
1 package (12 ounces) pitted prunes

Preheat the oven to 350°F. Coat a 2-quart casserole dish with nonstick cooking spray. In a large bowl, combine the orange juice, honey, butter, and salt; mix well. Add the remaining ingredients and toss until well coated. Spoon into the casserole dish and bake for 1½ to 2 hours, or until the apples are tender, stirring occasionally.

NOTE: This can also be made with fresh sweet potatoes and carrots. Just peel, cut into chunks, and boil until tender, then proceed as above.

Upside-down Apple Pie

6 to 8 servings

Okay, you heard it here first: This is no ordinary apple pie. It's gotten more raves than any other apple dessert I've made, so you just have to try it. Oh—be careful when carrying it to the table, 'cause if you drop it, it might become a right-side-up upside-down pie!

> 6 tablespoons (¾ stick) butter, melted, divided
> ½ cup firmly packed light brown sugar
> ½ cup chopped pecans
> 1 package (15 ounces) folded refrigerated pie crusts
> 1 cup granulated sugar
> ⅓ cup all-purpose flour
> ¾ teaspoon ground cinnamon
> 5 large Granny Smith or other apples, peeled, cored, and
>   cut into ½-inch wedges

Preheat the oven to 375°F. Coat a deep-dish pie plate with non-stick cooking spray and line it with waxed paper. Coat the waxed paper with cooking spray. In a small bowl, combine 4 tablespoons butter, the brown sugar, and pecans; mix well and spread evenly over the bottom of the pie plate. Unfold 1 pie crust and place it in the pie plate, pressing the crust firmly against the nut mixture and the sides of the plate; set aside. In a large bowl, combine the granulated sugar, flour, cinnamon, and the remaining 2 tablespoons butter; mix well. Add the apples and toss gently to coat. Spoon into the pie crust. Unfold the second pie crust and place over the apple mixture. Trim and pinch the edges together to seal, and flute, if desired. Using a knife, cut four 1-inch slits in the top crust. Bake for 1 to 1¼ hours, or until the crust is golden. Carefully loosen the waxed paper around the rim and invert the pie onto a serving plate while still hot. Remove the waxed paper and allow to cool slightly, then cut into wedges and serve warm, or allow to cool completely before serving.

NOTE: Here's a hint to make sure you don't have a mess on your hands in the oven: Position a cookie sheet on the bottom oven rack to catch any juices that may leak from the pie.

Simmering Cider

about 2 quarts, 8 to 10 servings

We serve this old-time favorite at our get-togethers with family and close friends. In fact, I'm wishing for cold weather already so we can fire up that fireplace. And don't forget the cinnamon sticks.

> ½ gallon apple cider
> 1 cup firmly packed light brown sugar
> 2 oranges, cut into ¼-inch slices
> 2 lemons, cut into ¼-inch slices
> 4 cinnamon sticks

In a large saucepan, combine all the ingredients; mix well. Cover and simmer over low heat for 30 minutes. Serve hot.

NOTE: I like to serve this from a slow cooker so that it can stay nice and hot all evening long.

WEEK 42

Columbus Day Discoveries

Although we celebrate our nation's birthday on July 4th, we also celebrate the birth of Christopher Columbus, who, it's said, discovered America. Upon his arrival in the New World, Columbus was greeted by people who ate very different foods from the ones he was used to. In honor of Columbus's native Italy, and his new native American friends, let's prepare a feast combining the foods and customs of both continents. Yes, they're all today-easy!

Rich and Creamy Fettuccine

Veal Cacciatore Stew

Sautéed Greens

Almond Gelato

Nutty Meringues

Rich and Creamy Fettuccine

4 to 6 servings

Not for the weakhearted, an appetizer-sized serving of this rich and creamy pasta dish is just the right "starter" for our big meal to come.

    1 pound fettuccine
    ½ cup (1 stick) butter
    2 cups (1 pint) heavy cream
    ½ teaspoon black pepper
    1 cup grated Parmesan cheese

Cook the fettuccine according to the package directions; drain and keep warm in a large serving bowl. Meanwhile, in a medium saucepan, melt the butter over medium-low heat and stir in the cream and pepper. Cook for 6 to 8 minutes, or until hot, stirring constantly. Stir in the cheese; mix well and cook for 3 to 5 minutes, or until thickened. Toss with the fettuccine and serve immediately.

NOTE: Top with additional Parmesan cheese, if desired. I like to use spinach fettuccine to give the dish nice color contrast.

Veal Cacciatore Stew

4 to 6 servings

You're really going to love this hearty dish that combines the flavors of the Old World with the fresh tastes of the New World.

½ cup all-purpose flour
1 teaspoon salt, divided
¼ teaspoon black pepper
2½ pounds veal stew meat
4 tablespoons vegetable oil, divided
1 pound fresh mushrooms, quartered
1 large green bell pepper, chopped
1 large onion, chopped
2 garlic cloves, minced
1 can (14½ ounces) ready-to-use beef broth
1 jar (28 ounces) spaghetti sauce
1 can (28 ounces) diced tomatoes, undrained

In a shallow dish, combine the flour, ½ teaspoon salt, and the black pepper. Roll the veal in the flour mixture, coating completely. Heat 3 tablespoons oil in a soup pot over high heat until hot; brown the veal on all sides for 5 minutes. Remove the veal from the pot and set aside. Add the mushrooms, green pepper, onion, garlic, and the remaining 1 tablespoon oil to the pot and cook for 5 minutes, or until the onions are tender, stirring occasionally. Add the remaining ingredients, including the remaining ½ teaspoon salt; return the veal to the pot and bring to a boil. Reduce the heat to low and simmer for 1½ to 2 hours, or until the veal is fork-tender, stirring occasionally.

Sautéed Greens

This dish has been passed down through generations of Italian kitchens and "Americanized" to use any kind of greens you have on hand—romaine, red leaf lettuce, even spinach works in this simple side dish.

- ¼ cup (½ stick) butter
- 2 garlic cloves, minced
- ⅛ teaspoon ground red pepper
- ½ teaspoon salt
- 2 medium heads escarole (about 3 pounds), trimmed, washed, and chopped
- 1 red bell pepper, diced
- ¼ cup water

In a soup pot, melt the butter over medium heat. Add the garlic, ground red pepper, and salt and sauté for 1 minute, or until the garlic is golden. Add the remaining ingredients and cook for 35 to 40 minutes, or until the escarole is tender, stirring occasionally.

NOTE: Although 2 heads of escarole look like a lot raw, when cooked, they reduce quite a bit in bulk, just like spinach.

Almond Gelato

6 to 8 servings

Rich and creamy, and very Italian—just like we love it! Who needs plain old ice cream when we can have this homemade dessert that goes together in a flash?

   1 cup sugar, divided
   ¼ cup plus 1 teaspoon light corn syrup, divided
   ½ cup slivered almonds, toasted
   2 cups milk
   1 cup (½ pint) heavy cream
   ⅓ cup nonfat dry milk
   ½ teaspoon unflavored gelatin

Coat a large rimmed baking sheet with nonstick cooking spray. In a small saucepan, combine ⅓ cup sugar and 1 teaspoon corn syrup over low heat until the sugar is melted and golden. Stir in the almonds and pour onto the baking sheet. Allow to cool, then crush into small pieces. In a medium bowl, combine the remaining ingredients, including the remaining ⅔ cup sugar and ¼ cup corn syrup; mix well. Add the crushed almond mixture; mix well. Cover or place in an airtight container and freeze for at least 8 hours, or until firm.

NOTE: For creamier ice cream, once the mixture is frozen, cut it into chunks and process in a food processor until creamy. Serve, or place in an airtight container and refreeze until ready to serve.

Nutty Meringues

about 4 dozen

Meringues look so fancy, yet they're really simple to make. Whip these up for serving with Almond Gelato and you'll have an Old World treat with New World appeal.

    4 egg whites
    ⅛ teaspoon salt
    1 cup sugar
    2 teaspoons grated lemon peel
    1 cup blanched almonds, finely chopped

Preheat the oven to 325°F. Lightly coat 2 large baking sheets with nonstick cooking spray. In a medium bowl, with an electric beater on high speed, beat the egg whites with the salt for 2 to 3 minutes, or until stiff and glossy. Gradually add the sugar and lemon peel and beat until the mixture forms soft peaks. Fold in the chopped almonds and drop by heaping teaspoonfuls onto the baking sheets. Bake for 10 minutes. Turn off the oven and leave in the oven for 1 hour with the door closed. Remove to a wire rack to cool completely.

NOTE: You can serve these with Almond Gelato (page 279) on the side, or, if you prefer, make the meringues slightly larger than directed, then flatten them out before baking so you'll be able to place the gelato right on top of them.

WEEK 43

Chocoholic Fantasies

Wow! Can you believe it? It's Worldwide Chocolate Month, so we get a whole month to honor that sweet treat that's known to drive a true "chocoholic" wild. Most of us love chocolate in one way or another, and this chapter covers all bases from a new approach to the traditional chocolate cake to a pie that's "to die for." It's hard to believe that all that flavor comes from a tiny bean, but we certainly should be thankful we have it and know how to use it!

Coconut Chocolate Cake

Fabulous Chocolate Walnut Fudge

Chocoholic's Parfait

Chocolate Pecan Fudge Pie

White Chocolate Macadamia Bars

Coconut Chocolate Cake

An alternative to traditional coconut cake, this tasty treat deserves an honor all its own. Don't forget a big glass of milk . . . trust me, you'll need it.

> 3 cups all-purpose flour
> 2 cups sugar
> ½ cup unsweetened cocoa
> 2 teaspoons baking soda
> 1 teaspoon salt
> 2 cups cold black coffee
> ⅔ cup vegetable oil
> 2 tablespoons white vinegar
> 2 teaspoons vanilla extract
> 1 package (14 ounces) sweetened flaked coconut, chopped
> ¾ cup light corn syrup
> 1 container (16 ounces) chocolate frosting

Preheat the oven to 350°F. Coat two 9-inch round cake pans with nonstick cooking spray. In a large bowl, combine the flour, sugar, cocoa, baking soda, and salt. Add the coffee, oil, vinegar, and vanilla. Stir until the batter is well combined. Pour into the cake pans and bake for 30 to 35 minutes, or until a wooden toothpick inserted in the center comes out clean. Allow to cool slightly, then remove to wire racks to cool completely. In a medium bowl, combine the coconut and corn syrup; mix well. Place 1 cake layer upside down on a serving plate and spread the coconut mixture over the top. Place the second layer over the coconut mixture. Heat the chocolate frosting in a microwave for 10-second intervals, stirring until smooth and pourable (see Note). When the frosting is pourable but not too runny, pour and spread it over the top and sides of the cake, forming a thick glaze. Chill for at least 2 hours, then serve, or cover and keep chilled until ready to serve.

NOTE: Although it's easiest to uncover the frosting and microwave it right in its plastic container (of course, first make sure to remove the foil seal completely), you can also heat the frosting in a saucepan over low heat until smooth and pourable.

Fabulous Chocolate Walnut Fudge

about 3 dozen pieces

Most of us associate fudge with the holidays. Well, I want you to try this one now so you'll savor each bite and make it again and again throughout the year. Remember, it's great for gift-giving, too.

> 2 cans (14 ounces each) sweetened condensed milk
> 1 package (12 ounces) semisweet chocolate chips
> 1 package (12 ounces) milk chocolate chips
> 1 cup chopped walnuts

In a medium saucepan, bring the sweetened condensed milk to a rolling boil over medium heat. Remove from the heat and add the semisweet and milk chocolate chips, stirring until smooth. Add the walnuts; mix well. Spread into an 8-inch square baking dish and chill for 3 to 4 hours, or until firm. Cut into squares and serve.

NOTE: Before chilling the fudge, you can press some miniature marshmallows and additional walnuts into the top to create Rocky Road Fudge.

Chocoholic's Parfait

8 to 10 servings

Chocolate, chocolate, and more chocolate! This promises to be addicting, so if you aren't ready to take that step . . . you'd better not get started!

> 2 cups cold chocolate milk
> 1 package (4-serving size) instant chocolate pudding and pie filling
> ½ cup (3 ounces) mini semisweet chocolate chips
> 1 container (8 ounces) frozen whipped topping, thawed
> 1½ cups coarsely crushed chocolate chip cookies

In a medium bowl, combine the chocolate milk and pudding mix; mix until well combined and thickened. Add the chocolate chips to the whipped topping; mix well. Place ½ cup of the crushed cookies in a glass serving bowl; top with half of the pudding, then half of the whipped topping mixture. Repeat the layers once more and sprinkle the remaining cookie crumbs over the top. Cover and chill for at least 3 hours before serving.

NOTE: These can also be made as individual parfaits by layering everything equally in 6 to 8 dessert or parfait glasses.

Chocolate Pecan Fudge Pie

8 to 10 servings (see Note)

Boy, is this a rich and tempting dessert. In fact, it's so good it should come with a warning: "Eat at your own risk!"

½ cup water
1 tablespoon cornstarch
3 squares (1 ounce each) unsweetened chocolate
1 can (14 ounces) sweetened condensed milk
2 eggs
¼ cup (½ stick) butter, softened
⅛ teaspoon salt
1 cup pecan halves
One 9-inch chocolate graham cracker pie crust

Preheat the oven to 350°F. In a small bowl, combine the water and cornstarch; set aside. In a medium saucepan, melt the chocolate in the sweetened condensed milk over low heat, stirring occasionally. Add the cornstarch mixture, the eggs, butter, and salt; mix until smooth. Remove from the heat and add the pecan halves; mix well. Pour into the crust and bake for 30 to 35 minutes, or until a knife inserted in the center comes out clean. Allow to cool on a wire rack, then cover and chill for at least 2 hours before serving.

NOTE: This is so rich, it can even be cut into smaller wedges than a regular pie to make 12 to 16 servings.

White Chocolate Macadamia Bars

15 to 18 bars

Most self-proclaimed chocolate lovers are cautious about trying anything made with white chocolate, but I assure you it's just as good as the dark stuff—and these bars prove it.

1 package (18 ounces) refrigerated sugar cookie dough
3 packages (8 ounces each) cream cheese, softened
3 eggs
¾ cup sugar
1 teaspoon vanilla extract
1 package (12 ounces) white baking chips (see Note)
1 cup coarsely chopped macadamia nuts

Preheat the oven to 350°F. Coat a 9" × 13" baking dish with nonstick cooking spray. Press two thirds of the cookie dough into the bottom of the baking dish. In a medium bowl, with an electric beater on medium speed, beat the cream cheese, eggs, sugar, and vanilla until creamy. Stir in the baking chips and nuts and pour into the baking dish. Crumble the remaining cookie dough and sprinkle it evenly over the cream cheese mixture. Bake for 40 to 45 minutes, or until the topping is golden and the center is set. Allow to cool completely, then cover and chill for at least 4 hours. Cut into bars and serve.

NOTE: Any type of white baking chips or even bars can be used, including imported ones. If using bars, though, coarsely chop them to the desired size.

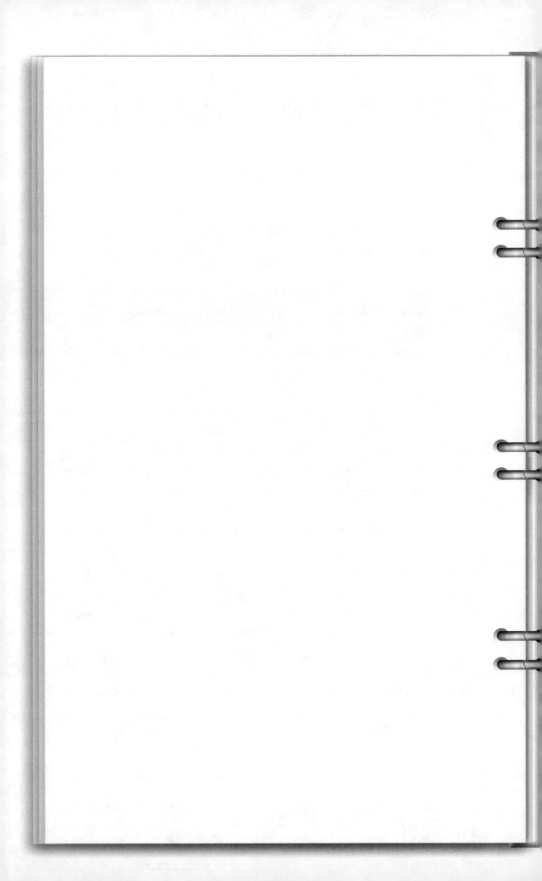

WEEK 44

Halloween Treats

BOO! It's time to get out those witch's hats and skeletons and get right down to the spooky stuff—goblin stew and witch's brew. Nah, I'm just kidding. But let's prepare some special treats for kids of all ages to enjoy. Trick or treat!

Halloween Pasta Salad

Jack-o'-Lantern Sandwiches

Candied Popcorn Balls

Pumpkin Patch Chocolate Chip Cookies

Witch's Butterscotch Brew

Halloween Pasta Salad

6 to 8 servings

Planning to take a hayride on Halloween? Well, this dish made with wagon wheel pasta is the perfect side dish to get everybody in the mood for the Halloween hayride and celebration.

½ pound wagon wheel pasta (see Note)
¾ cup Italian dressing
1 can (15¼ ounces) whole kernel corn, drained
1 can (15½ ounces) red kidney beans, rinsed and drained
1 can (15 ounces) black beans, rinsed and drained
1 medium red bell pepper, chopped
1 small red onion, chopped
2 carrots, diced
½ teaspoon black pepper

Cook the pasta according to the package directions; drain, rinse, drain again, and place in a large bowl. Add the remaining ingredients; mix well. Cover and chill for at least 2 hours before serving.

NOTE: Wagon wheel pasta can usually be found in the supermarket pasta section, and certainly in specialty markets. It's nice to use in salads like this 'cause the vegetables tend to get stuck in the spokes of the wheels. But sure, any kind of pasta can be used.

Jack-o'-Lantern Sandwiches

4 sandwiches

A colorful twist on one of our old favorites, these spooky sandwiches are just right for serving with some tomato soup for an out-of-this-world lunch or fast dinner before all the trick-or-treating begins.

    8 slices pumpernickel bread
    1 container (7½ ounces) pimiento cheese spread (see Note)
    2 tablespoons butter, softened, divided

Using cookie cutters or a knife, cut a simple jack-o'-lantern face from each of 4 slices of bread, as illustrated. Spread the cheese spread on the remaining 4 slices of bread. Top with the cut-out bread, and butter the tops with 1 tablespoon butter. Melt the remaining 1 tablespoon butter in a large skillet over medium-high heat and cook the bottom of the sandwiches. Turn over and cook the cut-out sides for 1 minute. Turn again and continue grilling until the cheese is melted and the bread is toasted. Serve immediately.

NOTE: Don't like pimientos? No problem—just use slices of orange American cheese—it tastes good and the color works perfectly!

Candied Popcorn Balls

about 3 dozen

This gooey treat is one that trick-or-treaters are sure to love. They're fun for everyone, but be sure to have lots of soap and water ready for washing those sticky hands!

16 cups popped popcorn (see Note)
1 package (15 ounces) candy corn
½ cup sugar
1 package (4-serving size) orange-flavored gelatin
1 cup light corn syrup

Coat a large bowl with nonstick cooking spray. Add the popcorn and candy corn; mix well and set aside. In a small saucepan, dissolve the sugar and gelatin mix in the corn syrup over medium heat. Bring to a boil and let boil for 1 minute, stirring constantly. Add to the popcorn mixture; mix well. Quickly form into 2-inch balls, packing well. Place on waxed paper–lined baking sheets. Allow to harden, then serve, or store in an airtight container until ready to serve.

NOTE: One regular package of microwaveable popcorn will yield 7 to 8 cups of popcorn. By adding different kinds and colors of candies and/or using different flavors of gelatin, these popcorn balls can be made for any holiday celebration or party.

Pumpkin Patch Chocolate Chip Cookies

about 2 dozen

Gather the kids around this pumpkin patch, 'cause it's the perfect cookie for them to help put together.

> 2¼ cups all-purpose flour
> 1 teaspoon baking soda
> 1 teaspoon salt
> 1 cup (2 sticks) butter, softened
> ¾ cup granulated sugar
> ¾ cup firmly packed light brown sugar
> ½ teaspoon red food color
> ½ teaspoon yellow food color
> 1 teaspoon vanilla extract
> 2 eggs
> 1 cup (6 ounces) semisweet chocolate chips

Preheat the oven to 375°F. In a small bowl, combine the flour, baking soda, and salt; mix well and set aside. In a large bowl,

"I'M NO TRICK!"

"I'M A TREAT!"

with an electric beater on medium speed, beat the butter, both sugars and food colors, and the vanilla until creamy. Beat in the eggs, then gradually beat in the flour mixture until well combined. Drop by heaping tablespoonfuls 2 inches apart onto ungreased cookie sheets. Bake for 9 to 11 minutes, or until the edges are golden. Remove from the oven and immediately press the chocolate chips firmly into the cookies, as illustrated, forming pumpkin eyes, nose, and a mouth in each while the cookies are still hot. Remove to a wire rack to cool.

NOTE: For best results, bake only a few cookies at a time so that you can add the chocolate chips while the cookies are still hot. That way, as the cookies cool, the chips will stay in the cookies.

Witch's Butterscotch Brew

about 1 quart, 4 to 6 servings

Fire up those cauldrons for one spectacular drink. This is the perfect brew for our favorite little ghosts and goblins.

   4 cups (1 quart) milk
   1 cup (6 ounces) butterscotch chips
   ½ cup miniature marshmallows

In a medium saucepan, combine all the ingredients over medium heat. Whisk until the chips and marshmallows are melted and the mixture is heated through. Serve immediately.

NOTE: Serve in mugs and top with some additional marshmallows.

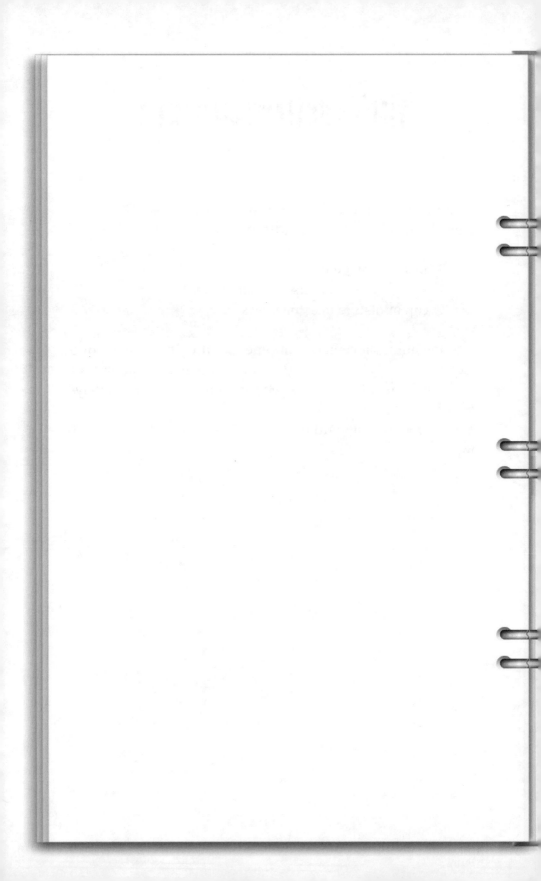

WEEK 45

National Sandwich Week

It's time to honor the Earl of Sandwich! After all, back in 1762, he invented our favorite timesaving noontime—or anytime—meal. And, boy, have sandwiches come a long way since then! From hot to cold, pocket to open-faced, where sandwiches are concerned, there's definitely something for everyone! So let's remember the Earl during National Sandwich Week by trying a few easy sandwiches. . . . As a matter of fact, we should remember to enjoy these and other fun sandwiches all year long.

Croissant Club

Monte Cristo

Fresh Veggie Pita

Italian Focaccia Sandwich

Baked Stuffed Tuna Sandwich

Croissant Club

8 sandwiches

It's time to try something different! For this take on the traditional club sandwich, we have a shortcut bacon mayonnaise that's made without frying bacon! It's a true time-saver—and isn't that what sandwiches are all about?

> 1 cup mayonnaise
> 2 tablespoons real bacon bits
> 8 large croissants, split
> 8 romaine lettuce leaves
> 1 pound thinly sliced deli turkey
> 1 large tomato, cut into 8 slices (see Note)

In a small bowl, combine the mayonnaise and bacon bits; mix well and spread evenly over the croissant halves. Layer the lettuce, turkey, and tomato over the bottom croissant halves; replace the tops of the croissants and serve.

NOTE: Cut each slice of tomato in half—that way they'll surely fit on the croissants.

Monte Cristo

8 sandwiches

This sandwich has been around for a long time, but have you ever wondered what it is? You're not alone! It's really just a chicken, ham, and cheese sandwich that's panfried like French toast. Sound good? Now you've gotta try it, right?

6 eggs
½ cup milk
½ pound thinly sliced deli chicken roll
½ pound thinly sliced deli ham
16 slices egg bread (challah)
8 slices (8 ounces) Swiss cheese
About 4 tablespoons (½ stick) butter

In a medium bowl, whisk the eggs and milk until well combined; set aside. Place the chicken and ham over 8 bread slices, dividing them equally. Place the slices of cheese over the chicken and ham, then top with the remaining 8 bread slices. Melt 1 tablespoon butter in a large skillet over low heat. Dip 2 sandwiches, one at a time, in the egg mixture, coating completely. Place in the skillet and cook for 2 to 3 minutes per side, or until golden and the cheese is melted, adding more butter as needed. Repeat with the remaining sandwiches. Serve immediately.

NOTE: Give these a flavor boost by cutting each sandwich in half diagonally and serving with cranberry sauce on the side.

Fresh Veggie Pita

6 sandwiches

Fresh and simple, this garden veggie pocket is versatile enough for all year round. Maybe enjoy it now with a bowl of hot soup for a light dinner, or pack it in a lunch box on those days when you're on the go. And this time of year it's ideal. Why? 'Cause you know how we all try to watch our waistlines before we indulge in all the Thanksgiving goodies coming soon!

> 2 large cucumbers, peeled, seeded, and finely chopped
> 1 container (16 ounces) plain yogurt
> 1 tablespoon sugar
> 1 teaspoon garlic powder
> ⅛ teaspoon salt
> ⅛ teaspoon black pepper
> ½ of a medium head iceberg lettuce, coarsely chopped
> 1 package (6 ounces) alfalfa sprouts
> 1 large tomato, seeded and chopped
> 1 medium carrot, grated
> 1 medium red bell pepper, diced
> ½ of a small onion, diced
> 6 whole wheat or regular pita breads, cut in half

In a medium bowl, combine the cucumbers, yogurt, sugar, garlic powder, salt, and black pepper; mix well. In a large bowl, combine the remaining ingredients except the pita breads; mix well. Stuff the pita halves with the lettuce mixture, then top with the cucumber sauce and serve.

NOTE: If I have a ripe avocado on hand, I add a couple of slices to each sandwich before topping with the cucumber sauce.

Italian Focaccia Sandwich

8 sandwiches

Don't miss this Italian favorite! Sure, lots of restaurants serve it, but now we can make it at home for a lot less money—and with all our own favorite flavors.

¼ cup mayonnaise
Two 10-ounce prepared thin pizza shells (see Note)
1 pound thinly sliced deli mortadella (Italian-style bologna)
1 package (6 ounces) sliced mozzarella cheese
3 tablespoons prepared yellow mustard

Preheat the oven to 450°F. Spread the mayonnaise over the top of 1 pizza shell. Layer the mortadella over the mayonnaise, then top with the mozzarella. Spread the mustard over the top of the second pizza shell, then place it mustard side down over the cheese. Place on a pizza pan that has been coated with non-stick cooking spray and coat the top of the pizza shell with nonstick cooking spray. Bake for 8 to 10 minutes, or until the crusts are crispy and the cheese is melted. Cut into wedges and serve.

NOTE: Use Italian bread pizza shells that have ingredients like olive oil, garlic, Parmesan, and mozzarella cheeses baked in.

Baked Stuffed Tuna Sandwich

6 sandwiches

This is the perfect sandwich to serve the hungry gang because not only is it easy, it's warm and filling, too! It's perfect for those Sunday football games and other times when you want something really hearty and good-looking. Rah, rah, rah! (That's for the game *and* the sandwich!)

> 1 can (12 ounces) chunk white tuna, drained and flaked
> ½ cup (2 ounces) shredded Cheddar cheese
> ½ cup mayonnaise
> 1 scallion, thinly sliced
> ⅛ teaspoon garlic powder
> ⅛ teaspoon black pepper
> One 1-pound loaf pumpernickel bread, unsliced (see Note)

Preheat the oven to 350°F. In a medium bowl, combine all the ingredients except the bread; mix well and set aside. Make 11 crosswise cuts in the bread, cutting to within ¼ inch of the bot-

MAKE ELEVEN CUTS...

FILL EVERY OTHER CUT!

PUMPERNICKEL... RYE... 7 GRAIN

tom of the loaf; be sure not to cut all the way through. Fill the spaces between every other cut with equal amounts of the tuna mixture. Wrap in aluminum foil and bake for 30 to 35 minutes, or until the cheese melts. Unwrap, slice completely through the unfilled cuts, and serve warm.

NOTE: This can be made with either long or round pumpernickel bread, or with rye, seven-grain, or any other whole firm loaf.

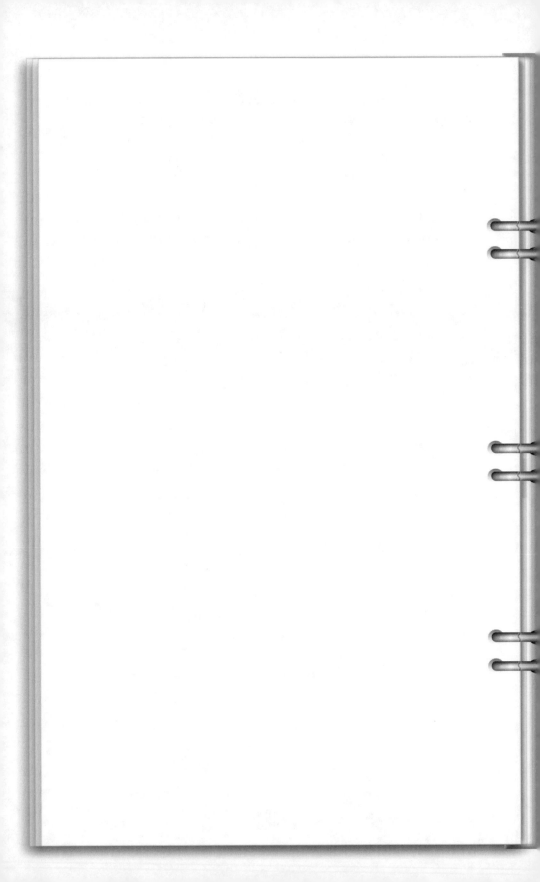

WEEK 46

Veterans Day

This is the time when our country honors those who've fought bravely to defend our freedom. Every day we should be thankful to them, as well as to those who made tremendous sacrifices at home in support of war efforts. You know, some of my earliest memories are of life during World War II when there was rationing of most of our daily necessities. Everything from gasoline and shoes to butter, sugar, meat, and coffee was in short supply . . . so, though those were particularly tough times, we made substitutions and made do with whatever we had. These recipes can surely stand on their own, but they mean so much more when we think about what they represent.

Honey Corn Bread

Tossed Garden Salad

Victory Garden Soup

Honey Mousse

Honey Corn Bread

6 to 8 servings

Since sugar was rationed during World War II, I thought it would be appropriate to include a bread made with honey instead of sugar. Why not make it this week to express your thankfulness for being able to share it with *your* honey?

>   1 cup all-purpose flour
>   ½ cup yellow cornmeal
>   1 tablespoon baking powder
>   ½ teaspoon salt
>   1 cup milk
>   1 egg, well beaten
>   ½ cup honey
>   1 tablespoon vegetable shortening, melted

Preheat the oven to 400°F. Coat an 8-inch square baking pan with nonstick cooking spray. In a large bowl, combine the flour, cornmeal, baking powder, and salt; mix well. Stir in the milk and egg until thoroughly combined. Add the honey and shortening; mix well. Pour into the baking pan and bake for 20 to 25 minutes, or until a wooden toothpick inserted in the center comes out clean.

Tossed Garden Salad

6 to 8 servings

During World War II, many Americans who didn't ordinarily grow their own produce planted small kitchen gardens to produce their own vegetables. This fresh veggie salad can remind us of these victory gardens . . . and, no, you don't have to make it with homegrown vegetables—unless you have them on hand!

½ cup vegetable oil
½ cup apple cider vinegar
1 tablespoon finely chopped fresh dill
1 teaspoon salt
1 teaspoon black pepper
½ pound fresh green beans, trimmed, cooked, and chilled
6 hard-boiled eggs, cut into wedges
6 radishes, thinly sliced
1 medium head iceberg lettuce, torn into bite-sized pieces
1 large tomato, cut into 1-inch chunks
1 medium green bell pepper, cut into 1-inch chunks
1 large cucumber, thinly sliced
1 small onion, finely chopped

In a small bowl, whisk the oil, vinegar, dill, salt, and pepper until well combined. Place the remaining ingredients in a large serving bowl; toss lightly. Drizzle with the oil and vinegar dressing and serve immediately.

Victory Garden Soup

8 to 10 servings

Know one of the things I love most about soup? It goes a long way. That was a really good thing when Mom was trying to stretch our rationing stamps in the early forties—and it's still a good thing today! Everything goes into one big pot, and before we know it we have a hearty, flavorful meal or go-along.

6 cups water
6 medium potatoes, peeled and cut into 1-inch chunks
4 large tomatoes, cored and cut into 1-inch chunks
4 medium carrots, peeled and cut into 1-inch chunks
3 medium zucchini, cut into 1-inch chunks
2 medium green bell peppers, coarsely chopped
2 medium onions, coarsely chopped
3 garlic cloves, minced
1½ teaspoons salt
1 teaspoon black pepper

In a soup pot, combine all the ingredients; mix well. Bring to a boil over high heat; reduce the heat to medium and cook for 1 hour, or until the vegetables are tender.

Honey Mousse

6 to 8 servings

Smooth and creamy, this is a dessert treat that's sure to mark the beginning of good, sweet times. It's nice served as is in a fancy glass, or dolloped over pound cake or even fresh berries. Mmm!

¾ cup honey
2 egg yolks
1 pint heavy cream

In a small saucepan, whisk the honey and egg yolks over medium-low heat for 3 to 5 minutes, until well combined and heated through. Remove from the heat and let cool completely. Meanwhile, in a large bowl, with an electric beater on high speed, beat the cream until stiff peaks form. Fold the honey mixture into the whipped cream until thoroughly combined. Spoon into a serving bowl or individual serving dishes, cover, and chill for at least 2 hours before serving.

WEEK 47

Autumn Harvest Dinner

Fall means the harvest season is here. And what better way to celebrate than with a dinner combining all those hearty seasonal tastes and flavors? As the cooler weather sets in, we know we can start heating things up in the kitchen again. So let's welcome the soups, casseroles, and stews we all love so much!

Carrot and Parsnip Soup

Reuben Casserole

Sour Cream and Chive Biscuits

Pecan Toffee Bars

Pineapple Wassail

Carrot and Parsnip Soup

4 to 6 servings

This can be a harvest in itself! By dinnertime they'll be drooling from the aroma. Better keep a close eye on the pot, though, 'cause otherwise there may not be any soup left for supper!

2 cans (14½ ounces each) ready-to-use chicken broth
5 medium carrots, cut into 1-inch chunks
1 large parsnip, peeled and cut into 1-inch chunks
1 medium potato, peeled and cut into 1-inch chunks
1 medium onion, diced
2½ cups milk
¼ teaspoon dried dill (see Note)
¼ teaspoon black pepper

In a soup pot, bring the chicken broth, carrots, parsnip, potato, and onion to a boil over medium-high heat. Reduce the heat to medium and simmer for 20 minutes, or until the vegetables are tender. Remove from the heat and mash. Add the milk, dill, and pepper; mix well and simmer over medium-low heat for 6 to 8 minutes, or until heated through.

NOTE: If I have some fresh dill, I like to chop about 1 table-spoon of it for the soup (instead of the dried dill) and sprinkle a bit more over each serving.

Reuben Casserole

6 to 8 servings

We all love those big melty Reuben sandwiches. I mean, who can resist the combination of meat, cheese, and creamy dressing? Now I've taken those same great tastes and reworked the form . . . into a casserole! Served as a side or on its own, however we do it, it's a thumbs-up hit!

1 can (27 ounces) sauerkraut, rinsed and drained
1 pound sliced deli corned beef, coarsely chopped
1 can (10¾ ounces) condensed cream of mushroom soup
1 bottle (8 ounces) Thousand Island dressing
1¼ cups milk
1 medium onion, chopped
1 teaspoon dry mustard
9 oven-ready ("no boil") lasagna noodles (see Note)
1 cup (4 ounces) shredded Swiss cheese
½ cup plain bread crumbs
1 tablespoon butter, melted

Preheat the oven to 350°F. Coat a 9" × 13" baking dish with nonstick cooking spray. In a medium bowl, combine the sauerkraut and corned beef; mix well. In another medium bowl, combine the soup, dressing, milk, onion, and mustard; mix well. Place 3 lasagna noodles in the baking dish. Top with half of the corned beef mixture, then half of the soup mixture. Add 3 more lasagna noodles and then the remaining corned beef mixture. Add the remaining 3 lasagna noodles, then cover with the remaining soup mixture. Top with the Swiss cheese, then sprinkle with the bread crumbs and drizzle with the butter. Cover with aluminum foil and bake for 45 to 50 minutes, or until bubbly. Uncover and bake for 5 to 10 more minutes, or until golden. Allow to sit for 5 to 10 minutes, then cut and serve.

NOTE: Oven-ready lasagna noodles are thinner than traditional lasagna noodles, so they don't need to be boiled before using. You can usually find them alongside the regular lasagna noodles at the supermarket.

Sour Cream and Chive Biscuits

about 1 dozen

No meal is truly complete without fresh-baked biscuits or bread. And the sour cream here adds a rich touch to these traditional biscuits. They're perfect for dunking in soup or eating right out of the oven.

> 2½ cups biscuit baking mix
> 1 tablespoon chopped fresh parsley
> 1 cup sour cream

Preheat the oven to 450°F. Coat a rimmed baking sheet with nonstick cooking spray. In a large bowl, combine the biscuit mix and parsley; mix well. Add the sour cream and knead for 2 to 3 minutes, or until the dough forms a soft ball. Place on a lightly floured surface and use a rolling pin to roll out to a ½-inch thickness. With a 3-inch biscuit cutter or round cookie cutter, cut the dough into biscuits and place on the baking sheet. Bake for 15 to 18 minutes, until light golden.

NOTE: I like to serve these biscuits with parsley butter, which is just a mix of softened butter and chopped fresh parsley. It sure is easy, but it looks so fancy!

Pecan Toffee Bars

15 to 18 bars

No harvest celebration is complete unless dessert is involved. And no matter how you cut 'em, these bars are tops!

   2 cups all-purpose flour
   ¾ cup sugar
   ½ cup (1 stick) butter, softened
   1 can (14 ounces) sweetened condensed milk
   1 egg
   1 teaspoon vanilla extract
   1 cup chopped pecans
   1 package (7½ ounces) almond brickle chips

Preheat the oven to 325°F. Coat a 9" × 13" baking dish with nonstick cooking spray. In a large bowl, combine the flour, sugar, and butter until crumbly. Press evenly into the baking dish. Bake for 15 minutes. In a medium bowl, combine the remaining ingredients; mix well and spread evenly over the crust, covering the surface completely. Bake for 25 to 30 minutes, or until bubbly. Allow to cool completely, then cut into bars and serve.

NOTE: To make these extra sinful, sprinkle 1 cup of semisweet chocolate chips over the top immediately after removing them from the oven.

Pineapple Wassail

about 2½ quarts, 8 to 10 servings

Wassail? What's that?! I'll tell you—it's a steaming-hot fruit punch that's just right for after dinner and before dessert. As a matter of fact, it's okay almost anytime!

1 can (46 ounces) pineapple juice
2 cans (12 ounces each) frozen orange juice concentrate, thawed
2 cups water
¾ cup corn syrup
2 teaspoons fresh lemon juice
4 cinnamon sticks
4 whole cloves

In a soup pot, bring all the ingredients to a boil over high heat. Reduce the heat to low, cover partially, and simmer for 30 minutes, stirring occasionally. Remove the cinnamon sticks and cloves, then pour into mugs and serve hot.

NOTE: I like to fancy this up a bit by garnishing each mug with a slice of fresh pineapple.

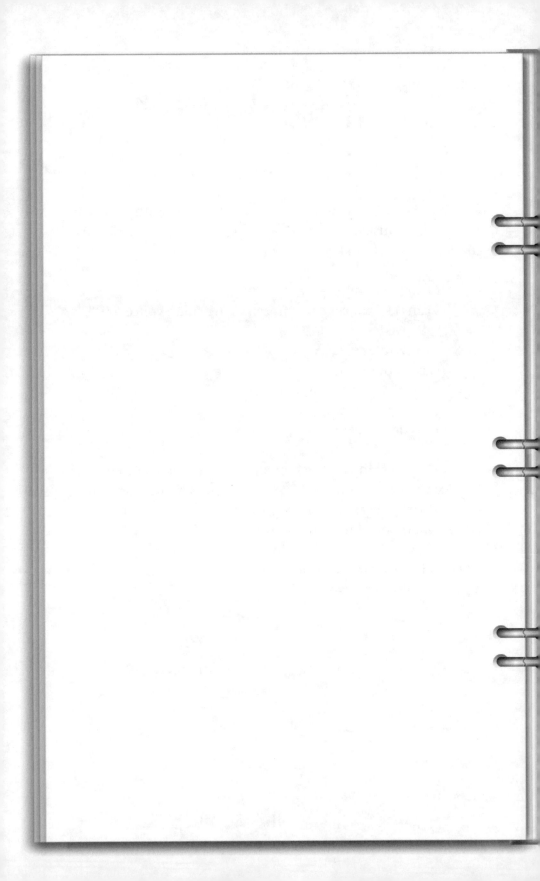

WEEK 48

Turkey Time

Just like the Pilgrims and Native Americans did so many years ago, it's our turn to give thanks. It's also a time for us to gather with friends and family to share good times and, of course, to follow in those traditional footsteps and feast away! We can't wait to enjoy the classic favorites of turkey and dressing on Thanksgiving, but why not sample a few new things this year? And whatever we do, let's not forget to appreciate all the good things we have!

Mincemeat-Crusted Turkey

Popcorn Dressing

Homemade Cranberry Sauce

Mashed Turnips

Pumpkin Custard Pie

Mincemeat-Crusted Turkey

8 to 10 servings

I wish mincemeat had a better name, 'cause it's so tasty. Today's version is a mixture of chopped fruits, spices, and nuts, and since mincemeat was quite popular in Colonial America, I thought we should give it a try with our traditional holiday turkey. What a match!

> One 12- to 15-pound turkey
> ¼ cup (½ stick) butter
> 2 medium onions, chopped
> 1 garlic clove, minced
> 1 jar (29 ounces) mincemeat with brandy
> 1 cup water

Preheat the oven to 350°F. Place the turkey in a foil-lined roasting pan. Melt the butter in a medium skillet over high heat. Add the onions and garlic and sauté for 6 to 8 minutes, or until the onions are golden, stirring constantly. Remove from the heat and stir in the mincemeat. Spoon 1 cup of the mixture into the cavity of the turkey. Spread the remaining mixture over the outside of the turkey. Pour the water into the pan around the turkey and cover loosely with aluminum foil. Bake for 3½ hours, basting with the pan juices every 30 minutes. Uncover and bake for 30 more minutes, or until no pink remains and the juices run clear. Allow to sit for 15 minutes before carving.

NOTE: When the turkey registers 180° to 185°F. on a meat thermometer, it should be cooked through. The best and safest way to thaw turkey is to put it in the refrigerator for 2 to 3 days before cooking.

Popcorn Dressing

6 to 8 servings

When I was experimenting with this week's menu, I searched for the type of ingredients the Pilgrims would have used at their first Thanksgiving and discovered that the Native Americans introduced popcorn to the Pilgrims way back then. It hit me that I should try it in a dressing and, what do you know, now we have a tasty, authentic-flavored popcorn side dish!

6 cups crumbled corn bread or corn muffins (see Note)
3 cups popped popcorn (see Note)
1 medium onion, finely chopped
1 can (14½ ounces) ready-to-use chicken broth
½ cup (1 stick) butter, melted
2 eggs
1½ teaspoons rubbed sage

Preheat the oven to 375°F. Coat an 8-inch square baking dish with nonstick cooking spray. In a large bowl, combine all the ingredients; mix well. Spoon into the baking dish. Bake for 40 to 45 minutes, or until the center is set.

NOTE: Ready-made corn bread or muffins can be found in the bakery section of your supermarket, or you can start from scratch and use your favorite corn bread recipe. One regular package of microwave popcorn will yield 7 to 8 cups of popcorn.

Homemade Cranberry Sauce

about 2 cups

If you've never had homemade cranberry sauce, boy, are you in for a real treat! It's a bit on the tart side, so pucker up . . . or add an additional half cup of sugar!

> 1 package (12 ounces) fresh cranberries (see Note)
> 1½ cups sugar
> ¼ cup water

In a large saucepan, combine all the ingredients; mix well and bring to a boil over medium-high heat. Reduce the heat to medium-low and simmer for 8 to 10 minutes, or until thickened. Serve warm, or allow to cool, then cover and chill until ready to use.

NOTE: If fresh cranberries aren't available, you can use a 12-ounce package of frozen cranberries for a taste that's just as good as fresh.

Mashed Turnips

6 to 8 servings

Wow 'em with this alternative to mashed potatoes. They're just as smooth and creamy, so I bet your gang won't even miss the spuds.

    4 pounds turnips, peeled and cut into 1-inch chunks
    ⅓ cup butter, softened
    3 tablespoons half-and-half (see Note)
    ½ teaspoon onion powder
    1 teaspoon salt
    ½ teaspoon black pepper

Place the turnips in a soup pot and add just enough water to cover them. Bring to a boil over high heat and boil for 30 minutes, or until tender; drain. In a large bowl, with an electric beater on medium speed, beat the turnips and the remaining ingredients until well combined; the mixture will be lumpy. Serve immediately.

NOTE: No half-and-half in the refrigerator? Don't worry—you can use milk instead. Whole, 2%, or skim . . . it's your choice.

Pumpkin Custard Pie

6 to 8 servings

We always seem to eat the same ol' pumpkin pie for dessert, so one year I decided to do things a little differently. The result . . . pumpkin custard pie, a little creamier than the one we grew up with—and now a whole lot more popular.

     1 can (15 ounces) solid pack pumpkin
     ½ cup honey
     ½ cup half-and-half
     3 eggs
     ¾ teaspoon ground cinnamon
     ½ teaspoon ground nutmeg
     ¼ teaspoon ground ginger
     One 9-inch frozen ready-to-bake pie shell, thawed

Preheat the oven to 375°F. In a large bowl, whisk together all the ingredients except the pie shell. Pour into the pie shell and bake for 55 to 60 minutes, or until set. Allow to cool for 30 minutes, then cover and chill for at least 4 hours before serving.

NOTE: For a more festive look, top each slice with a dollop of whipped cream and a sprinkle of cinnamon.

WEEK 49

Recipes for Romance

Because of all the holidays and parties in December, my wife and I usually try to celebrate our anniversary a little earlier than its actual date, December 26. Sure, we love sharing special times with our family and friends, but there are certain times that should be celebrated without the gang—and our wedding anniversary is one of them! So, whenever it's *your* special day, here's a romantic feast that's so easy to make you'll have plenty of time to enjoy it with your sweetie.

Steaming Artichoke Dip

Mediterranean Green Salad

French Country Chicken

Double Stuffers

Chocolate Mousse Tarts

Steaming Artichoke Dip

2 to 4 servings

This creamy dip is the perfect predinner nibbler. Serve it up with almost anything from fresh veggies to bread sticks or crackers. Don't worry about how much it makes—the leftovers are great reheated tomorrow! (And I want you to save room for dinner . . . there's lots more to come!)

    1 can (14 ounces) artichoke hearts, drained and finely
        chopped
    1 package (8 ounces) cream cheese, softened
    ¼ cup (1 ounce) shredded Swiss cheese
    1 tablespoon fresh lemon juice
    ¼ teaspoon salt
    ⅛ teaspoon black pepper

Preheat the oven to 350°F. In a medium bowl, combine all the ingredients; mix well. Spoon into a small baking dish and bake for 25 to 30 minutes, or until heated through and bubbly. Serve immediately.

Mediterranean Green Salad

2 servings

With a big meal ahead, let's keep our salad light and, of course, crispy. The dressing? Well, that's an all-time favorite.

> ½ cup olive oil
> ¼ cup balsamic vinegar
> ½ teaspoon dried oregano
> ½ teaspoon salt
> ½ teaspoon black pepper
> 1 small head romaine lettuce, cut into bite-sized pieces
> 4 cherry tomatoes, cut in half

In a small bowl, whisk together the oil, vinegar, oregano, salt, and pepper until well blended. Place the lettuce and tomatoes in a serving bowl. Add the dressing to taste and toss until well coated. Serve immediately.

NOTE: I love cheese and like to add some whenever possible; a sprinkle of crumbled blue cheese or Gorgonzola makes this salad truly outstanding.

French Country Chicken

2 servings

Bursting with so many different flavors, this wine, cheese, and chicken combination promises to be a special anniversary dish for years to come.

    2 boneless, skinless chicken breast halves (about ½ pound
        total), pounded to ½-inch thickness
    ¼ cup seasoned bread crumbs
    2 slices Muenster cheese
    2 tablespoons dry white wine (see Note)

Preheat the oven to 350°F. Coat an 8-inch square baking dish with nonstick cooking spray. Coat the chicken with the bread crumbs, turning to coat completely. Place in the baking dish and bake for 15 minutes. Remove from the oven, top with the cheese, and pour the wine evenly over the top. Bake for 15 minutes, or until no pink remains in the chicken and the cheese is bubbly and golden.

NOTE: Whether the wine is French or American and whether it comes in a bottle, jug, or box, as long as you like it, it'll make your chicken special.

Double Stuffers

Double-stuffed means double flavor, especially with these tasty 'taters. They're better than plain baked potatoes any day! And on your anniversary, you surely want to shower your honey with the very best.

> 6 large baking potatoes
> ¼ cup sour cream
> 3 tablespoons butter, softened
> 1 tablespoon chopped fresh parsley
> ¼ teaspoon onion powder
> ½ teaspoon salt
> ¼ teaspoon black pepper
> Paprika for sprinkling

Preheat the oven to 400°F. Scrub the potatoes and pierce the skins with a fork. Bake for 55 minutes, or until tender. (Leave the oven on.) Cut a 1-inch lengthwise slice off the top of each potato; discard the tops. Scoop out the pulp and place in a medium bowl. Add the sour cream, butter, parsley, onion powder, salt, and pepper to the potato pulp. Beat with an electric beater on medium speed until smooth. Spoon back into the potato shells and lightly sprinkle the tops with paprika. Bake for 30 minutes, or until the potatoes start to brown on top.

NOTE: Since it's just as easy to make a bunch of these as it is to make 2, this recipe makes 6 servings. You can bake 2 to serve with your anniversary dinner and wrap the remaining potatoes after you've stuffed them, before the final baking. You can bake and enjoy them the next day with the rest of the family, or double-wrap and freeze them so you'll have a handy side dish on hand for another time. All you'll need to do is allow them to thaw in the fridge, sprinkle with paprika, and bake for 30 minutes.

Chocolate Mousse Tarts

6 tarts

Make these ahead of time so you have a few to give to the kids before shipping them off to Grandma's or out to a movie. Then, when your romantic main course is complete, you can simply get out those long-handled ice cream spoons and share this sweet with your sweetie.

> 1 package (4-serving size) instant chocolate pudding and pie filling
> 1½ cups cold milk
> 2 cups frozen whipped topping, thawed, divided
> 6 single-serving graham cracker tart shells
> Shaved chocolate for garnish (see Note)

In a large bowl, whisk the pudding mix and milk together until thickened and smooth. Stir in 1 cup whipped topping and mix well. Spoon evenly into the tart shells and top with the remaining 1 cup whipped topping, covering the pudding mixture completely. Garnish with the shaved chocolate, then cover loosely and chill for at least 2 hours before serving.

NOTE: It's easy to shave chocolate. Just take a chocolate bar and grate it with a hand-held cheese grater, or, for larger chocolate curls, use a vegetable peeler.

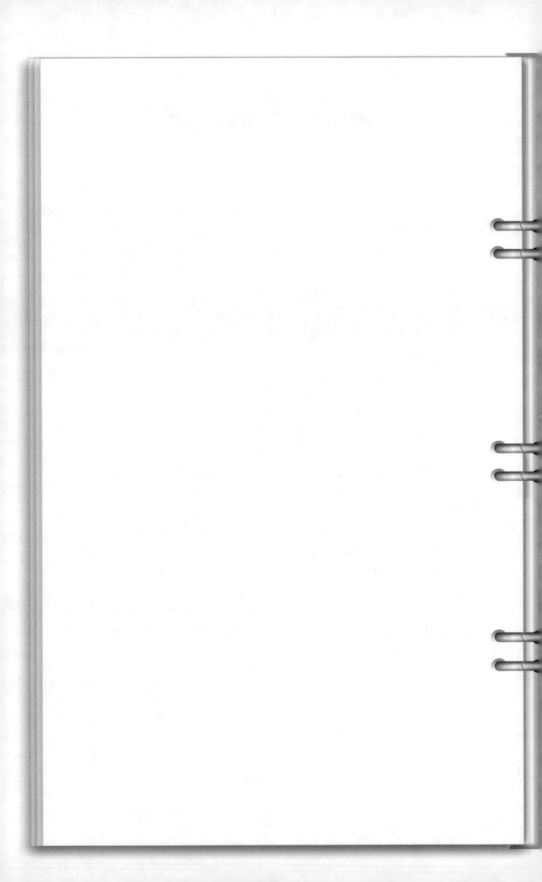

WEEK 50

Holiday Open-House Nibbles

The holidays are coming and you know what that means—parties and open houses galore. Whether we're the hosts or guests, we still need to prepare a few snacks that'll "wow" everybody. After all, we can't arrive empty-handed! Here are some of my favorite (and most popular!) holiday recipes. Now all we need are a few holiday decorations, some seasonal tunes, and our friends and family to help us celebrate!

Festive Crab Spread

Buttermilk Dip

Pumpkin Spice Bread

Sugar Plums

Apricot Macadamia Snowballs

Festive Crab Spread

10 to 12 servings

You don't have to worry about the high price of crabmeat, 'cause I have the solution here! I bet nobody'll even know the difference.

> 2 packages (8 ounces each) cream cheese, softened
> ½ pound imitation crabmeat, flaked
> 1 teaspoon lemon juice
> 1 teaspoon dried dill

Preheat the oven to 350°F. In a medium bowl, combine all the ingredients; mix well. Spoon into a 9-inch pie plate and bake for 25 to 30 minutes, or until hot and bubbly. Serve immediately.

NOTE: Serve with crackers or homemade pita chips. For homemade pita chips, just cut large pitas into 8 wedges each, separate the halves, and bake on a baking sheet in a preheated 350°F. oven until crisp and golden.

Buttermilk Dip

about 1½ cups

Our holiday buffets might be packed with all sorts of fancy goodies, but one of the most popular choices will still be the fresh veggies and dip. With the dip served in a hollowed-out loaf of bread, it'll look as special as everything else on the table!

    1 cup mayonnaise
    ½ cup buttermilk
    1 tablespoon lemon juice
    ½ teaspoon garlic powder
    ¼ teaspoon dry mustard
    ¼ teaspoon salt
    ¼ teaspoon black pepper

In a small bowl, whisk all the ingredients together until well combined. Serve, or cover and chill until ready to serve.

NOTE: For a special Christmas treat, I "decorate" a Styrofoam cone by covering it with assorted cut-up vegetables stuck on toothpicks, then filling in any spaces with parsley. Then we have a colorful, festive display of veggie dippers for our party dips.

"ANYBODY UP FOR A DIP?"

Pumpkin Spice Bread

7 mini loaves

Looking for something to bring along to the office, or maybe to give to your guests as a little "thank you for coming" take-home treat? Here it is! Not only does this bread taste great, but it looks great, too, which makes it an ideal holiday gift.

> Eight 1-pint widemouthed canning jars (see Note)
> 3½ cups firmly packed light brown sugar
> ½ cup (1 stick) butter, softened
> 1 can (15 ounces) solid pack pumpkin
> 4 eggs
> 3½ cups all-purpose flour
> 1½ teaspoons baking powder
> 1 teaspoon baking soda
> 1 teaspoon ground cinnamon
> ½ teaspoon ground ginger
> 1 cup chopped pecans

Preheat the oven to 325°F. Coat the canning jars with nonstick cooking spray. In a large bowl, with an electric beater on medium speed, beat the brown sugar and butter for 3 to 4 minutes, or until well blended. Add the pumpkin and eggs and beat for 2 minutes, or until well blended. Add the flour, baking powder, baking soda, cinnamon, and ginger. Beat for 1 to 2 minutes, or until well blended. Stir in the pecans. Spoon evenly into the canning jars. Place the jars on a baking sheet and bake for 45 to 50 minutes, or until a wooden toothpick inserted in the center comes out clean. Carefully place the lids on the jars and seal while still hot; allow to cool completely before opening. To serve, remove from the jars and slice.

NOTE: This batter can also be baked in two 9" × 5" loaf pans, but the nice thing about making it in canning jars is that they make great take-along gifts. Add some ribbon and a label for the perfect way to show somebody special that you care.

Sugar Plums

about 5 dozen

As the old holiday poem goes, "The children were nestled all snug in their beds, while visions of sugar plums danced in their heads." Now we don't have to be satisfied by visions, 'cause it's as simple as can be to make sugar plums a tasty addition to our holiday tables.

> 1 package (24 ounces) large pitted prunes
> 1 cup sweetened flaked coconut
> ½ cup blanched almonds, finely chopped
> ½ cup confectioners' sugar

With a knife, make a small slit in each prune. In a small bowl, combine the coconut and almonds; mix well. Stuff the coconut mixture evenly into the prunes. In a large resealable plastic storage bag, toss the stuffed prunes in the confectioners' sugar in batches until all the prunes are well coated. Serve, or store in an airtight container layered between sheets of waxed paper.

NOTE: If you're not serving these right away, you may need to sprinkle them with additional confectioners' sugar before serving because the prunes will absorb the sugar as they sit. (They're full of sugar, so I guess that's how they got their name!)

Apricot Macadamia Snowballs

2 dozen

What a fun way to decorate the table *and* serve a wintry treat at the same time! This no-bake goodie is sure to become an annual guest at your holiday get-togethers.

>   6 ounces dried apricots
>   ¼ cup apricot jam
>   1 tablespoon sugar
>   1 cup macadamia nuts
>   ½ cup flaked coconut (see Note)

In a food processor, blend the apricots, jam, sugar, and nuts, pulsing the motor until the mixture forms a mass. Form rounded teaspoonfuls of the mixture into 1-inch balls; roll each ball in the coconut until well coated. Chill for at least 1 hour before serving.

NOTE: If you prefer a nuttier flavor, you can toast the coconut before using it. Just spread it out on a cookie sheet and place the sheet in a 300°F. oven for a few minutes, until the coconut is lightly browned. Watch it carefully so it doesn't burn!

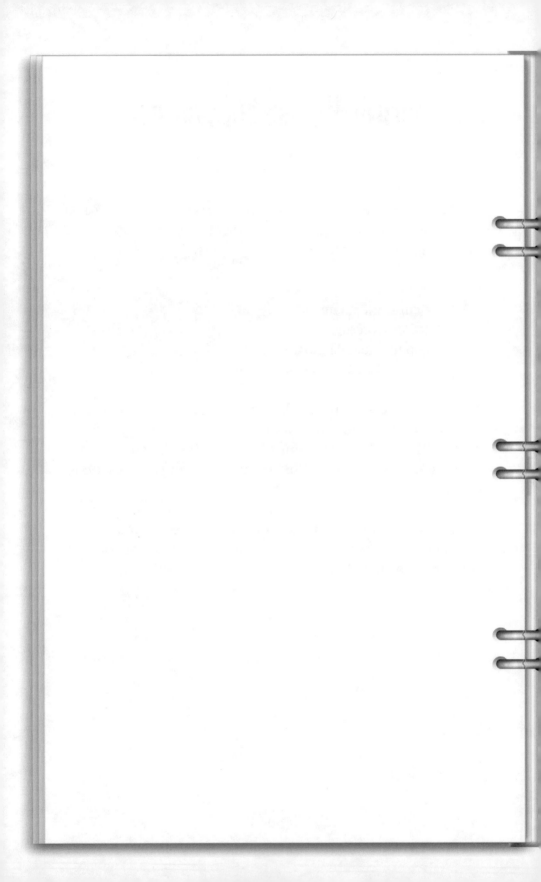

WEEK 51

Hanukkah Traditions

It's time to spin the dreidel and light the candles on the menorah. Yes, Hanukkah, also known as the Jewish Festival of Lights, is here. As we celebrate the miracles of Hanukkah, we have eight days to enjoy these traditional holiday favorites.

Potato Pancakes

Chunky Applesauce

Jelly Donuts

Hanukkah Butter Cookies

Potato Pancakes

about 1½ dozen

Latke is the Yiddish word for pancake, and this dish is also called potato latkes. It's a tradition to eat these at Hanukkah time because they're cooked in oil, and oil symbolizes the miracle of Hanukkah: Although there was what looked like just enough oil to burn for one day in the holy temple, instead the oil lasted for eight days! And that's why we celebrate Hanukkah for eight days.

> 8 medium potatoes (about 3 pounds), peeled and grated
> 1 large onion, finely chopped
> 2 eggs, beaten
> 1 cup all-purpose flour
> 2 teaspoons baking powder
> 1½ teaspoons salt
> 1 teaspoon black pepper
> About ¾ cup vegetable oil

Place the grated potatoes and chopped onions in a strainer. Press down on them with the back of a large spoon to extract excess moisture. (If they're still watery after doing this, wrap them in a clean old dish towel and squeeze out the remaining moisture.) Place the strained potatoes and onions in a large bowl and add the eggs, flour, baking powder, salt, and pepper; mix well. In a large deep skillet, heat ½ cup oil over medium-high heat. Using about ¼ cup of batter for each pancake, cook them in batches, being careful not to crowd the pan. Fry until the pancakes are golden and flecked with brown on both sides, adding additional oil as needed. Drain on a paper towel–lined platter and serve hot.

NOTE: Place the cooked pancakes on a rimmed cookie sheet and keep warm in a 200°F. oven until ready to serve. Make sure to serve with Chunky Applesauce (page 344) and/or sour cream for topping.

Chunky Applesauce

about 4 cups

We can't serve our potato pancakes without sour cream or applesauce, can we? And once you have them with this chunky homemade applesauce, you won't want them any other way!

8 apples, peeled, cored, and cut into thin slices (see Note)
¾ cup apple juice
½ cup firmly packed light brown sugar
1 cinnamon stick

In a soup pot, combine all the ingredients. Bring to a boil over medium-high heat. Reduce the heat to medium-low, cover, and simmer for 50 to 60 minutes, or until the desired texture, stirring occasionally. Remove the cinnamon stick. Allow to cool, then cover and chill until ready to serve.

NOTE: Use whatever type of apples you prefer. For suggestions, check out the Apple Chart on pages 268–69. If you prefer smooth applesauce, cook this until the apples have cooked down to a purée. Since apples vary in moisture content, you may need to add a bit more water during the cooking in order to get the right consistency.

Jelly Donuts

1 dozen

Donuts known as *sufganiyot* are fried in oil, a significant Hanukkah symbol. This simplified version of the traditional holiday treat allows us to spend less time in the kitchen and more time with our families. After all, that's what holidays are about! Right? Of course, right!

> 1 container (17½ ounces) refrigerated butter-flavored
>   biscuits (8 biscuits)
> ¼ cup strawberry jam
> 2 cups vegetable oil
> ¼ cup confectioners' sugar

Carefully separate each biscuit into 3 pieces. Place the jam in the centers of half the biscuit pieces, using an equal amount for each, then top with the remaining biscuit pieces. Pinch the edges together to seal well. In a large deep skillet, heat the oil over medium-low heat until hot but not smoking. Cook the donuts in batches for 4 to 5 minutes, turning to brown on both sides. Drain on a paper towel–lined platter. Sprinkle with the confectioners' sugar and serve warm, or allow to cool completely before serving.

NOTE: If you prefer, you can use a mixture of granulated sugar and cinnamon instead of the confectioners' sugar as a topping for the donuts.

Hanukkah Butter Cookies

about 3 dozen

Cut these tasty treats into dreidels, menorahs, and other Hanukkah shapes, or simply enjoy them round as the butteriest butter cookies you'll ever eat!

    1 cup (2 sticks) butter, softened
    ¾ cup sugar
    2 eggs
    1 teaspoon vanilla extract
    3½ cups all-purpose flour

Preheat the oven to 350°F. In a large bowl, with an electric beater on medium speed, cream the butter and sugar. Add the eggs and vanilla; beat for 1 to 2 minutes, until light and fluffy. Gradually add the flour and beat for 2 minutes, or until well blended. Form the dough into 2 balls; cover and chill for at least 2 hours. On a work surface that has been lightly floured,

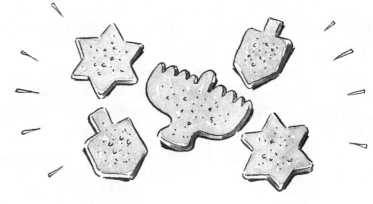

using a rolling pin, roll 1 ball of dough ¼ inch thick. Using cookie cutters or a knife, cut into Hanukkah shapes, as illustrated. Place the shapes 1 inch apart on ungreased cookie sheets. Repeat with the remaining ball of dough. Bake for 10 to 12 minutes, or until golden around the edges. Remove to a wire rack to cool completely.

NOTE: You can enjoy these plain, but you might also want to sprinkle them with colored sugar or sprinkles before baking, or frost and decorate the cooled cookies. Do your own thing!

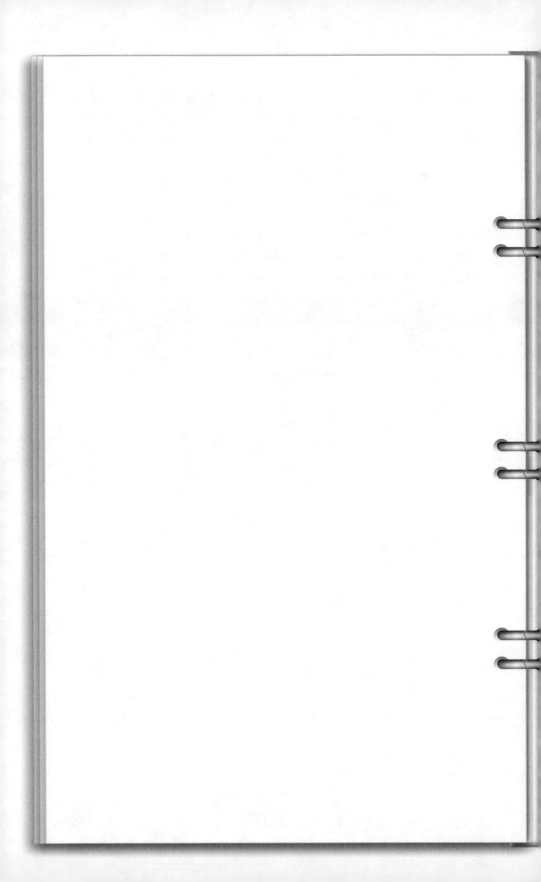

WEEK 52

Christmas Dinner

Hooray! Christmas is finally here! We've shopped and wrapped and decorated, and the special day is upon us. Now comes the dinner the whole family has been looking forward to. Will it be the same old dishes or will there be something new? Maybe try a little of both, 'cause we shouldn't give up some traditions, yet a little change is good for us now and then. The gang won't care, as long as it's served with TLC. And make sure to save a plate for Santa! Delivering all those presents sure does work up an appetite.

Creamy Pumpkin Soup

Roasted Holiday Prime Rib

Christmas Peas

Praline Sweet Potatoes

Peppermint Swirl Cheesecake

Creamy Pumpkin Soup

6 to 8 servings

Sure, we usually think of pumpkins at Halloween and Thanksgiving time, but why not try this soup with our Christmas dinner? It's a super way to start off the festive meal.

    1 can (29 ounces) solid pack pumpkin
    1 can (14½ ounces) ready-to-use chicken broth
    ½ cup water
    ¼ cup firmly packed light brown sugar
    ½ teaspoon ground nutmeg
    ½ teaspoon salt
    ⅛ teaspoon black pepper
    2 cups (1 pint) half-and-half

In a large saucepan, combine all the ingredients except the half-and-half; mix well. Bring to a boil over medium heat, stirring frequently. Reduce the heat to low and stir in the half-and-half until well blended. Cover and simmer until heated through. Serve immediately.

NOTE: Make this extra festive by swirling a dollop of sour cream into each bowl before serving. For a really spectacular presentation, serve the soup in hollowed-out individual small pumpkins or acorn squash.

"Now that's a real pumpkin soup!"

Roasted Holiday Prime Rib

6 to 10 servings

Rev up the traditional holiday roast with some new flavors and the whole family will practically hail you as a Christmas saint! Know the best part? The oven does all the work!

> One 4- to 6-pound boneless beef prime rib roast
> 3 tablespoons all-purpose flour
> 2 tablespoons vegetable oil
> 1 tablespoon Dijon-style mustard
> 1 tablespoon light brown sugar
> ½ teaspoon ground allspice
> 1 teaspoon salt
> 1 teaspoon black pepper

Preheat the oven to 350°F. Coat a roasting pan with nonstick cooking spray. Place the beef fat side up in the roasting pan. In a small bowl, combine the remaining ingredients; mix well. Rub the mixture evenly over the beef. Roast the beef for 1 to 1½ hours (or 15 minutes per pound), until a meat thermometer reaches 140°F. for medium-rare, or until desired doneness beyond that. Remove the beef to a cutting board and let stand for 15 minutes before carving across the grain.

NOTE: To give the roast a crispier crust, broil it for the last few minutes of cooking.

Christmas Peas

6 to 8 servings

What side dish is pretty enough for our Christmas table? This one! It's my version of classic peas . . . dressed up for the holidays.

1 package (16 ounces) frozen peas, thawed
1 can (10¾ ounces) condensed cream of mushroom soup
1 can (8 ounces) sliced water chestnuts, drained
1 can (2.8 ounces) French-fried onions, divided
1 small red bell pepper, finely chopped (see Note)
¼ cup (½ stick) butter, melted
¼ teaspoon black pepper

Preheat the oven to 350°F. In a large bowl, combine all the ingredients except 1 cup French-fried onions; mix well. Pour into an 8-inch square baking dish and sprinkle the reserved 1 cup French-fried onions around the edges. Bake for 25 to 30 minutes, or until heated through and bubbly.

NOTE: The red bell pepper makes this a very colorful red and green Christmas dish, but any color bell pepper will do.

Praline Sweet Potatoes

6 to 8 servings

Since we're so busy making dinner, wrapping gifts, and doing the last-minute decorating, this dish is our time-saving solution. It'll be full of the flavor of a hearty homemade dish, even though we took a few shortcuts.

> ½ cup firmly packed light brown sugar, divided
> ⅓ cup chopped pecans
> ¼ cup sweetened flaked coconut
> 3 tablespoons all-purpose flour
> ¼ cup plus 2 tablespoons butter, softened, divided
> 2 cans (29 ounces each) yams or sweet potatoes, drained (see Note)
> ¼ teaspoon ground nutmeg
> ½ cup milk
> 2 eggs

Preheat the oven to 350°F. In a medium bowl, combine ¼ cup brown sugar, the pecans, coconut, flour, and 2 tablespoons butter; mix until crumbly, then set aside. In a large bowl, mash the yams and the remaining ¼ cup butter. Stir in the remaining ingredients, including the remaining ¼ cup brown sugar; mix well. Pour into a 2-quart casserole dish and sprinkle the pecan mixture evenly over the top. Bake for 45 to 50 minutes, or until heated through. Serve immediately.

NOTE: If you have time to start from scratch, then you can make this with 2 pounds sweet potatoes, boiled, peeled, and mashed—but, trust me, no one will know that you used canned instead of fresh!

Peppermint Swirl Cheesecake

8 to 10 servings

Oh, do we love our holiday cookies, gingerbread men, and fruitcakes. . . . Well, two out of three ain't bad! So when we bring out this cheesecake sporting the colors of Christmas, expect all the "Ho! Ho! Ho!" to quickly turn into a chorus of "OOH IT'S SO GOOD!!®"

1½ cups finely crushed chocolate graham crackers
1 cup plus 1 tablespoon sugar, divided
¼ cup (½ stick) butter, melted
3 packages (8 ounces each) cream cheese, softened
4 eggs
1 teaspoon vanilla extract
½ teaspoon peppermint extract, divided
5 drops red food color
5 drops green food color

Preheat the oven to 350°F. In a medium bowl, combine the graham cracker crumbs, 1 tablespoon sugar, and the butter; mix well. Press into the bottom of a 9-inch springform pan to form a crust; set aside. In a large bowl, with an electric beater on medium speed, beat the cream cheese and the remaining 1 cup sugar until creamy. Add the eggs one at a time, beating well after each addition. Add the vanilla extract; mix well. Reserve ½ cup batter and pour the remaining batter over the prepared crust. Divide the ½ cup batter between 2 small bowls and add ¼ teaspoon peppermint extract to each bowl. Add the red food color to one bowl and the green food color to the other bowl; mix each one well. Spoon each colored batter onto the white batter in dollops. Using a knife, swirl the batters together to

354

create a marbled effect. Bake for 40 to 45 minutes, or until almost set in the center. Allow to cool completely, then cover and chill for at least 6 hours before serving.

NOTE: Complete the holiday theme by garnishing each slice of cheesecake with a blizzard of whipped cream and a miniature candy cane.

Index

almond(s):
  in cheese ball pinecone, 88
  chocolate truffles, 111
  cookies, 57
  gelato, 279
  in sugar plums, 338
apple(s):
  baked beans, 235
  candy, old-fashioned, 255–256
  cider, simmering, 274
  -glazed chicken, 270
  orchard goodies, 267–274
  in orchard sweet potato bake, 271
  pie, upside-down, 272, 273
  sauerkraut, 261
  types of, 268–269
applesauce, chunky, 344
apricot macadamia snowballs, 339
April Fool's Day menu, 87–93
artichoke dip, steaming, 326
artichoke hearts:
  in hash-brown bake, 4
  in marinated salad, 34
  with veal, 41
asparagus, herb-marinated, 84
autumn harvest dinner, 311–317

back-to-school favorites, 239–244

bacon:
  'n' blue-cheese burger, 168
  corn bread, 14
  'n' potato salad, hot, 29
banana-strawberry smoothie, 244
barbecue(d):
  Bastille Day, 185
  Father's Day, 167–172
  Joe, 157
  spareribs, tangy, 141–142
  -style chicken, 28
bean(s):
  baked, apple, 235
  baked, in campfire hot diggity dogs, 182
  black, salsa, steak sandwiches with, 121
  in Halloween pasta salad, 290
  in marinated salad, 34
  red kidney, in bread bowl chili, 21
  soup, speedy, 10
beef:
  in bacon 'n' blue-cheese burger, 168
  in barbecue Joe, 157
  bourguignon, 188
  in bread bowl chili, 21
  brisket, Passover, 99
  corned, and carrots, 75
  corned, in Reuben casserole, 313–314

beef *(continued)*
  in hamburger soup, 8
  in hot-shot meatball hoagies,
    70
  kung pao, 56
  in meat loaf cake, 89–90
  and National Beef Month, 155
  prime rib, roasted holiday, 351
  stew, cozy, 35
  tenderloin, tarragon, 158
  in traditional German braten
    stew, 260
  see also steaks
beefed-up dinners, 155–160
beet mashed potatoes, 109
beignets, quick, 63
berry(ies):
  and cream, picture-perfect,
    126
  salad, mixed, 174
beverages:
  café mochaccino, 153
  eye of a hurricane, 60
  frozen virgin margaritas, 123
  minted lemonade, 32
  mint julep iced tea, 117
  patriotic milk shakes, 177
  pineapple cran-orange
    refresher, 238
  pineapple wassail, 317
  simmering cider, 274
  witch's butterscotch brew, 295
  see also punch; smoothies
birthday bash, red, white and
    blue, 173–177
biscuits:
  light 'n' flaky, 220
  sour cream and chive, 315
black-and-white soda, 257
Black Forest cake roll, 264–265

blueberry(ies):
  bonanza, 213–218
  cobbler, 215
  muffins, 214
  in patriotic milk shakes, 177
  pie, awesome, 216
  pie, custard, 218
  shortcake, toasted, 217
bourbon parfaits, Kentucky, 116
bourguignon, beef, 188
braten stew, traditional German,
    260
bread(s):
  beignets, quick, 63
  bowl chili, 21
  buns, hot cross, 103–104
  corn, bacon, 14
  corn, honey, 306
  donuts, jelly, 345
  honey-mustard-swirl, 208
  onion straws, 236
  popovers, mint-laced, 80
  pumpkin spice, 336–337
  scones, teatime, 226
  shortnin', 47
  soda, cranberry Irish, 74
  sticks, dunkin', 12
  strawberry 'n' cream roll-
    ups, 3
  see also biscuits; muffins; rolls
breakfast in a cup, 5
Brie, hazelnut-crusted, 186
brisket, Passover, 99
brownie, s'more pie, 183
brunch:
  Mother's Day, 125–129
  New Year's Day, 1–6
buns, hot cross, 103–104
butter cookies, Hanukkah,
    346–347

buttermilk:
  dip, 335
  fried chicken, 15
butterscotch brew, witch's, 295

cabbage veggie slaw, 143
cacciatore stew, veal, 277
Caesar salad, easy, 204
café mochaccino, 153
cake(s):
  Black Forest, roll, 264–265
  chocolate coconut, 282–283
  easy king, 64–65
  fruit cocktail, 37
  graduation, 135–136
  layered watermelon, 172
  meat loaf, 89–90
  strawberry sweetheart, 43–44
  Super Bowl pennant, 23
  wedding basket, 151–152
campfire cookin', 179–184
candy(ied):
  apples, old-fashioned,
    255–256
  popcorn balls, 292
canned food creations, 33–37
  and National Canned Food
    Month, 33
caramel(ized):
  corn, nutty, 71
  grilled onions, 171
  ice cream balls, 31
carrot(s):
  corned beef and, 75
  and parsnip soup, 312
  -pineapple slaw, 222
casserole, Reuben, 313–314
cheese:
  ball, pinecone, 88
  blue-, 'n' bacon burger, 168

Cheddar, in hot potato
    packets, 181
cream, in disappearing stuffed
    French toast, 127
cream, in festive crab spread,
    334
hazelnut-crusted Brie, 186
macaroni and, soup, 240
nacho, and ham roll-ups, 241
Parmesan-garlic oil, 202
pretzel sandwiches, 242
in steaming artichoke dip,
    326
cheesecake:
  dreamy orange swirl, 206
  peppermint swirl, 354–355
cherry(ies):
  lasagna, 92–93
  pie, tart, 50
  in presidential honey walnut
    salad, 46
chicken:
  apple-glazed, 270
  barbecue-style, 28
  buttermilk fried, 15
  cordon bleu, simple, 149
  French country, 328
  in halftime hoagies, 22
  pizza muffins, upside-down,
    162
  with root vegetables, 108
  salad, fruity, 133
  saucy, 247
  soup, homemade, 97
  wings, touchdown, 20
chili, bread bowl, 21
Chinese New Year, 51–57
chive and sour cream biscuits,
    315
chocoholic's parfait, 285

chocolate:
  almond truffles, 111
  chip bars, 237
  chip cookies, pumpkin patch, 293–294
  in chocoholic's parfait, 285
  coconut cake, 282–283
  fantasies, 281–287
  fondue, tropical, 6
  in frozen peanut butter cups, 195–196
  hot, mix for, 184
  mousse tarts, 331
  pecan fudge pie, 286
  raspberry tarts, 100
  walnut fudge, fabulous, 284
  white, macadamia bars, 287
chowder, creamy clam, 203
Christmas dinner, 349–355
cider, simmering, 274
Cinco de Mayo celebration, 119–123
citrus twist pasta, 223
clam(s):
  chowder, creamy, 203
  linguine and, in red sauce, 205
cobbler, blueberry, 215
coconut:
  in apricot macadamia snowballs, 339
  chocolate cake, 282–283
  cream pie ice cream, 197
  in praline sweet potatoes, 353
  in sugar plums, 338
coffee, Irish, 78
collard greens, slow-cookin', 16
college graduation party, 131–137

Columbus Day discoveries, 275–280
cookies:
  almond, 57
  chocolate chip, pumpkin patch, 293–294
  chocolate chip bars, 237
  fruit pinwheels, 250
  fruity egg nests, 106
  Hanukkah butter, 346–347
  'n' ice cream, 166
  lemon tart, 85
  meringues, nutty, 280
  peanut butter and jelly bars, 243
  peanut butter chippies, 72
  peanut M&M bars, 165
  pecan toffee bars, 316
  red, white and blue ribbon, 176
  snowflake tea, 230–231
  white chocolate macadamia bars, 287
cordon bleu, simple chicken, 149
corn:
  bread, bacon, 14
  bread, honey, 306
  on the cob, grilled, 170
  on the cob, herbed, 30
  nutty caramel, 71
  and potato soup, creamy, 9
  salad, toss-together, 180
  soup, velvet, 54
corned beef:
  and carrots, 75
  in Reuben casserole, 313–314
couscous, spring vegetable, 83
crab spread, festive, 334

cranberry:
Irish soda bread, 74
-orange pineapple refresher,
238
sauce, homemade, 322
cream(ed)(y):
berries and, picture-perfect,
126
clam chowder, 203
corn and potato soup, 9
fettuccine, rich and, 276
mushroom soup, 11
pumpkin soup, 350
salsa two-step, 68
spinach, autumn, 262
'n' strawberry roll-ups, 3
crepes suzette, light and easy,
190–191
croissant club, 298
cucumber tea sandwiches, 229
custard:
pie, blueberry, 218
pie, pumpkin, 324

desserts:
apricot macadamia snowballs,
339
blueberry cobbler, 215
candied popcorn balls, 292
cherry lasagna, 92–93
dreamy orange swirl
cheesecake, 206
éclairs, quick mini, 112
honey mousse, 309
nutty caramel corn, 71
old-fashioned candy apples,
255–256
peppermint swirl cheesecake,
354–355
simple peach sorbet, 36

Spanish flan, 122
sugar plums, 338
toasted blueberry shortcake,
217
see also cakes; chocolate;
cookies; ice cream; parfaits;
pies
deviled eggs, picnic-time, 140
dip(ping):
buttermilk, 335
sauce, Parmesan-garlic oil, 202
steaming artichoke, 326
donuts:
jelly, 345
quick beignets, 63
dressing:
popcorn, for turkey, 321
salad, maple mustard, 209
drumsticks, walkaway turkey, 252
dumplings, "sweet potato," 263

Earth Day, 107–112
Easter traditions, 101–106
éclairs, quick mini, 112
egg(s):
in breakfast in a cup, 5
colored, 102
deviled, picnic-time, 140
nests, fruity, 106
egg rolls, easy, 52
English:
rose jelly, 227
tea, 225–231
étouffée, "jazzed-up" shrimp, 61

Father's Day barbecue, 167–172
fettuccine, rich and creamy, 276
fish and shellfish:
crab spread, festive, 334
lobster boil, New England, 175

fish and shellfish *(continued)*
  tuna sandwich, baked stuffed,
    302–303
  see also clams; salmon; shrimp
flan, Spanish, 122
flank steak salad, marinated, 156
fluffwich, grilled, 163
focaccia sandwich, Italian, 301
fondue, tropical chocolate, 6
Fourth of July birthday bash,
    173–177
French:
  buffet, 185–191
  country chicken, 328
  toast, disappearing stuffed, 127
fries, seasoned, 254
fruit(y):
  chicken salad, 133
  cocktail cake, 37
  egg nests, 106
  pinwheels, 250
  see also specific fruits
fudge:
  chocolate walnut, fabulous,
    284
  pie, chocolate pecan, 286

garlic-Parmesan oil, 202
gelato, almond, 279
German braten stew, traditional,
    260
graduation party, college,
    131–137
Grandparents' Day dinner,
    245–250
grapefruit, glazed, 246
greens:
  collard, slow-cookin', 16
  sautéed, 278
  see also spinach

Halloween treats, 289–295
ham:
  maple-glazed, and sweet
    potatoes, 105
  and nacho cheese roll-ups, 241
hamburger soup, 8
Hanukkah traditions, 341–347
hash-brown bake, 4
hazelnut-crusted Brie, 186
herb(ed):
  corn on the cob, 30
  -marinated asparagus, 84
hoagies:
  halftime, 22
  hot-shot meatball, 70
honey:
  corn bread, 306
  mousse, 309
  -mustard-swirl bread, 208
  walnut salad, presidential, 46
hot dogs:
  campfire, diggity, 182
  in taco dogs, 164

ice cream:
  almond gelato, 279
  balls, caramel, 31
  in black-and-white soda, 257
  coconut cream pie, 197
  'n' cookies, 166
  in frozen mochaccino, 199
  in frozen peanut butter cups,
    195–196
  and National Ice Cream
    Month, 193
  in patriotic milk shakes, 177
  pie, minty, 77
  pistachio, 194
  sampler, 193–199
  spumoni, 198

Irish:
    coffee, 78
    potatoes, 76
    soda bread, cranberry, 74
Italian focaccia sandwich, 301

jelly:
    bars, peanut butter and, 243
    donuts, 345
    English rose, 227
July Fourth birthday bash,
        173–177

kebabs, grilled veggie, 144
Kentucky Derby day, 113–117
kung pao beef, 56

Labor Day get-together,
        233–238
lamb, roasted leg of, 81
lasagna:
    cherry, 92
    noodles, in Reuben casserole,
        313–314
lemonade:
    minted, 32
    -poached salmon, 221
lemon tart cookies, 85
lime, chilled shrimp with, 120
limesicle pie, 145
linguine and clams in red sauce,
        205
lobster boil, New England, 175
lo mein, pork, 55

macadamia:
    apricot snowballs, 339
    white chocolate bars, 287
macaroni and cheese soup,
        240

maple:
    -glazed ham and sweet
        potatoes, 105
    mustard dressing, 209
March madness buffet, 67–72
Mardi Gras feast, 59–65
margaritas, frozen virgin, 123
marinated:
    asparagus, with herbs, 84
    flank steak salad, 156
    salad, 34
marshmallow creme:
    in grilled fluffwich, 163
    in s'more brownie pie, 183
Martin Luther King, Jr. Day,
        13–17
matzo balls, Aunt Sarah's, 98
meat:
    loaf cake, 89–90
    see also specific meats
meatball hoagies, hot-shot, 70
Mediterranean green salad, 327
Memorial Day, 139–145
meringues, nutty, 280
midwinter picnic, 27–32
milk shakes, patriotic, 177
mimosas, sunrise, 2
mincemeat-crusted turkey, 320
mint(y):
    fresh, roasted leg of lamb
        with, 81
    ice cream pie, 77
    julep iced tea, 117
    -laced popovers, 80
    lemonade, 32
mochaccino:
    café, 153
    frozen, 199
Monte Cristo, 299
Mother's Day brunch, 125–129

mousse:
  honey, 309
  tarts, chocolate, 331
mud pie, 110
muffins:
  blueberry, 214
  English, in upside-down
    chicken pizza muffins,
    162
  upside-down pineapple,
    224
mushroom(s):
  in marinated salad, 34
  soup, extra-creamy, 11
mustard:
  -honey-swirl bread, 208
  magic with, 207–211
  maple dressing, 209
  and National Mustard Day,
    207
  orange pork tenderloin, 211
  in parsley buttered potatoes,
    210

nacho cheese and ham roll-ups,
    241
National:
  Beef Month, 155
  Canned Food Month, 33
  Ice Cream Month, 193
  Mustard Day, 207
  Sandwich Week, 297–303
  Soup Month, 7–12
New England lobster boil, 175
New Year, Chinese, 51–57
New Year's Day brunch, 1–6
nutty:
  caramel corn, 71
  meringues, 280
  see also specific nuts

Oktoberfest, 259–265
onion(s):
  grilled caramelized, 171
  sausage, and pepper sandwich,
    253
  straws, 236
open-house goodies, 333–339
orange:
  cran-, pineapple refresher,
    238
  -grilled strip steaks, 234
  mustard pork tenderloin, 211
  smoothie, 129
  swirl cheesecake, dreamy, 206

palm, hearts of, in two-hearts
    salad, 40
pancakes, potato, 342–343
parfaits:
  chocoholic's, 285
  Kentucky bourbon, 116
Parmesan-garlic oil, 202
parsley buttered potatoes, 210
parsnip and carrot soup, 312
Passover seder, 95–100
pasta:
  citrus twist, 223
  salad, Halloween, 290
  shrimp salad, winner's circle,
    115
  see also specific pastas
peach sorbet, simple, 36
peanut(s):
  in kung pao beef, 56
  M&M bars, 165
peanut butter:
  chippies, 72
  cups, frozen, 195–196
  and jelly bars, 243
peas, Christmas, 352

pecan(s):
  chocolate fudge pie, 286
  in fruity chicken salad, 133
  in praline sweet potatoes,
    353
  toffee bars, 316
pepper(s):
  red, pilaf, 42
  sausage, and onion sandwich,
    253
peppermint swirl cheesecake,
    354–355
pickle, sweet-, potato salad, 169
picnic:
  midwinter, 27–32
  -time deviled eggs, 140
pies:
  apple, upside-down, 272–273
  blueberry, awesome, 216
  blueberry custard, 218
  brownie s'more, 183
  cherry, tart, 50
  chocolate pecan fudge, 286
  limesicle, 145
  minty ice cream, 77
  mud, 110
  pumpkin custard, 324
  sweet potato, 17
pilaf, red pepper, 42
pineapple:
  -carrot slaw, 222
  cran-orange refresher, 238
  muffins, upside-down, 224
  wassail, 317
pistachio ice cream, 194
pita, fresh veggie, 300
pizza:
  muffins, upside-down
    chicken, 162
  super stuffed, 134

plums, sugar, 338
popcorn:
  balls, candied, 292
  dressing, for turkey, 321
  in nutty caramel corn, 71
popovers, mint-laced, 80
pork:
  lo mein, 55
  spareribs, tangy barbecued,
    141–142
  tenderloin, orange mustard,
    211
  see also ham
potato(es):
  'n' bacon salad, hot, 29
  baked mashed, 249
  beet mashed, 109
  and corn soup, creamy, 9
  in cozy beef stew, 35
  double stuffers, 329–330
  dumplings, "sweet," 263
  in hash-brown bake, 4
  Irish, 76
  mashed, in meat loaf cake,
    89–90
  packets, hot, 181
  pancakes, 342–343
  parsley buttered, 210
  roses, 150
  salad, sweet-pickle, 169
  in seasoned fries, 254
  in "timeout" stuffed spuds,
    69
  in vichyssoise, 187
  see also sweet potatoes
poultry, see chicken; turkey
praline sweet potatoes, 353
President's Day salute, 45–50
pretzel cheese sandwiches,
    242

prime rib, roasted holiday, 351
prunes:
   in orchard sweet potato bake,
     271
   in sugar plums, 338
pumpkin:
   custard pie, 324
   soup, creamy, 350
   spice bread, 336–337
punch:
   cap-and-gown, 137
   kickoff, 25

raspberry chocolate tarts, 100
red pepper pilaf, 42
Reuben casserole, 313–314
Rhode Island sensations, 201–206
rice:
   festive, 62
   in red pepper pilaf, 42
rolls:
   Derby, 114
   Passover, 96
roll-ups:
   ham and nacho cheese, 241
   strawberry 'n' cream, 3
romance, recipes for, 325–331
rose jelly, English, 227

sage breakfast sausage, 128
St. Patrick's Day dinner, 73–78
salad dressing, maple mustard,
   209
salad(s):
   easy Caesar, 204
   fruity chicken, 133
   hot bacon 'n' potato, 29
   marinated, 34
   marinated flank steak, 156
   Mediterranean green, 327

mixed berry, 174
pasta, Halloween, 290
presidential honey walnut, 46
shrimp pasta, winner's circle,
   115
on a stick, 132
strawberry spinach, 148
sweet-pickle potato, 169
tossed garden, 307
toss-together corn, 180
two-hearts, 40
see also slaws
Salisbury steak, diner-style, 160
salmon:
   crusted baked, 49
   lemonade-poached, 221
   -watercress tea sandwiches,
     228
salsa:
   black bean, steak sandwiches
     with, 121
   two-step, creamy, 68
sandwiches:
   bacon 'n' blue-cheese burger,
     168
   barbecue Joe, 157
   campfire hot diggity dogs, 182
   cheese pretzel, 242
   croissant club, 298
   fresh veggie pita, 300
   grilled fluffwich, 163
   Italian focaccia, 301
   jack-o'-lantern, 291
   Monte Cristo, 299
   and National Sandwich Week,
     297–303
   sausage, pepper, and onion,
     253
   steak, with black bean salsa,
     121

taco dogs, 164
tuna, baked stuffed, 302–303
see also hoagies; roll-ups; tea
sandwiches
sauce:
cranberry, homemade, 322
dipping, Parmesan-garlic oil,
202
red, linguine and clams in,
205
saucy chicken, 247
sauerkraut:
apple, 261
in Reuben casserole, 313–314
sausage:
pepper, and onion sandwich,
253
sage breakfast, 128
in super stuffed pizza, 134
scampi, spaghetti squash, 91
scones, teatime, 226
Secretaries Week, 107–112
seder, Passover, 95–100
shellfish, *see* fish and shellfish
shortcake, toasted blueberry,
217
shortnin' bread, 47
shrimp:
étouffée, "jazzed-up," 61
with lime, chilled, 120
pasta salad, winner's circle,
115
slaws:
pineapple-carrot, 222
veggie cabbage, 143
smoothies:
orange, 129
strawberry-banana, 244
s'more brownie pie, 183
soda, black-and-white, 257

sorbet, simple peach, 36
soup(s):
bean, speedy, 10
carrot and parsnip, 312
chicken, homemade, 97
clam chowder, creamy, 203
corn, velvet, 54
corn and potato, creamy, 9
hamburger, 8
macaroni and cheese, 240
mushroom, extra-creamy, 11
and National Soup Month, 7
pumpkin, creamy, 350
vichyssoise, 187
victory garden, 308
sour cream and chive biscuits, 315
spaghetti, in pork lo mein, 55
spaghetti squash scampi, 91
Spanish flan, 122
spareribs, tangy barbecued,
141–142
spice, pumpkin, bread, 336–337
spinach:
autumn creamed, 262
colonial, 48
strawberry salad, 148
spread, festive crab, 334
spring, tastes of, 79–85
spumoni, 198
squash:
buttery, 248
spaghetti, scampi, 91
state fair fare, 251–257
steak(s):
diner-style Salisbury, 160
orange-grilled strip, 234
round, skillet, 159
salad, marinated flank, 156
sandwiches with black bean
salsa, 121

stew:
  cozy beef, 35
  traditional German braten, 260
  veal cacciatore, 277
strawberry(ies):
  -banana smoothie, 244
  'n' cream roll-ups, 3
  ice cream and preserves, in patriotic milk shakes, 177
  spinach salad, 148
  sweetheart cake, 43–44
stuffed:
  baked tuna sandwich, 302–303
  French toast, disappearing, 127
  pizza, super, 134
  potatoes, double, 329–330
  spuds, "timeout," 69
sugar plums, 338
summer celebration, light 'n' healthy, 219–224
summer fun food, 161–166
Super Bowl munchies, 19–25
sweet potato(es):
  bake, orchard, 271
  maple-glazed ham and, 105
  pie, 17
  praline, 353

taco dogs, 164
takeout, homemade Chinese, 51–57
tarragon tenderloin, 158
tart(s):
  chocolate mousse, 331
  chocolate raspberry, 100
  lemon, cookies, 85
tea:
  cookies, snowflake, 230–231

  English, 225–231
  iced, mint julep, 117
tea sandwiches:
  cucumber, 229
  watercress-salmon, 228
teatime scones, 226
tenderloin, tarragon, 158
Thanksgiving, 319–324
toffee pecan bars, 316
truffles, chocolate almond, 111
tuna sandwich, baked stuffed, 302–303
turkey:
  drumsticks, walkaway, 252
  mincemeat-crusted, 320
turnips, mashed, 323

Valentine's Day dinner, 39–44
veal:
  with artichoke hearts, 41
  cacciatore stew, 277
vegetable(s):
  couscous, spring, 83
  fresh veggie pita, 300
  grilled veggie kebabs, 144
  mixed-up roasted, 189
  root, chicken with, 108
  veggie cabbage slaw, 143
  in victory garden soup, 305
  see also specific vegetables
Veteran's Day, 305–309
vichyssoise, 187
victory garen:
  soup, 38
  tossed garden salad, 307
walnut:
  chocolate fudge, fabulous, 284
  honey salad, presidential, 46

wassail, pineapple, 317
watercress-salmon tea
    sandwiches, 228
watermelon cake, layered, 172

wedding:
    anniversary dinner, 325–331
    basket cake, 151–152
    welcome dinner, pre-, 147–153

Mr. Food®'s Library
Gives You More
Ways to Say. . .
"OOH IT'S SO GOOD!!®"

WILLIAM MORROW

Mr. Food
From My
Kitchen to Yours:
Stories and Recipes
from Home

Q

Easy Tex-Mex

R

Mr. Food
One Pot, One Meal

S

Mr. Food
COOL
CRAVINGS

T

Mr. Food's
Italian Kitchen
Quick, Easy, and Fun Recipes!

U

Mr. Food's
Simple Southern
Favorites

V

A Mr. Food
Christmas
Homemade and Hassle-Free

W

Mr. Food
Cooking by the
Calendar
Fifty-two Weeks of Year-Round Favorites

X

Mr. Food's
Meals in
Minutes
Quick, Easy, Fun Recipes!

Y

Mr. Food ® CAN HELP YOU BE A KITCHEN HERO!

Let **Mr. Food** ® make your life easier with Quick, No-Fuss Recipes and Helpful Kitchen Tips for

Family Dinners • Soups and Salads • Potluck Dishes • Barbecues • Special Brunches • Unbelievable Desserts

... and that's just the beginning!

Complete your **Mr. Food** ® cookbook library today. It's so simple to share in all the *"OOH IT'S SO GOOD!!®"*

✂---

TITLE	PRICE	QUANTITY	
A. **Mr. Food** ® Cooks Like Mama	@ $12.95 each	x _____	= $_____
B. The **Mr. Food** ® Cookbook, *OOH IT'S SO GOOD!!®*	@ $12.95 each	x _____	= $_____
C. **Mr. Food** ® Cooks Chicken	@ $ 9.95 each	x _____	= $_____
D. **Mr. Food** ® Cooks Pasta	@ $ 9.95 each	x _____	= $_____
E. **Mr. Food** ® Makes Dessert	@ $ 9.95 each	x _____	= $_____
F. **Mr. Food** ® Cooks Real American	@ $14.95 each	x _____	= $_____
G. **Mr. Food** ®'s Favorite Cookies	@ $11.95 each	x _____	= $_____
H. **Mr. Food** ®'s Quick and Easy Side Dishes	@ $11.95 each	x _____	= $_____
I. **Mr. Food** ® Grills It All in a Snap	@ $11.95 each	x _____	= $_____
J. **Mr. Food** ®'s Fun Kitchen Tips and Shortcuts (and Recipes, Too!)	@ $11.95 each	x _____	= $_____
K. **Mr. Food** ®'s Old World Cooking Made Easy	@ $14.95 each	x _____	= $_____
L. "Help, **Mr. Food** ®! Company's Coming!"	@ $14.95 each	x _____	= $_____
M. **Mr. Food** ® Pizza 1-2-3	@ $12.00 each	x _____	= $_____
N. **Mr. Food** ® Meat Around the Table	@ $12.00 each	x _____	= $_____
O. **Mr. Food** ® Simply Chocolate	@ $12.00 each	x _____	= $_____
P. **Mr. Food** ® A Little Lighter	@ $14.95 each	x _____	= $_____
Q. **Mr. Food** ® From My Kitchen to Yours: Stories and Recipes from Home	@ $14.95 each	x _____	= $_____
R. **Mr. Food** ® Easy Tex-Mex	@ $11.95 each	x _____	= $_____
S. **Mr. Food** ® One Pot, One Meal	@ $11.95 each	x _____	= $_____
T. **Mr. Food** ® Cool Cravings: Easy Chilled and Frozen Desserts	@ $11.95 each	x _____	= $_____
U. **Mr. Food** ®'s Italian Kitchen	@ $14.95 each	x _____	= $_____
V. **Mr. Food** ®'s Simple Southern Favorites	@ $14.95 each	x _____	= $_____
W. A **Mr. Food** ® Christmas: Homemade and Hassle-Free	@ $19.95 each	x _____	= $_____
X. **Mr. Food** ® Cooking by the Calendar	@ $14.95 each	x _____	= $_____
Y. **Mr. Food** ®'s Meals in Minutes	@ $14.95 each	x _____	= $_____

Send payment to:
Mr. Food ®
P.O. Box 9227
Coral Springs, FL 33075-9227

Book Total	$_____
+ Postage & Handling for *First Copy*	$ 4.00
+ $1 Postage & Handling for Ea. Add'l. Copy (Canadian Orders Add Add'l. $2.00 *Per Copy*)	$_____
Subtotal	$_____
Add 6% Sales Tax (FL Residents Only)	$_____
Total in U.S. Funds	$_____

Name _____

Street _____ Apt._____

City _____ State_____ Zip_____

BKX1

Method of Payment: ☐ Check or ☐ Money Order Enclosed

Please allow up to 6 weeks for delivery.